W9-BTZ-195

AN ARMED AMERICA
ITS FACE IN FICTION

An *Armed* America
Its Face in Fiction

A History of the American Military Novel

Wayne Charles Miller

New York
London

New York University Press
University of London Press Ltd
1970

MIDDLEBURY COLLEGE LIBRARY

2/1976
Am. Lit.

PS
374
M5
M5
1970

© 1970 by New York University
Library of Congress Catalog Card Number: 75-111521
SBN: 8147-0473-5
Manufactured in the United States of America

AN ARMED AMERICA
BY WAYNE C. MILLER

ACKNOWLEDGMENTS

THANKS ARE DUE THE FOLLOWING FOR THEIR KIND PERMISSION TO USE
PASSAGES FROM THE WORKS INDICATED.

FROM JAMES JONES' FROM HERE TO ETERNITY AND ERNEST HEMINGWAY'S
ACROSS THE RIVER AND INTO THE TREES. REPRINTED BY PERMISSION
OF CHARLES SCRIBNER'S SONS (PUBLISHERS).

FROM ARMS AND MEN: A STUDY IN AMERICAN MILITARY HISTORY BY
WALTER MILLIS. COPYRIGHT 1956 BY WALTER MILLIS. REPRINTED BY
PERMISSION OF G.P. PUTMAN'S SONS.

FROM JOSEPH HELLER'S CATCH 22. REPRINTED BY PERMISSION OF
SIMON AND SCHUSTER, INC., JONATHAN CAPE LTD., AND A.M. HEATH &
COMPANY LTD.

FROM JOHN P. MARQUAND'S MELVILLE GOODWIN, U.S.A. COPYRIGHT
1951 BY JOHN P. MARQUAND. COPYRIGHT 1951 BY JOHN P. MARQUAND
AND ADELAIDE H. MARQUAND. REPRINTED BY PERMISSION OF LITT.E,
BROWN AND COMPANY.

FROM WILLIAM WISTER HAINES' COMMAND DECISION. COPYRIGHT 1947,
1948 BY WILLIAM WISTER HAINES. COPYRIGHT IN CANADA 1948 BY
WILLIAM WISTER HAINES. REPRINTED BY PERMISSION HAROLD OBER
ASSOCIATES INCORPORATED.

FROM DALTON TRUMBO'S JOHNNIE GOT HIS GUN. REPRINTED BY
PERMISSION OF LYLE STUART, INC.

FROM EUGENE BURDICK AND HARVEY WHEELER'S FAIL-SAFE. REPRINTED
BY PERMISSION OF McGRAW-HILL.

FROM JOHN DOS PASSOS' FIRST ENCOUNTER. REPRINTED BY PERMISSION
OF THE PHILOSOPHICAL LIBRARY.

FROM JAMES GOULD COZZEN'S GUARD OF HONOR. COPYRIGHT 1958 BY JAMES
GOULD COZZENS. REPRINTED BY PERMISSION OF HARCOURT, BRACE AND
WORLD, INC. AND THE LONGMAN GROUP LTD.

FROM JOHN HORNE BURNS' THE GALLERY. COPYRIGHT 1947 BY JOHN HORNE
BURNS. REPRINTED BY PERMISSION OF HARPER & ROW, PUBLISHER,
INCORPORATED AND THE WILLIAM MORRIS AGENCY, INCORPORATED.

FROM FRED J. COOK'S THE WARFARE STATE. COPYRIGHT 1962 BY FRED J.
COOK. REPRINTED BY PERMISSION OF THE MACMILLAN COMPANY.

To Alison and Heather, who bring much joy, and to Mary Jane, who makes everything possible.

Acknowledgments

I would like to thank William M. Gibson for his invaluable advice and criticism during the research and writing, and my assistant, Susan Brennan, for her help in preparing the manuscript. Also, I must thank those career officers at the Air Force Academy with whom I argued constantly and for whom I have the greatest affection— Jesse Gatlin, Cort Auser, Jim McCarthy, Chuck Roades, Mike Mendelsohn, Joe Berthelot, and, of course, Colonel Peter Moody. Finally, for their conversation and criticism during the past two years, I record a note of gratitude to Merton Harris, Harry Bloom, and especially to the man who helped with all kinds of difficulties, Norm Wesley.

Contents

Introduction

One hundred years before World War II burned across Europe, Herman Melville shipped aboard an American man-of-war, the *United States,* on a journey home from the Hawaiian Islands. He experienced the life of a common sailor within the structured society of the military world, mulled it over, and recreated it in *White Jacket* (1850). Long before fear of Communism had permitted military ascendance in the United States, Melville warned of the dangers of the totalitarianism of the Right. He showed that in the structured world of the man-of-war, everyone loses his freedom. As he wrote *White Jacket,* Melville saw no immediate threat of a military take over in his native land, reasoning that a liberal constitution and a liberal political philosophy guranteed continuing democracy. By the time of the creation of *Billy Budd,* however, such faith had vanished. Melville knew as well as anyone that all too often men and nations are willing to sacrifice freedom for authority during times of crisis and to continue under totalitarian rule as long as economic conditions are tolerable. With this in mind, one wonders what Melville's hope for American democracy would be today in a politically polarized world ridden with crises and conflict, and with 7,500,000 workers at home dependent upon defense spending for their livelihoods. Are these, as Fred J. Cook suggests, the ingredients of the warfare state? Is this the world of which Melville warned?

It is undeniable that we have lived through a period of military ascendancy in the United States. We all know now the troubling facts: the massive dependence of the economy on weapons production, the impact of military thinking on national strategy, the image-at-any-price bungling of public relations problems such as the six thousand dead sheep in Utah and the transporting of nerve gas across the country, the waste in Pentagon procurement policies, the secret development of weapons for chemical and biological warfare, and the involvement of American men and matériel in clandestine military operations. All these things we know. Despite such knowledge, however, and despite marches on the Pentagon and speeches by prominent politicians, the continued growth of the military establishment seems assured. As long as Americans fear Soviet and Chinese intentions, they will be willing to spend billions and then more billions on weapons systems—systems that are quickly obsolete, thus guaranteeing new production and continued employment. As long as members of the House of Representatives are interested in bringing Federal funds into their districts, they will vote the funds necessary for such production.

The late Dwight David Eisenhower surprised the nation during his Farewell Address when he warned of the disturbing growth of what he termed the military-industrial complex. At that time defense spending totaled approximately forty billion dollars annually. Now, nine years later, it has doubled, and, according to Senator Eugent J. McCarthy, the defense establishment is "rapidly becoming a kind of republic within the Republic." [1] Indeed, the record of political intention at variance with accomplished fact has become part of the scenario of the growth of the military-industrial complex.

All too often, national leaders have asked us to listen to their words and not to examine their policies. After all, Eisenhower's warning came after his administration had overseen massive acceleration of defense spending. Furthermore, the acceleration continued under the late President Kennedy, who, it should be remembered, relied upon American military superiority (both strategic and tactical) to bring about the successful conclusion of the Cuban missile crisis of 1962. Two years later, President Johnson ran on a platform pledged to oppose escalation of the war in Vietnam; soon after, he talked of hanging the coonskin on the wall. President Nixon beat Hubert Humphrey primarily because of the latter's inability to extricate himself from apparent responsibility for Vietnam policies; yet, Nixon's first significant action in the defense area was to demand congressional approval of an ABM (anti-ballistic missile) system. If housewives protested, the military did not; and so deployment of Safeguard is planned, at least it was at first, around missiles instead of people. One thing is clear. Regardless of the president or his party or his personal style, the military-industrial complex continues to grow. Certainly, never before in the history of this nation has the military arm possessed such power within the system.

Melville is not alone among American novelists in warning of the military structure, the military mind, and

[1] "The Power of the Pentagon," *Saturday Review* (December 21, 1968), p. 8.

the conservative political philosophy they both represent. John William De Forest, writing of the Civil War, created a Regular Army officer who wished to make the state a Prussia. John Dos Passos and other World War I novelists wrote of military units as microcosms of the authoriatrian state; and, a generation later, Norman Mailer's General Cummings of *The Naked and the Dead,* a clever and clear-eyed purveyor of power, predicted that in the aftermath of World War II the United States would emerge as a great totalitarian power. Finally, Joseph Heller, in a significant use of symbolism, found in a military unit the means of examining the fabric of American society as it has developed since World War II.

It would be a mistake, however, to picture the history of the American military novel as one in which writer after writer condemns the military and the military definition of reality—a definition described in Samuel Huntington's *The Soldier and the State* as one which deems conflict and authoritarianism to be inevitable. Indeed, as early as James Fenimore Cooper and William Gilmore Simms, the nation had produced novelists essentially aristocratic and conservative; and, in the twentieth century, such skeptical "recorders" as John Marquand and James Gould Cozzens write of the military man as simply an integral part of the social structure. Clearly, they offer little criticism of his activities and attitudes. Furthermore, even writers who are opposed to the philosophical underpinnings of the military definition of reality often admire the courage and intelligence of the military men they create. Captain Vere, Colonel Carter, General Cummings, and General James Matton Scott are all memorable and commanding figures; and, indeed, even if it is an insane society of which Heller writes, it is Scheisskopf who comes to power within it.

This study, then, like any history, is a mixed bag of goods. Throughout it, I have sought resolutely to avoid oversimplification in one direction or the other in order to easily condemn or easily praise. The United States has engaged in many wars, perhaps too many. Out of the carnage have emerged many novelists, some of them significant, who have reported and recreated their responses to those national efforts. In tracing the thread of cultural history that they have produced, it is perhaps possible to understand the American character and the culture at large more clearly. For, despite the noble attitudes of those who wish that the American military would just disappear, it is clear that in the foreseeable future it will not. It is important, however, that it remain an arm of the state and not the brain at the center of the state's activities. In regard to this problem, President Kennedy's thoughts in the aftermath of the Cuban crisis seem significant in their very ambivalence. According to the late Robert F. Kennedy in *Thirteen Days, A Memoir of the Cuban Missile Crisis,* the President admired the technical capacity of the military to deploy weapons systems, men and matérial; however, he was also profoundly disturbed by the inability of the nation's military leaders to see beyond the simple use of force—particularly when the result could be nuclear holocaust.

But he was distressed that representatives with whom he met, with the notable exception of General Taylor, seemed to give so little consideration to the implications of steps they suggested. They seemed always to assume that the Russians and the Cubans would not respond or, if they did, that a war was in our national interest. One of the Joint Chiefs of Staff once said to me he believed in a preventive attack against the Soviet Union. On that fate-

ful Sunday morning when the Russians answered
they were withdrawing their missiles, it was suggested by one high military adviser that we attack
Monday in any case. Another felt that we had in
some way been betrayed.[2]

In Kennedy's account, some of the Joint Chiefs sound
remarkably like the caricature generals of *Dr. Strangelove,
or: How I Learned to Stop Worrying and Love the Bomb.*
Obviously, to feel "betrayed" by the fact that a nuclear
exchange with the Soviet Union had been avoided is to
be culturally suicidal. Interestingly, the novelists who
write of the possibilities of nuclear holocaust are generally
less gentle with the scientists who create the weapons than
with the military men who deploy them.

In any case, it is my hope that this book, in addition
to explicatiing a large number of American novels, also
provides a better historical and cultural perspective from
which the American military man and military machine
may be understood and controlled.

W. C. M.

[2] Kennedy, p. 119.

AN ARMED AMERICA
ITS FACE IN FICTION

1.

James Fenimore Cooper: The Historical Romance and the American Revolution

The Revolutionary War provided the basis for the first ideological conflict in America concerning what kind of military structure the nation would possess and how much power it would wield. A number of historians, political scientists, and sociologists currently see the final choice of a citizen-soldier reserve rather than a professional standing army as crucial to the nation's political development, and many express fears that recent changes in the American military establishment represent a turning from traditional policy of limiting military power toward a dangerous aggrandizement of it.

In recent years, primarily because of the immense expansion of military might caused by a world in continuous conflict, some scholars have concerned themselves with the Revolution as a harbinger of American attitudes

toward the military establishment. They include, among
others, so diverse a group as Walter Millis, Samuel Huntington, Fred J. Cook, Tristram Coffin, and C. Wright
Mills. Unfortunately, the authors' attitudes toward the
past are too often conditioned by their concern for the
present, and historical perspective suffers as a case is made
either for or against the military's role in the nuclear age.
For example, Cook verges on bellicosity in his condemnation of the current military-industrial complex in his
book, *The Warfare State,* and Tristram Coffin, though
readable and amusing, is often glib and impressionistic in
his treatment of the same subjects in *The Passion of the
Hawks: Militarism in Modern America.* Both are alarmed
by growing military influence, and, significantly, both
quote the Founding Fathers in order to disparage those
policies in the twentieth century that have led to the expansion of the role of the military in the United States.[1]
Huntington, on the other hand, seems to welcome this
expansion, and implies, in alluding to suggestions made
by Alexander Hamilton, that the nation should have established a large, centralized force after the Revolution.[2]
C. Wright Mills, primarily interested in the present impact of military power, looks back somewhat wistfully to
the period of the Revolution when "the means of violence remained decentralized" as an example of an era
when civilian dominance was assured.[3]

Walter Millis maintains greater objectivity throughout *Arms and Men: A Study in American Military History* and it is to him that one turns for a clarification of
the military's role both during the war and in its aftermath, particularly in terms of the political consequences
of the choice of the citizen-soldier as the backbone of the
nation's military strength. Differing from the school of
military thought generated by Emory Upton's admira-

tion for Prussian techniques,[4] he praises the militia's role both in terms of martial effectiveness and political consequence.

> While the regular armies marched and fought more or less ineffectively, it was the militia which presented the greatest single impediment to Britain's only practicable weapon, that of counterrevolution. The militia were often much less than ideal combat troops and they have come in for many hard words ever since. But their true military and political significance may have been underrated.[5]

John Richard Alden, Willard M. Wallace, Christopher Ward, Marvin A. Kreidberg and Merton G. Henry, and Richard A. Preston, Sydney F. Wise, and Herman O. Werner, in a variety of studies, are less enthusiastic.[6] They voice the usual criticism of the militia, emphasizing the problems of short-term enlistment and lack of discipline. Millis is less interested in immediate tactical issues and more concerned with the overall effects upon the developing nation, and while his findings generally favor the choice and its results, he does not oversimplify its effects. For instance, he evaluates the ultimate changes in warfare brought about by the emergence of the citizen-soldier in a somber light insofar as it expanded the number of participants.

> War had been democratized and "nationalized," as it were; finally it had been freed from its economic shackles, and primitive means had been discovered for circumventing the money system in the service of a national interest. By 1783 the principal seeds

had been sown from which were to spring the modern "socialization" of war and its development to those heights of total effort and total savagery to which we are now accustomed. The way had been opened for the confiscation of property as well as conscription of life in the name of the all-powerful modern deity—the state.[7]

Millis' breadth of view can be appreciated when one compares him to two of the scholars who deal exclusively with military histories of the Revolution. Howard H. Peckham's *The War for Independence*: *A Military History* and Christopher Ward's previously mentioned *The War of the Revolution* confine themselves almost exclu-' sively to consideration of tactical problems. Peckham, while presenting many of the militia's shortcomings in specific battles, idealizes the citizen-soldiers by emphasizing the idea that their success resulted from their commitment to democratic ideals. He envisions them as more competent in battle than mercenaries because they enjoyed more rights and responsibilities.[8] Ward's conclusions are more typical insofar as he finally suggests that a plodding professional is a better soldier than a poorly trained militiaman, however idealistic.[9] Neither author, however, considers the larger, and ultimately more important, political and social issues raised by the kind of military structure that emerged.

As revealed in Huntington, Coffin, Cook, Mills, and others, the issue of what kind of military policy the nation embraced during and after the Revolution is still currently a matter of concern. Millis, using some of the usual quotations from George Washington, James Madison, and the Congress, dramatizes the choice that the nation faced.[10]

Since 1781 Congress had been passing into the control of "nationalist" politicians, the conservative magnates who had been most hesitant over the plunge into independence, but who were now most desirous that independence should produce a strong central government, capable of servicing the national debt and of keeping unduly divisive or democratic tendencies under control with a national standing army.[11]

The Congress finally ordered Washington to furlough his men, but "never again did an American regular establishment come as near as that to using the power of its armies in domestic politics." [14] Millis goes on to state that the compromises of 1789 guaranteed freedom from military force capable of expansionist activity when the opportunity arose in 1812.[12]

Clearly, the historian, the political scientist, and the sociologist find matters of great importance in the military situation during and after the Revolution—matters, in some cases, basic to democratic processes. For the most part, one looks in vain for a comparable seriousness of consideration on the part of American novelists who have dealt with the war. Although one would not wish for propaganda, the novel of the American Revolution possesses, for the most part, neither significant ideas nor serious development of character. Besides avoiding issues endemic to the Revolution, the novelists generally fail to develop theses and themes that would emerge to distinguish the novelists of other wars and other military situations. For instance, no one creates, as Herman Melville does in *White Jacket* and *Billy Budd,* a sense of the threats to freedom and justice that a totalitarian military rule would engender. With one or two exceptions, no

one writes, as John William De Forest does, of the brutality and corruption that war produces. With the possible
exception of Howard Fast, no one suggests a sense of the
ultimate pointlessness and futility of war as one finds in
the World War I novels of Dalton Trumbo, Ernest Hemingway, John Dos Passos, William March Campbell,
William Faulkner, and others. Finally, no one uses the
military structure in order to investigate the inadequacies
of American society as the best of the World War II
novelists, such as Norman Mailer, John Horne Burns,
and Joseph Heller, would do.

Of course, no De Forest, Dos Passos, or Heller
emerges from the war to present a fictional recreation of
the Revolution. Moses Coit Tyler's *The Literary History
of the American Revolution 1763–1783* and Lillie Deming Loshe's *The Early American Novel* reveal an absence
of any participant's serious consideration of the war in
fiction, although Miss Loshe points out that the Revolution was occasionally used for stock Gothic or romantic
purposes. Alexander Cowie blames the dearth of material
on the sparsity of research facilities and on the popularity
of the Gothic and the sentimental novel.[13] In any case,
not until the publication of James Fenimore Cooper's
The Spy does there appear an important piece of fiction
that might be termed a military novel.

Although Arvid Shulenberger, in *Cooper's Theory
of Fiction,* points out that Cooper did not consider *The
Spy* researched and detailed enough to be called an historical novel,[14] such critics as Cowie, Brander Matthews,
and Warren S. Walker describe it as such.[15] Certainly the
period of thirty-eight years that elapsed from the end of
the Revolution to the publication of the novel seems
sufficient to qualify the book according to Ernest E.
Leisy's definition: "A historical novel is a novel the action

of which is laid in an earlier time—how much earlier remains an open question, but it must be a readily identifiable past time." [16] Thus, beginning with Cooper's work, one is exclusively dependent upon the historical novel for fictional interpretations of the war; and, unfortunately, the genre is not noted for its profound treatment of any subject. Lion Feuchtwanger in *The House of Desdemona or the Laurels and Limitations of Historical Fiction* states that the historical novel is generally "a plush meadow for those authors who strive for effect rather than for truth," and that the vast majority of writers who deal with eras other than their own do so in order to make money.[17] In words easily applied to even the most recent of the novels of the Revolution, Feuchtwanger goes on: "The authors transfer some cheap romantic plot to an epoch which they believe interests the readers. They differ in only one respect from earlier writers of this kind, for they paint the historical background with an industrious brush and seek to substitute diligent study for genuinely creative talent." [18] Unlike writers like Kenneth Roberts to whom Feuchtwanger alludes, Cooper burdens neither *The Spy* nor *The Pilot* with overwhelming detail; but, at least partially because of his debt to Sir Walter Scott, he does establish some unfortunate precedents for later novelists of the Revolution. These include the use of caricature and the avoidance of serious consideration of social issues.

Three of the most recent novelists dealing with the Revolution, Bruce Lancaster, David Taylor, and John Brick, although writing during the same years as the political and sociological writers mentioned earlier, fulfill the most unfortunate of Feuchtwanger's descriptions, and are in the Cooper tradition in their creation of character and treatment of the war. No serious intent pervades their novels. Lancaster's *Guns of Burgoyne,* *Phantom Fortress, The Secret Road,* and *Blind Journey* deal in pure adventure; although a galaxy of historical figures including Burgoyne, St. Leger, Morgan, Arnold, Franklin, Lafayette, and Martha Washington appears, Lancaster concentrates on courageous young men and usually full-blown young women who find love in the midst of heroic action. The Revolution is little more than a setting—a series of sumptuous or awesome tableaux against which heroes and heroines move and pose. Taylor, whose list of famous personages is of approximately the same length, offers the same kind of escape literature in *Lights Across the Delaware, Farewell to Valley Forge,* and *Storm the Last Rampart.* Brick occasionally criticizes the militia and does realistically depict the winter camp at Valley Forge, but he too deals for the most part in sentimental and romantic motivation.[19] Not one of these novelists considers with any seriousness either the problems of life in a military structure or the political problems surrounding the military; and they, unlike Cooper, had the advantage of the examples of Melville, De Forest, Crane, and the writers of two world wars. One must look back along the isolated line of the American historical novel beginning with Cooper and *The Spy* for the characteristics found in these recent novels.

Because of the subject of this history, Harvey Birch, the most frequently discussed figure in *The Spy,* will receive less attention than the characters more directly involved in the military situation. One of the precedents Cooper establishes for most of his successors is that he deals with an élite group in *The Spy,* in this case officers from both sides who can discuss their differences in the Wharton home—a home which, while torn by divided allegiance and located in the Neutral Ground, still permits the social niceties. In fact, most of the onslaughts in the novel are verbal rather than military, as Colonel Wellmere, Captain Wharton, Mister Wharton, Doctor Sitgreaves, Captain Lawton, Major Dunwoodie, and, of course, the ladies discuss issues such as allegiance versus rebellion while enjoying rather resplendent dinners. The common soldier, the enlisted man in the ranks, serves almost exclusively as a comic foil. He appears in the battle mass and seems from afar happy, content, and well adjusted. Sergeant Hollister epitomizes Arthur Hobson Quinn's observation that Cooper's common man is good if he is loyal to his leader.[20] He is simplicity itself, faithfully following orders, enjoying frequent "potations" at the Hotel Flanagan, and carrying on a seemingly platonic relationship with the hotel's proprietress, Betty Flanagan. He has no ambitions within the military structure; he accepts the hierarchal system unquestioningly; he does not question the war; he does not quail at killing; he goes to battle happily. In short, he is divested of all complexity and emerges as a caricature.

Paralleling this oversimplification of the enlisted man, Cooper provides little detailed description of battle. Marvin Klotz, in *The Imitation of War 1800–1900: Realism in the American War Novel*, describes Cooper's treatment of the battles of Lexington and Concord in *Lionel Lincoln*: ". . . it reveals a common view which pervades the early historical novel that war provides an opportunity for attaining glory."[21] Certainly, this is so in *The Spy*. The first confrontation of British-Hessian and Continental forces takes place near the Wharton home, permitting the captive loyalist, Captain Wharton, and his rebellious sister, Frances, to view the tableau. Elements of romance appear which would be approximated fre-

quently in later novels of the Revolution. As he anticipates the fight, Wharton yearns to be part of it. "He
longed, with the ardour of youth, to join in the glorious
fray, but was compelled to remain a dissatisfied spectator
of a scene in which he would so cheerfully have been an
actor." [22] Moments before engagement, Frances' beloved
Major Dunwoodie leaves his troops in order to gallop to
her to steal one last embrace (pp. 92–93), and the battle
soon takes place in terms of flourishing trumpets, wheel-
ing columns of troops, waving sabres, and the blaring of
martial music (p. 96). The British Colonel Wellmere exclaims, after his capture, that " 'Danger is but an unseemly
word for a soldier' " (p. 103). Like all the officers on both
sides, he is forthright, courageous, and guided by a good
conscience. The officers, while receiving much more detailed attention from Cooper, seem, like the enlisted
men, two-dimensional figures pasted on a series of well-
painted tableaux. Cooper's idealization of both officer
and enlisted men is revealed later in the novel when he
presents his ideal army in battle.

> Led on by Lawton, the men followed, destitute alike
> of fear and reflection. Whether it was a party of the
> refugees, or a detachment from the royal army, that
> they were to assail, they were profoundly ignorant;
> but they knew that the officer in advance was dis-
> tinguished for courage and personal prowess; and
> these are virtues that are sure to captivate the
> thoughtless soldiery. (p. 301)

One hesitates for a moment over the word *thoughtless* to consider the possibility of irony; however, no
pattern of irony is traceable and, following Quinn's suggestion, one must conclude that none is intended. Cooper

expects from his common men only unflinching and thoughtless dedication to their leader with none of the ambiguity of Melville's *Benito Cereno* concerning the ultimate results of such faithfulness. Throughout the novel he treats his soldiery in a tone of undiluted romanticism. His description of Lawton's heroic death is typical. " 'Come on!' shouted the trooper, as a body of English appeared on the rock, and threw in a close fire; 'Come on!' he repeated, and brandished his sabre fiercely. Then his gigantic form fell backward, like a majestic pine yielding to the axe; but still, as he slowly fell, he continued to wield his sabre, and once more the deep tones of his voice were uttering, 'Come on!' " (pp. 444–445). Lawton is a caricature of the dashing, courageous soldier. With a full stomach and a stout heart and a clear conscience, he bids defiance to anything the world can do (p. 137); he is a cavalier figure who at one point in the novel offers the toast: " 'A speedy peace, or a stirring war' " (p. 189).

Despite his overall glorification of battle and war, Cooper occasionally offers a brief criticism of the military and touches on one issue that Melville and later writers would explore as one of the major problems for the individual living within a military structure—the problem of attempting to find justice within a totalitarian framework. But, unlike Melville in *White Jacket* and *Billy Budd,* he does not seriously analyze the problem, or, rather, he does not present it in a way that encourages serious consideration on the part of the reader. In fact, Cooper skirts the issue twice. In the first instance, Major Dunwoodie abruptly sentences Harvey Birch to death but then allows a time lag which conveniently permits Birch's escape. " 'No,' said the Major, recoiling in horror at his own justice. 'My duty requires that I order you to be executed, but surely not so hastily; take until nine to-morrow to prepare for the awful change' " (pp. 225–226). Birch escapes and the "awful change" and the consequence of military jurisdiction are avoided. The second situation occurs in the trial of Captain Wharton. One of the court of officers self-consciously defends the fairness of the court-martial: " '. . . although we are a court of martial law, yet in this respect, we own the principles of all free governments' " (p. 344). After an emotional outburst in which Frances exhorts Colonel Singleton to be merciful, the members of the court deliberate in language that at least parallels the court's discussion in *Billy Budd*.

> "Still, gentlemen, we have our duty as officers to discharge;—our feelings as men may be indulged hereafter. What is your pleasure with the prisoner?"
>
> One of the judges placed in his hand a written sentence that he had prepared while the colonel was engaged with Frances, and declared it to be the opinion of himself and his companion.
>
> It briefly stated that Henry Wharton had been detected in passing the lines of the American army as a spy, and in disguise. That thereby, according to the laws of war, he was liable to suffer death, and that this court adjudged him to the penalty; recommending him to be executed by hanging, before nine o'clock on the following morning. (p. 353)

Harvey Birch, however, acting as an instrument of the godlike Harper-Washington, enables Wharton to escape. Thus, in the fashion of romance, the dire consequence disappears, Cooper again avoids the issue of justice within a military structure, and the reader is not encouraged to consider the issue seriously.

This is not to say, however, that Cooper was not interested in the issue of military justice. Commenting on the famous Somers affair, the incident that triggered Melville's imagination toward the creation of *Billy Budd,* he condemns the manner in which Commander Alexander Slidell MacKenzie denied the sailors accused of mutiny their rights. In fact, in a critique of the entire court-martial, Cooper is most critical:"While the court of inquiry was in session, the prisoners remained in confinement, ironed most of them, without any charges being brought against them. The truth is not to be concealed, they were dealt with as sailors and not as citizens." [23] Unlike Melville, Cooper did not see the issue in terms of a universal problem concerning freedom and authority. Rather, his concern is limited to the practical and immediate issue of a single miscarriage of justice, and, ultimately, he states that military discipline often necessitates the abrogation of civil rights.[24]

In another of his novels, *The Pilot,* one finds an avoidance of issues similar to that in *The Spy.* Thomas Philbrick, in *James Fenimore Cooper and the Development of American Sea Fiction,* justly credits Cooper with the role of innovator in this genre. He has much praise for *The Pilot,* particularly for what he terms Cooper's realism, but he applies the term within strict limitations, intending only "the strictest accuracy in all matters involving nautical technicalities." [25] George Snell, in *Shapers of American Fiction: 1798–1947,* expresses similar appreciation of Cooper's control of the argot of the sea and his magnificent seascapes.[26] More to the point in terms of this history, however, is Philbrick's statement: "But still more powerful influences demanded the materials and tone of romance. Prime among them, of course, was Cooper's desire to give appropriate fictional expression to his doctrine of maritime nationalism." [27] Perhaps Louis H. Bolander, in "The Naval Career of James Fenimore Cooper," overstates his case in insisting that Cooper's brief naval career "made a definite and ineffaceable impression on his mind and altered the course of his entire life," [28] but certainly the Navy was for him an interesting and often attractive institution, as his scholarly works on the subject and his late membership in the U.S. Naval Lyceum indicate. Cooper was strongly committed to the idea that the nation needed a large naval force, and his sentimental dedication of the late edition of *The Pilot* to one of the men with whom he served aboard *The Wasp* also attests a longstanding affection.

Cooper served as an officer and this experience, one can assume without much risk, contributed to his patrician view of ship society and the need for discipline.

It is not easy to make the public comprehend all the necessities of a service afloat. With several hundred rude beings confined within the narrow limits of a vessel, men of all nations and of the lowest habits, it would be to the last degree indiscreet, to commence their reformation by relaxing the bonds of discipline, under the mistaken impulses of a false philanthropy. It has a lofty sound, to be sure, to talk about American citizens being too good to be brought under the lash, upon the high seas; but he must have a very mistaken notion who does not see that tens of thousands of these pretending persons on shore, even, would be greatly benefited by a little judicious flogging.[29]

His history of the Navy [30] tends to substantiate such aristocratic and patriotic leanings. In large measure a series of well-written and heroic accounts of battles, the book is also openly biased in its insistence on the necessity of a large naval force to insure national pride and dignity for the United States. In fact, Robert Spiller sees in Cooper's attitudes an early example of a later American militarism.[31]

Marius Bewley sees a conflict between Cooper's aristocratic tendencies and his writing of a democratic revolution,[32] and Donald A. Ringe seems to concur when he points out the anomaly of the novelist's insistence upon absolute obedience within a military structure whose very existence was an act of disobedience against the king and authority.[33] In any case, Cooper creates in *The Pilot* a distinctly stratified society which provides an orderliness he seems to regard as ideal. The military arrangement of social levels is unquestioned throughout, and everyone is pictured as happily performing the duties of his level. Enlisted men, even in circumstances as dire as Manual's surrender to Borroughcliffe, follow their commander unhesitatingly (p. 248). Similarly, when Barnstable and his charges, without firearms, face a well-armed British contingent led by Borroughcliffe, the American exclaims:

"As for the trifles in your hands, gentlemen, you are not to suppose that men who are trained to look in at one end of a thirty-two pounder, loaded with grape, while the match is put to the other, will so much as wink at their report, though you fired them by fifties. What say you, boys, is a pistol a weapon to repel boarders?"

The discordant and disdainful laughs that burst from the restrained seamen were a sufficient pledge of their indifference to so trifling a danger. (pp. 377–378)

The view is much the same as that expressed when Lawton's men follow him into battle in *The Spy*. Leisy's suggestion that *The Pilot* transposed the action of *The Spy* to the sea seems near the mark.[34] Again, Cooper treats an élite group with Colonel Howard's home replacing Mr. Wharton's as a center for conversation; and, although in this novel physical conflict penetrates the house, there remains plenty of time for dinners and discussion. He continues to glamorize the idea of combat with leaders always itching for action and their men always ready to follow. Specific, detailed descriptions of battle are nonexistent, and death, particularly Long Tom Coffin's, is glorified in the manner of Captain Lawton's. The John Paul Jones figure embodies characteristics of the demigod similar to those possessed by Harper-Washington and, again, there is little concern for the common man, here the seaman, except as a loyal follower. He exists, much like his counterpart in *The Spy,* only to drink and fight.

Many critics have seen Long Tom Coffin in *The Pilot* as a sea-born Natty Bumpo; in Long Tom, Cooper seems to present his idealized common man. This idealization reveals something of the author's attitudes toward the nature of the enlisted man and the masses in general. Tom possesses prodigious physical strength which he puts at the service of his superiors (pp. 223 ff.); he reveals his physical and nautical superiority to his commander without ever considering usurping his leader's privileged position (pp. 315–320); he is an inspiration to his fellowmen in battle (p. 229); he is morally straight as in his indignation over Kit Dillon's lies (pp. 298, 302); he is absolutely fearless (p. 229); and he dies heroically in the line of duty (p. 328). His death, like the escapes of Birch

and Captain Wharton in *The Spy,* seems a narrative device used in order to avoid a thematic problem.

Since Long Tom Coffin, with the possible exception
of the Pilot himself, is the most commanding and heroic
figure in the novel, one must ask why he is not rewarded
within the system of which he is a part. Cooper creates in
him a member of an aristocracy of worth who does not
enter the military aristocracy; instead, he dies. Clearly,
Coffin possesses those qualities that Bolander attributes
to Cooper as indicative of a good commander: self-confi-
dence, initiative, dauntless courage, and intense patriotism.[35] The explanation seems to be that Long Tom is a
common man, however idealized, and common men in
Cooper's fiction do not move from the masses of the enlisted rank to the aristocracy of the officer corps.

In the spirit of Quinn's comment concerning the
issue of enlisted men's loyalty, Philbrick sees Cooper ad-
miring the discipline and subordination of sailors, and
Kay Seymour House in *Cooper's Americans* specifically
investigates Coffin to discover that "his unquestionable
merits do not indicate that he has been unjustly denied
command; Tom fits his station as naturally as a line-tub
fits a whale boat." [36] The point is that in Cooper's idealized shipboard society everyone fits properly in his place
—so much so that Ringe sees the novel's central theme as
one of obedience to authority, and House concurs in suggesting that "when ruled by a good captain, the ship is,
as we have said, an ideal community." [37] This is, of
course, little different from the concept of feudal agrari-
anism Cooper finally came to see as the ideal social structure on land.

Cooper, then, would seem to suggest that the military
structure, ruled by a benevolent leader, exists without

antagonism within its social classes. It is true that during the years in which he produced *The Spy* and *The Pilot* the novelist paid little attention to criticism of American society,[38] but one can see in his idealization of the military structure in these novels the seeds of an aristocratic view of social structure that would eventually envision ultimate destructiveness in the democratic levelers in *The Crater*. Donald Ringe asks the reader to pause over Cooper's reliance upon authority in his early works.

> To be sure, the Pilot himself imposes order and extricates the characters from their difficulties. We can take him, in other words, as "the man who knows and can act," the man to whom obedience is due. But the twentieth century reader distrusts this solution; for, if such a man be twisted by his passions, he could easily introduce the tyrannical dictatorship that Colonel Howard foresees as the logical end of the rebellion. . . .[39]

In summary, Cooper's John Paul Jones parallels his Harper-Washington in *The Spy*. Both are always calm, always right, always ready, always mysterious, and always obeyed. Cooper envisions the military structure as one in which everyone is happy, obedient, and willing to sacrifice for his leader; he oversimplifies the common man in the name of romance, and avoids such issues as the problem of justice within the military. He pays no attention to the political consequences of his idealization of the benevolent dictator, and generally seeks to entertain his reader rather than to enlighten him. He glorifies combat and uses the Revolution primarily as a setting for his tales of adventure. In all of these things, he sets an example that most historical novelists would follow when treating the war. Alexander Cowie suggests that

he [Cooper] became the first and greatest of a long
line of American writers of the historical romance,
extending from 1821 to the present. The genre has
altered in some important respects—witness the new
methods employed by Kenneth Roberts and others—
but its essentials remain the same; a tale of high adventure set in the past, centering in a situation
crucial in the life of a nation or a people, involving
persons, places, and actions partly invented and
partly historical.[40]

Although this is not the place to investigate every
novel dealing with the Revolution, a survey of representative authors reveals great conformity in the avoidance of
issues and the pursuit of adventure from Cooper to
Taylor, Lancaster, and Brick. The romances of the Revolution penned by William Gilmore Simms parallel
Cooper's work.[41] Although he occasionally presents a bit
more blood than Cooper, he too spends much time presenting sentimental love relationships and characters in
debate over the problems of conflicting loyalties. He also
shares Cooper's fundamentally conservative, static view of
society. While the two works concerned with the war
written in the 1850's, *The Forayers* and *Eutaw,* may be
seen as thinly veiled rationalizations for the possible
southern secession, he nevertheless values a structured
world in which everyone is content with his lot and in
which everyone works for the common good. Joseph V.
Ridgely seems on the mark when he describes the basic
intention throughout this group of novels. "Simms had
portrayed all levels of society and he had interconnected
them by one central theme: the responsibility of each to
all in the establishment of a lasting system." [42] While
Ridgely makes a good case for considering the body of

Simms' work seriously, the romances of the Revolution add little to the development of the American military novel.

Silas Weir Mitchell's *Hugh Wynne, Free Quaker* (1897), which Quinn calls "the greatest novel of the Revolution," [43] is essentially a novel of character, told in the first person in order to trace the maturation of the young hero during his war experiences. After revealing an emotional commitment to the new nation and, in effect, denying the pacifist tenets of his religion, Hugh decides to fight. The war becomes the means through which he discovers the world. Despite some hair-raising experiences, he is not shattered by it. Rather, Mitchell makes it clear that the war is ultimately good for his hero. Upon his return to civilian life and home, Hugh thinks: "I was no longer the mere lad I had left it. Command of others, the leisure for thought in the camp, the sense that I had done my duty well, had made of me a resolute and decisive man." [44] The author interjects some minor criticism of the militia (p. 251), but the novel contains neither consideration of the military as social structure nor in a political context. Unlike Cooper, the author does offer some of the horrors of battle (pp. 303–304, 309–314), prison life (pp. 317–321), and the conditions at Valley Forge (pp. 354 ff.), but the central story line of the absurd love relationship between Hugh and Darthea and Hugh's final battle with his arch enemy, Arthur Wynne, reveals the dominant tone of the work as adventurous escape.

Of lesser merit as a novel, Winston Churchill's *Richard Carvel* contains the usual love interest and glorification of the Founding Fathers. Most of the military action is crammed into short space with John Paul Jones and Richard emerging as stock heroes on two different levels of responsibility. The book contains no analysis of the military situation of the Revolution nor any of the themes that have emerged as important in the history of the military novel. Harold Frederic's *In the Valley* presents the war in terms of freedom versus slavery with the Americans idealistically fighting for their liberty. Frederic, in an aside, describes the militia as undisciplined,[45] but, by and large, follows Cooper's precedent in using most instances of war as opportunities for heroics. His narrator-hero is all good, and the villain, Philip Cross, all evil. So Frederic, a groundbreaker for realism in *Seth's Brother's Wife* and *The Damnation of Theron Ware*, writes his historical novel in a totally different manner, offering little realistic description of battle and no consideration of military structure.

Edward Bellamy, in *The Duke of Stockbridge: A Romance of Shay's Rebellion*, reveals some insight into the unfortunate circumstances of the returned veteran, Captain Hamlin, but the theme does not remain central in the novel. Joseph Hergesheimer's hero in *Balisand*, Richard Bale, recalls his war experiences as disenchanting, but this is just a passing consideration. James Boyd's *Drums* includes some criticism of the militia [46] but after the hero, John Fraser, listens to his emotions in order to enter the war on the rebel side, such criticism fades and the book becomes for the most part glorification of John Paul Jones as a courageous freedom fighter.

F. van Wyck Mason offers some realistic battle description in *Three Harbors* and details some of the real problems involved in raising a militia army,[47] but he avoids consideration of military structure and political questions. His *Rivers of Glory* and *Stars on the Sea* introduce greater concentration on sexual exploits and offer pure adventure in dealing with the war and the military.

The former, dedicated to his wife whom he describes as the kind of woman red-blooded Americans would always fight for, is intended to present the Continental Army as an example for American troops entering World War II.[48] Despite this intention, however, most of the novel is concerned with spying and skullduggery on the island of Jamaica. The latter novel is also intended as an inspiration, this time for young Americans in the Navy, and presents romantic sea action.[49] Generally speaking, Mason writes juvenile books spiced with sex which reveals that unbuttoned bodices do not alone elevate a book into serious consideration. Robert Gessner's *Treason* presents an interesting portrait of Benedict Arnold and some realistic description of destruction and death,[50] but relies on the Cooperesque conflict of divided loyalty and does not consider any of the major themes of the military novel or any of the political problems of the Revolution.

Two novelists of the war who are sometimes mentioned as transcending the genre are Kenneth Roberts and Howard Fast. Leisy finds Roberts' *Arundel* and *Rabble in Arms* the "most satisfactory account of the Revolution in New England and Canada," and praises the novelist's "knowledge of woodcraft, vivacity, humor, and originality."[51] While it is true that Roberts displays great command of historical detail and creates an authentic sense of an era, his treatment of the military is standard. Fast's works differ radically from the mainstream of the American novel of the Revolution insofar as he attempts to present the war not for purposes of romantic escape but rather as an example of class warfare. In such novels as *Conceived in Liberty, The Unvanquished,* and *The Proud and the Free,* he approaches the conflict in a manner that parallels that taken by many of the World War I novelists. Like Dos Passos and Trumbo, he portrays the war and the officer/enlisted man antagonism in terms of Marxist doctrine. As a Marxist, he occasionally finds himself hard pressed in his treatment of officers. On the one hand, they are members of an élite group that normally contributes to the suppression of the masses; on the other hand, they are the leaders of the revolt.

Much of *The Unvanquished* concerns itself with the problem of how Washington, an aristocrat, can be a leader of a people's war. Fast presents the general as simple, naïve, and reliant upon appearance rather than capability to muddle through difficult situations. This depiction of the general officer is common to many novels dealing with the American military and is perhaps presented in most detail in John Marquand's *Melville Goodwin, USA*.[52] In fact, Fast suggests that Washington's simplicity prevented him from assuming dictatorial control of the country.[53] He criticizes the militia at some length in *The Unvanquished*, but it is in *Conceived in Liberty* that he offers his most realistic creation of battle scenes and in which he most resembles the World War I novelists.

The narrator, Allen Hale, becomes a cog in a military machine: "I don't think any more. My mind is gone. Only my body moves, and my body is a machine apart from me. It will go on until the spark of life in it flickers out." He describes his experience in battle in vivid, often horrifying detail: "I drive my bayonet into a fleeing man, tear it free and leap past him. I am a machine to kill— ice inside. I am no longer a man."[54] But despite the realistic details in his work, Fast is often caught in his own Marxist straitjacket, particularly in having his heroes of the proletariat accept their officers. For instance, it is suggested that von Steuben in *Conceived in Liberty* is a hero merely because he permits his troops to rest on a drill field; and early in the novel one of the most class conscious of characters, a sympathetically drawn Jew, exclaims about Washington: "There's a man. No officer, but a man to lead men.' " [55] Despite such obviousness, however, Fast is a novelist who, unlike most of the writers of novels of the Revolution, learned from techniques outside the tradition of the historical romance and used them effectively.

For the most part one looks in vain within the host of novels dealing with the American Revolution for a focus on the military or for a seriousness of intent paralleling that evinced in recent nonfiction dealing with the same subject. The example of Cooper, the general tradition of the historical novel, and the desire to appeal to a large audience demanding escape, all have worked against it. There is, however, a nineteenth-century novel of the Revolution that stands outside the tradition both in tone and intent. Herman Melville's *Israel Potter,* while not concerned with the military as fully as *White Jacket* and *Billy Budd,* does introduce elements of Melville's handling of the subject and will be considered in the next chapter, which deals exclusively with Melville.

Notes

1. Cook, pp. 35–39; Coffin, pp. 26, 35–37.
2. Samuel P. Huntington, *The Soldier and the State: The Theory and Politics of Civil–Military Relations,* p. 194.
3. Mills, *The Power Elite,* p. 178.
4. Millis, pp. 140–141.
5. *Ibid.,* pp. 34–35.
6. Alden, *The American Revolution: 1775–1783;* Wallace, *Appeal to Arms: A Military History of the American Revolution;* Ward, *The War of the Revolution,* ed. John Richard Alden; Kreidberg and Henry, *History of Military Mobilization in the United States Army: 1775–1945;* and Preston, Wise, and Werner, *Men in*

Arms: A History of Warfare and its Interrelationships with Western Society.

7. Millis, pp. 40–41.
8. Peckham, pp. 43, 50, 54; 4, 180, 204; 26.
9. Ward, p. 521.
10. Millis, pp. 43, 50, 46.
11. *Ibid.*, p. 41.
12. *Ibid.*, pp. 42, 70.
13. Cowie, *The Rise of the American Novel*, p. 29.
14. Shulenberger, p. 36.
15. Matthews, *Americanisms and Briticisms: With Other Isms*, p. 99; Walker, *James Fenimore Cooper: An Introduction and Interpretation*, p. 25.
16. Leisy, *The American Historical Novel*, p. 5.
17. Feuchtwanger, pp. 26, 25.
18. *Ibid.*, p. 30.
19. *The King's Rangers*, pp. 17, 42; *The Rifleman*, p. 181; *The Strong Men*, pp. 27, 113, 317.
20. Quinn, *American Fiction: An Historical and Critical Survey*, p. 74.
21. Klotz, p. 20.
22. P. 91, in the New York, 1871 ed. (Subsequent references are also to this edition, and are indicated by page numbers in the text.)
23. Review in *Proceedings of the Naval Court Martial in the Case of Alexander Slidell MacKenzie, a Commander in the Navy of the United States, &c Including the Charges and Specification of Charges. Preferred against Him by the Secretary of the Navy. To Which Is Annexed, an Elaborate Review, by James Fennimore [sic] Cooper* (New York, 1844), p. 273.
24. *Ibid.*, p. 272.
25. Philbrick, pp. 51, 52.
26. Snell, p. 18.
27. Philbrick, p. 52.
28. *United States Naval Institute Proceedings*, April, 1940, pp. 541, 550.
29. *The Pilot* (New York, 1872), p. xi. (Subsequent references are also to this edition, and are indicated by page numbers in the text.)
30. *The History of the Navy of the United States of America*, 2 vols.
31. Spiller, *Fenimore Cooper: Critic of His Times*, p. 277.
32. Bewley, *The Eccentric Design: Form in the Classical American Novel*, pp. 77–81.

33. Ringe, *James Fenimore Cooper*, p. 38.
34. Leisy, p. 95.
35. Bolander, p. 543.
36. House, p. 188.
37. Ringe, p. 38; House, p. 202.
38. Ringe, pp. 54, 68–69, 91–92; Walker, p. 25.
39. Ringe, p. 40.
40. Cowie, p. 116.
41. The romances are: *The Partisan*, 1835; *Mellichampe*, 1836; *The Kinsman*, 1841; *Katharine Walton*, 1851; *Woodcraft*, 1854; *The Forayers*, 1855; and *Eutaw*, 1856.
42. Ridgely, *William Gilmore Simms*, p. 118.
43. Quinn, p. 312.
44. *Hugh Wynne, Free Quaker: Sometime Brevet Lieutenant-Colonel on the Staff of His Excellency General Washington*, p. 386 in the New York 1922 ed. (Subsequent references are also to this edition, and are indicated by page numbers in the text.)
45. Frederic, p. 358.
46. Boyd, pp. 239–240.
47. Mason, *Three Harbors*, pp. 342–348.
48. *Rivers of Glory*, p. 1.
49. *Stars on the Sea*, pp. 5, 531–550.
50. Gessner, pp. 108–109.
51. Leisy, pp. 73, 74.
52. See Chap. 6.
53. Fast, *The Unvanquished*, pp. 290–292.
54. *Conceived in Liberty*, pp. 101–102, 374.
55. *Ibid.*, pp. 299–300, 52.

2.

Herman Melville and the Dissection of the Military World: A Warning to America

In almost every way, Herman Melville's *Israel Potter* is the antithesis of the typical historical novel of the American Revolution. Surprisingly, many critics of Melville's work give it only slight notice. Lion Feuchtwanger, a German writing on the genre rather than exclusively on Melville, sees the novel as "grossly underestimated," and offers some of the best analysis of it. He insists:

The melancholy fate of Israel Potter consistently points to the social problem. The contrast between the brilliance of the ideology and the leadership and the misery of the masses of men who fought for this ideology becomes a magnificent parable of human

29

life. Israel Potter is the true hero of the Revolution, the unknown Soldier, the People, and his fate becomes for Melville a parable of the fate of all unfortunates, of the downtrodden, and of the oppressed.[1]

Instead of adventure and escape, then, Melville offers considerations of character and of a social problem. Throughout the novel, one feels the tragic disparity between the American dream of democracy and the plight of the common man in America, and this is just one of the striking differences between Melville's and Cooper's approaches to treating the Revolution.

Melville does not glamorize combat, but offers instead some realistic description of warfare, including the horror of dismemberment.[2] He makes a common man the center of his attention, a man who gained nothing either from his participation in the war or from the country for which he fought. Although not consistently so throughout the military novel in America, works which present a disenchanted enlisted man as hero normally contain some consideration of class conflict. This is the case in *Israel Potter*. While Israel suffers in London, Melville describes war making not as heroic adventure but as an economic function to rid a nation of its poor. He presents London at the end of the American Revolution as a city glutted with returned soldiers for whom there are no jobs and who soon find themselves engulfed in poverty. Melville presents the remedy. "In 1793 war again broke out, the great French war. This lighted London of some of its superfluous hordes . . ." (p. 216). In addition, he differs radically from Cooper in his treatment of historical figures. While Cooper idealized, Melville toys with the heroes of the American past. Lewis Mumford catches some of the satirization of Benjamin Franklin; Leon Howard sees John Paul Jones, Franklin, and Nathan Hale as satirized to some degree; Harry Levin characterizes Melville's Franklin as an example of "successful philistinism"; Richard Chase finds him a prototype for the confidence man, and suggests that Jones embodies what Melville feared the nation would become—"inorganic, unstable, possessed by an enormous impatience which would lead it to plunge violently into undertakings for which it was unprepared." [3] James E. Miller, Jr., while disagreeing with most in his interpretation of Franklin, agrees with Chase on Melville's intention for Jones and sees in the combination of Jones' savageness and Ethan Allen's self-righteous defiance a sense of Ahab and a warning for America that if Allen and Jones embody the American character "America might, like Ahab, go in defiance to her doom." Miller generalizes further in suggesting that the presence of these national figures provides a means whereby Melville could probe the national character, and Feuchtwanger agrees: "*Israel Potter* is in truth an historical novel. The novel is the history of the first fifty years of America seen through the grim and bitter temperament of a great realistic artist." [4]

Certainly, Melville announces in his preface to *Israel Potter* that he will not write romance when he vows to forebear "anywhere to mitigate the hard fortunes of my hero," and to avoid "the artistic recompense of poetical justice" (p. vi). Unlike Cooper in his concentration on élite groups, Melville anticipates Arthur Miller's arguments for Willy Loman as tragic hero by asserting that Israel may be a "plebeian Lear or Oedipus" (p. 214). He intends that the reader sympathize with Israel's material defeat in contrast to such successful Americans as the penny-pinching, self-seeking Franklin and the savage and barbaric Jones. Israel is victimized by a rigidly structured society. Within the military, he leads a rebellion against authority and is put in chains (p. 16); he battles against the cruelty of officers (p. 117); he is critical of a structure in which a lieutenant can offer his men to another officer "as if they were a parcel of carcasses of mutton" (pp. 113–114). The military, in its rigidity, serves as a microcosm of a cruel world which finally reduces Israel to poverty and death. That Melville particularly intends to damn American society is suggested by the ironic tone of his dedication to the Bunker Hill monument: ". . . a private of Bunker Hill, who for his faithful services was years ago promoted to a still deeper privacy under the ground, with a posthumous pension, in default of any during life, annually paid him by the spring in ever-new mosses and sward" (p. v). Just how bitter Melville is over the fate of his common-man hero he reveals in a statement similar to one of Harry Morgan's in Hemingway's *To Have and Have Not*. Israel has subsisted by working in a brick yard and, in effect, becoming clay himself, when Melville, near the end of the novel, comments: "Man attains not to the nobility of a brick, unless taken in the aggregate" (p. 207).

Besides pointing out differences between Melville and Cooper, one may note certain elements in *Israel Potter* that reappear and develop further in *White Jacket* and *Billy Budd*. Melville sees the military as a microcosm of stratified society at large; he pictures that world through the eyes of an enlisted man and is interested in the tragic effects of that world on his hero; he presents class conflict between the enlisted and officer ranks; and, finally, he sees in the authoritarian military world, despite his sympathy for the common man and for the ideals of democracy, a tragic victory of tyranny and tradition over freedom and innovation.

Frederic Ives Carpenter, in *American Literature and the Dream*, within the context of a consideration of Melville's lack of faith in the fulfillment of the dream of a democratic America, analyzes his use of a military world:

Because he believed that war was the one constant fact of human history, he wrote of the world as a man-of-war. And because he believed that this constant of war made it inevitable that martial law should prevail, he embodies the law in the authoritarian discipline of the ship, whose captain's orders were final. About half of his novels were set in actual men-of-war where martial law was absolute, and about half in whaling ships where authoritarian discipline prevailed in a modified form. But all his novels excepting *Pierre* suggested that the authoritarian life of the ship was the microcosm of the life of the nation, and ultimately the world as a whole.[5]

In *White Jacket* Melville hints at the ultimate prospect of totalitarian rule in the United States. As a common seaman sailing upon a United States Navy ship, the *United States,* his thoughts must have paralleled those of his alter ego White Jacket aboard the *Neversink,* as the latter considers the possibility of shipboard military rule becoming the kind of government that the country as a whole would embrace. "But in a nation under a liberal constitution, it must ever be unwise to make too distant and peculiar the profession of either branch of its military men. True, in a country like ours, nothing is at present to be apprehended of their gaining political rule; but not a little is to be apprehended concerning their perpetuating or creating abuses among their subordinates. . . ."[9] In this passage, Melville warns of two things:

the aggrandizement of the military arm and the need for
the nation to maintain a liberal political philosophy. Although he sees no *present* military threat to democratic
government, he does see the military world as a microcosm of a cruel authoritarian state, and he uses *White
Jacket* as the vehicle for dissecting that world.

Melville's analysis of the command or corporate pyramid pictures a world in which the captain is dictator, the
various ranks of officers do his bidding for position and
prestige, the marines aboard ship are the captain's police
force, the seamen are bondmen or slaves, and the mid-
shipmen are children receiving training which will per-
petuate the system. At various points in the novel Melville
describes the ship as a Parisian lodging house (p. 95), a
town (pp. 95, 109), a city (pp. 68, 94), a nation (p. 27),
and finally the world itself (p. 204). At every point he insists upon its structure as totalitarian. "It is no limited
monarchy, where the sturdy Commons have a right to
petition, and snarl if they please; but almost a despotism,
like the Grand Turk's. The captain's word is law; he
never speaks but in the imperative mood. When he stands
on his quarterdeck at sea, he absolutely commands as far
as the eye can reach. Only the moon and stars are beyond
his jurisdiction. He is lord and master of the sun" (p. 27).
As a democratic American,[7] Melville chafes at the captain's authority and power over the personal lives of the
crew. In this man-of-war world his right to absolute censorship is evidenced by his ability to order a seaman's
journal confiscated and thrown overboard (p. 53); and,
when he must review Lemsford's Fourth of July play in
order to "see whether it contained anything calculated to
breed disaffection against lawful authority among the
crew" (p. 116), Melville's satire is evident. Further, the
captain can order his men to attend church services (pp.

195–196), and even dictate which games they may play (pp. 344–345). He has the right to punish arbitrarily—even unto death through manipulation of the court-martial.

How the individual seaman prospers under such conditions is one of Melville's major concerns throughout *White Jacket*. In an episode which suggests emasculation, he offers his conclusions. The captain has arbitrarily ordered all the men's beards cut off before they are permitted ashore. It is clear that most of the crew regard their beards as symbolic of their uniqueness and masculinity. As his is cut, Jack Chase exclaims to the barber: ". . . you are about to sheer off my manhood" (pp. 454–455). Ushant (You Shan't) becomes a hero for preferring a flogging to a shearing. It is clear that in this world the masses of men do have their manhood taken from them as they are transformed into parts of a gigantic, well-oiled machine to which they must be subservient and in which they are relegated to positions of slaves.

Melville may see docility within the system as an expedient for survival, but in *White Jacket* he certainly does not admire it. In sharp contrast to Coffin, Cooper's idealized seaman, Melville presents Landless, a favorite of the officers, and shows why he is their favorite. They like him precisely because he is their slave, their dupe; precisely because he follows blindly and causes no trouble. Never a threat, totally agreeable, he is made to order.

> This Landless was a favourite with the officers, among whom he went by the name of *"Happy Jack."* And it is just such Happy Jacks as Landless that most sea-officers profess to admire; a fellow without shame, without a soul, so dead to the least dignity of manhood that he could hardly be called a man. Whereas,

a seaman who exhibits traits of moral sensitiveness, whose demeanor shows some dignity within; that is the man they, in many cases, instinctively dislike. The reason is they feel such a man to be a continual reproach to them, as being mentally superior to their power. He has no business in a man-of-war; they do not want such men. To them there is an insolence in his manly freedom, contempt in his very carriage. He is unendurable, as an erect, lofty-minded African would be to some slave-driving planter. (pp. 485–486)

Landless, the happy seaman, is a kind of moral eunuch— an unthinking automaton within the system. That he is not alone is indicated when Melville generalizes about the men-of-war: ". . . men are to be found in them, at times, so used to a hard life, so drilled and disciplined to servitude, that, with an incomprehensible philosophy, they seem cheerfully to resign themselves to their fate. They have plenty to eat; spirits to drink; clothing to keep them warm; a hammock to sleep in; tobacco to chew; a doctor to medicine them; a parson to pray for them; and, to a penniless castaway, must not all this seem as a luxurious Bill of Fare?" (p. 483). It would seem that for the security of bread and board these men forego their freedom.

Most commentators on *White Jacket* concentrate on such specific issues as flogging in analyzing Melville's objections to military life, but he has a more general intent and flogging is but an incident in a system which denies justice in almost all instances. He sees the practice of forcing the crew member to witness floggings as a "terrible hint of the omnipotent authority under which he lives" (p. 167). "You see a human being, stripped like a slave; scourged worse than a hound. And for what? For

it means to lose. Although Melville may have accepted the idea that war is the most constant and predictable event in human history, he does so sorrowfully with sidelong glances at that condition as chaotic, meaningless, evil.

As quoted in Chapter One, Donald Ringe, hinting at Cooper's lack of political sophistication, states that the twentieth-century reader must be skeptical about Cooper's reliance upon authority.[8] In this, he closely parallels a description in *White Jacket* in which Melville in the nineteenth century looks at the possibility of totalitarian control: ". . . if some brainless bravo be captain of a frigate in action, he may fight her against invincible odds, and seek to crown himself with the glory of the shambles, by permitting his hopeless crew to be butchered before his eyes, while at the same time that crew must consent to be slaughtered by the foe, under penalty of being murdered by the law" (p. 395).

But while Melville's view of the military world is pessimistic, he does not oversimplify the officers as "bad guys" and the enlisted men as "good guys" in the manner in which some of the World War I and World War II novelists would do. In fact, he emphasizes the crew's cowardice, lethargy, and perversion along with the officers' cruelty and conceit. His interest ultimately is in the effect that life within a totalitarian system has on all its members. Lewis Mumford, in an early study, sums up Melville's intention in *White Jacket* as well as anyone.

> Melville dealt with the effect of regimentation, with the relation of superior to underling, with the accidents and mischances and the ordinary routine of a man-of-war's life, in such a fashion that he included other institutions as well: the human truths

and relationships would remain, though all the navies of the world were scrapped next week. The malevolence of the Articles of War, the essential degradation of the whole military process, the hectoring, the arrogance of station (the quarter-deck face!), the military necessity of converting all the variable human potentialities into submissive mechanisms— that is, human defectives—are here once and for all coolly observed and demonstrated.[9]

Finally, it would seem that in *White Jacket* Melville pictures the military establishment as a world in which the strong and the cunning and the privileged dominate the weak and the docile and in which the masses forego self-determination for the comforts of dependence upon authority.

If one were to remain a part of such a world, all he could hope for would be a benevolent dictatorship. "There are some vessels blessed with patriarchal, intellectual captains, gentlemanly and brotherly officers, and docile and Christianized crews" (p. 486). However, if to be "Christianized" means that one should be like Landless, then certainly Melville intends irony in presenting this ideal—perhaps because he realized that a world without social conflict was impossible. The two primary sympathetic figures in *White Jacket,* White Jacket himself and Jack Chase, offer two different solutions to the personal dilemma of life within such a world. Chase, after a period of rebellion, rejoins the man-of-war world and attempts to work out his place in it even if it does mean giving in to having one's manhood cut away. White Jacket-Melville detaches himself to write a book which he hopes will bring about changes in the system, and it seems clear that Melville, at the time of *White Jacket's* composition, still had hopes for ultimate amelioration. The mere fact that the book has an overt purpose in terms of bringing about reforms in the Navy reveals that he believed in the possibility of change, and *White Jacket* was indeed influential in calling attention to some Navy abuses. In addition to these limited objectives, however, Melville held out greater promises. At one point, White Jacket looks forward to a time when war will be abolished (p. 260), and he feels that the conservative Navy has harbored barbaric traditions which otherwise would have been changed by "the general amelioration of other things" (p. 290). Finally, he hopes that someday his story will be "the history of an obsolete barbarism" (p. 355).

Melville hints that both the unjust laws and the unjust structure must be altered in order to bring about real reform. Although, as mentioned above, he does not idealize the "people," his sympathy for their condition leads to his conclusion that it is the environment in which they live that is responsible for the problem: ". . . it cannot admit of a reasonable doubt, in any unbiased mind conversant with the interior life of a man-of-war, that most of the sailor iniquities practised therein are indirectly to be ascribed to the morally debasing effects of the unjust, despotic, and degrading laws under which the man-of-war's man lives" (p. 382). In addition, despite the ironic ending of the novel in which he shuns revolution, Melville appears not averse to using violence if other measures fail. For instance, White Jacket ultimately chooses to write a book in order to foster change, but when about to be humiliated by Captain Claret, he considers killing him despite the fact that it would mean an end to his own life as well (pp. 352–353). From the incident grows a theory of revolution as White Jacket thinks: "The privilege, inborn and inalienable, that every man has, of dying himself, and inflicting death upon another, was not given to us without a purpose. These are the last resources of an insulted and unendurable existence" (p. 353). It is a theory of revolution that desperation breeds in groups in the United States today. Of course, a "Christianized" crew would never resort to violence, but Melville at least dangles the possibility before the reader that this "Christianization" makes it possible for the officer-élite to dominate the crew-masses, and, indeed, the present rejection of Christianity among militant blacks echoes Melville's voice. White Jacket, however, does not choose revolution; he writes instead, hoping for evolutionary change through nonviolent means.

Thus, *White Jacket* is the first novel in which Melville used the military world as a microcosm of the totalitarian state. He presented it as unjust, ruthless, arbitrary, and destructive of the dignity of the individual. Although in a country like the United States, he saw no immediate danger of the military's gaining political control, he examined what that kind of martial control would mean to the nation by exposing the conditions he had encountered aboard a ship named the *United States,* and, indeed, not a little was to be apprehended in view of the abuses in the system.

Although, technically, *Billy Budd* does not fall into the domain of this history because it does not deal with Americans, the book is so important to an understanding of Melville that it must receive some consideration. The amount of criticism it has already received, as well as the diversity of opinions proffered, is staggering. Over the issue of whether or not the tone of the book is ironic, scholars and critics line up like contending football teams, ready to strike a blow for their side. On the team of Melville's acceptance of necessity one finds Leon Howard, Newton Arvin, James E. Miller, Milton R. Stern, F. O. Matthiessen, D. E. S. Maxwell, William Braswell, F. Barron Freeman, Charles Weir, and Edward H. Rosenberry;[10] on the side of irony and rejection of expediency are Harry Levin, Richard Chase, Merlin Bowen, Alfred Kazin, Lawrance Thompson, Charles Robert Anderson, John Bernstein, Joseph Schiffman, and, like a specter hovering in the background, the instigator of the debate, Gay Wilson Allen, who suggested to Schiffman that Melville might have intended irony throughout *Billy Budd*.[11] Two all-star teams indeed! It is not the purpose here to pursue the intricacies of the argument. Rather it is *Billy Budd* as it reveals Melville's analysis of a military world that is our concern. However, it is best to recognize that one's interpretation of the novel is at least partially determined by the direction from which one arrives at it. Having traveled the road of *Israel Potter* and *White Jacket* with their sympathy for the common man and their criticism of structure and authority, this study naturally tends toward alignment with those that view Melville as ironic in *Billy Budd*. It is interesting to note that while Charles Weir, one of the first who saw the novel as Melville's testament of acceptance, called for an approach to it through the earlier work, he mentions neither *Israel Potter* nor *White Jacket;* and Edward H. Rosenberry, the most recent of those who favor the theory of acceptance, rejects some obvious parallels between *Pierre* and *Billy Budd* in favor of quotations and parallels from Johnson Jones Hooper's *Some Adventures of Captain Simon Suggs* and Ignazio Silone's *Bread and Wine* in order to prove that Melville intended no irony in the story.[12] But Rosenberry is not alone. The arguments on both sides occasionally seem farfetched as attempts are made to explain away ambiguity and to arrive at a single interpretation.

Again, this study admits its angle of approach as at least partially determining its conclusion.

The similarities between *White Jacket* and *Billy Budd* are many. Both are set on warships; both present essentially innocent heroes persecuted, in different degrees, by the masters of arms, Bland and Claggart; both are concerned with officer/enlisted man relationships and the problem of justice in a totalitarian military world. The Somers incident, central to the problem in *Billy Budd* and of peculiar interest to Melville because of the involvement of a relative,[13] is alluded to in *White Jacket,* and in this earlier work Melville is opposed to expediency. In pointing out the arbitrary nature of military justice, he states: "The well-known case of a United States brig furnishes a memorable example, which at any moment may be repeated. Three men, in a time of peace, were then hung at the yard-arm, merely because, in the captain's judgment, it became necessary to hang them. To this day the question of their complete guilt is socially discussed" (p. 380). He then admits that sea commanders should have extraordinary powers, but adds that these powers have "undoubtedly furnished warrant for clothing modern sea-commanders and naval courts-martial with powers which exceed the due limits of reason and necessity" (p. 381).

For most students of *Billy Budd,* interpretations hinge on whether the captain is presented as exceeding "the due limits of reason and necessity." Lawrance Thompson pays particular attention to the peculiarly military structure in which Vere operates, pointing out that the captain sets up an unfair confrontation between Billy and Claggart insofar as the officer's word must always take precedence over the enlisted man's in any dispute between them in a military world.[14] He sees Vere as a totalitarian figure who manipulates Billy's death in order to preserve a structure which he rules. Merlin Bowen goes a step further in picturing Vere as one "who has abdicated his full humanity in the interests of a utilitarian social ethic and postponed the realization of truth and justice to some other and more convenient world. Neither the Christian gospel nor the modern doctrine of the rights of man has, in his opinion, any place in the government of this man-of-war world." [15] To Bowen, Vere is a figure who may dabble in ideas, but one who has sold his rights to free thought for the attainment of position and power.

> Vere is, to begin with, no simple impressed seaman but an officer and therefore a volunteer. He is also, as Melville is at some pains to emphasize, a mature, thoughtful, and morally sensitive man who presumably knew what he was doing when he accepted his commission and so placed himself in the service of a military code whose brutishness he abhors. If, as he now intimates, his buttons and epaulets were purchased at the cost of his independence as a moral being, it must be admitted that the bargain was his own.[16]

Thus, Vere as a professional officer, despite any "starry" private protestations to the contrary, is first an officer and commander in a totalitarian world and second a man interested in personal and social justice. Like the seaman Melville pictured in *White Jacket,* though operating at a different level, he has sold his right to free thought and, in a sense, his manhood, for security. His security may involve position and prestige rather than bread and board, but the principle is the same. It is true

that Melville sympathizes with Vere's situation: that of
the essentially well-intentioned, if self-deluding, man who
discovers too late that he has lost all freedom of action
to a life style most particularly destructive of such freedom; it is also true that Melville implies that this is the
fate of most men if they wish to avoid that of a passive
resister like Bartleby.

Therein lies the rub. In the world that Melville
creates and in the world at large, almost everyone, at every
level, gives up his freedom for security: the crew for
bread, the lesser officers on the court in order not to cross
the captain, the captain himself in order not to destroy
his own authority which he views as the key to social
stability. That Melville chose a military society in which
to treat this subject was no accident. The totalitarian
form of military government, so inimical to democratic
processes as he proved in *White Jacket,* best sums up the
tragic view that tradition and authority must triumph
over innovation and experimentation.

It is Melville's peculiar attitude toward this triumph
that causes difficulties in interpretation. Many seem anxious to welcome him to the school of political conservatism. Those who are not so anxious insist, like Bowen,
that after so long and deeply considered a life it seems
impossible that Melville should be left with merely "this
sorry wisdom of resignation to a forced complicity in
evil." [17] To accept an either/or answer to *Billy Budd* as
political testament, however, is to oversimplify. After all,
Melville does not aggrandize Vere. One may sympathize
with the captain's position and one may understand the
compromises he makes; one does not admire him. He
takes the path of least resistance, choosing manipulation
of the existing social order and his position in it rather
than pursuit of a world of greater equality and justice. And

although Billy Budd is killed, he transcends death insofar as he is remembered among the masses as an innocent
victim of an unjust system. Bernstein, who oversimplifies
in one direction as much as the conservatives in another,
sees the story as a call for rebellion, and suggests that "if
a system can exist only if its most innocent and just members must be sacrificed, then this system is not worth pre-
serving." [18] The fact that a sensitive reader can come away
from *Billy Budd* with this thought suggests the impossibility of any simple answer to its mystery. Melville seems
to say that throughout history ("horological time" if you
will) he discovers men and societies giving up their freedom for reliance upon authority. Despite the fact that
this process seems inevitable, he also shows that it inevitably produces abuses of justice, expediency, and the death
of innocence and ideals. Men like Claggart, useful to
authority, cunning and calculating, are its ultimate
product.

That the United States was involved in a political
experiment whose hopes ran counter to reliance upon
authority Melville understood. That he hoped for its
success without believing it possible has been main-
tained.[19] That *Billy Budd* serves as warning to America
is at least a possibility. Frederic Ives Carpenter hints at
this line of reasoning: "Melville remains the greatest
critic of the democratic dream. Whether our democracy
ultimately triumphs and proves his forebodings false de-
pends in part on how well it heeds Melville's own warnings in *Moby-Dick*. But the submission to traditional
authority and the rejection of individual responsibility
which Melville approved in *Billy Budd* runs counter both
to American experience and to American idealism." [20]
The key word in the passage is *approved*. For rather than
an approval of such abdication, *Billy Budd* seems, like

Moby-Dick, more of a warning—a warning that if the American dream of democracy is to succeed, the nation's leaders must choose a path other than expediency. Melville seems to make it clear that it is not enough to die with "Billy Budd" on your lips after you have been the chief agent in bringing about his death.[21] This warning stems from the somber tone of the work itself, an elegiac statement of the death of man's political hope for democracy. For it seems that Carpenter is correct, despite his citing of Melville's "approval," when he states that "the story describes the military execution of the good man, who has previously been deprived of his civil rights without his own consent." [22] If the "good man" is killed in the name of expediency, Melville seems to say, then the hopes for political and social justice are dead. He may seem to insist that he does not mourn the death, but *Billy Budd* is testament that he refuses to mourn in the same manner as Dylan Thomas refused to mourn the death by fire of that London child. This sense of *Billy Budd* as elegy is at least suggested in a recent article by Ralph W. Willett. In commenting on Melville's attitude toward Vere, Willett concludes: "Small wonder that Melville, in his last years, should have shown compassion and understanding for a character who illustrates the complexity of human hopes and behavior in a tense and uncertain world." [23]

In *White Jacket* Melville announced that he saw no present threat of a military takeover in the United States, but he would explore life within a military structure in order to expose its effects upon an individual thinking man. In *Billy Budd,* with less of his earlier optimism for American political development, he looked again at the same subject. Not very much had changed. There was still much to fear, much to be "apprehended," particularly when so benevolent a dictator as Captain Vere, well intentioned as he might be in the effort to preserve social order in the face of change, could manipulate justice in order to bring about the death of an innocent victim in the name of expediency.

In summary, Herman Melville emerges as a prime innovator in the history of the American military novel. He is the first to concentrate his attention on the fate of the common man within a military structure. He is the first to analyze that structure as a microcosm of the authoritarian state. He is the first to mention seriously the possibility that such a form of government ever could gain power in the United States. One looks in vain in Cooper and others in the tradition of the historical novel for serious consideration of social issues and the creation of complex character: one finds both in Melville. He initiates the military novel as a vehicle for serious thought concerning American political and social issues, and, like many who follow him, he warns the country of the consequences inevitable in an unquestioning reliance upon the military.

It is perhaps an additional indication of his genius that Melville's poems in *Battle-Pieces* provide a most fitting introduction to the best of the fiction of the Civil War. In some of them he praised the courage and fortitude of soldiers of both sides;[24] in others he explored the horror of pointless death and destruction.[25] In "A Utilitarian View of the Monitor's Fight," however, Melville provides a most insightful description of the peculiar nature of the Civil War—a conflict that was to revolutionize the techniques of organized violence, particularly in the employment of vast firepower, and was to reduce the individual human being to the position of a mere cog in a vast and terrifying machine of destruction.

Hail to victory without the gaud
　　Of glory; zeal that needs no fans
Of banners; plain mechanic power
Plied cogently in War now placed—
　　　　Where War belongs—
Among the trades and artisans.

Yet this was battle, and intense—
　　Beyond the strife of fleets heroic;
Deadlier, closer, calm 'mid storm;
No passion; all went on by crank,
　　　　Pivot, and screw,
And calculations of caloric.

.　　.　　.　　.　　.　　.　　.　　.　　.　　.　　.　　.　　.

War yet shall be, and to the end;
　　But war-paint shows the streaks of weather;
War yet shall be, but warriors
Are now but operatives; War's made
　　　　Less grand than Peace,
And a singe runs through lace and feather.[26]

Notes

1. *The House of Desdemona or the Laurels and Limitations of
   Historical Fiction,* pp. 91, 94.
2. *Israel Potter: His Fifty Years of Exile,* p. 15 in the London
   1923 ed. (Subsequent references are also to this edition, and are
   indicated in the text.)
3. Mumford, *Herman Melville: A Study of His Life and Vision,*
   p. 166; Howard, *Herman Melville: A Biography,* p. 214; Levin,
   The Power of Blackness: Hawthorne, Poe, Melville, p. 191; Chase,
   Herman Melville: A Critical Study, pp. 178, 182.
4. Miller, *A Reader's Guide to Herman Melville,* pp. 148, 143;
   Feuchtwanger, p. 96.
5. Carpenter, p. 76.
6. *White Jacket or the World in a Man-of-War,* p. 289 in the
   London 1922 ed. (Subsequent references are also to this edition,
   and are indicated by page numbers in the text.)

7. See Henry W. Wells, "An Unobtrusive Democrat: Herman Melville," *South Atlantic Quarterly*, XLIII (January 1944), 46–51.

8. See note 39, Chapter One.

9. Mumford, p. 78.

10. Howard, p. 328;

Arvin, *Herman Melville,* pp. 292–199;

Miller, p. 228;

Stern, *The Fine Hammered Steel of Herman Melville,* pp. 234–238;

Matthiessen, *American Renaissance: Art and Expression in the Age of Emerson and Whitman,* pp. 509–510;

Maxwell, *American Fiction: The Intellectual Background,* pp. 176–177;

Braswell, "Melville's *Billy Budd* as 'An Inside Narrative'," *American Literature*, XXIX (May 1957), 133–146;

Freeman, *Melville's* BILLY BUDD;

Weir, "Malice Reconciled: A Note on *Billy Budd,*" *University of Toronto Quarterly*, XIII (April 1944), 276–285;

Rosenberry, "The Problem of *Billy Budd,*" *PMLA*, LXXX (December 1965), 489–498.

11. Levin, pp. 194–197;

Chase, *Herman Melville,* p. 258. In *The American Novel and Its Tradition,* Chase insists that the novel is essentially political, pp. 113–115;

Bowen, *The Long Encounter: Self and Experience in the Writings of Herman Melville,* pp. 217–233;

Kazin, "Ishmael in His Academic Heaven," *New Yorker* (February 12, 1949), pp. 84–89;

Thompson, *Melville's Quarrel with God,* pp. 120–121, 356–409;

Anderson, "The Genesis of *Billy Budd,*" *American Literature,* XII (November 1940), 329–346;

Bernstein, *Pacifism and Rebellion in the Writings of Herman Melville,* pp. 202–213;

Schiffman, "Melville's Final Stage, Irony: a Re-examination of *Billy Budd* Criticism," *American Literature*, XXII (May 1950), 128–136.

12. Weir, pp. 276–285; Rosenberry, p. 493.

13. Howard, p. 90.

14. Thompson, p. 382.

15. Bowen, p. 217.

16. *Ibid.,* pp. 222–223.

17. *Ibid.,* p. 217.

18. Bernstein, pp. 211, 209.

19. Carpenter, p. 74.

20. *Ibid.,* p. 82.

21. *Billy Budd, Sailor (An Inside Narrative)*, p. 129.

22. Carpenter, p. 79.

23. Ralph W. Willett, "Nelson and Vere: Hero and Victim in *Billy Budd, Sailor*," *PMLA*, LXXXII (October 1967), 376.

24. *Battle-Pieces*, in Howard P. Vincent, ed., *Collected Poems of Herman Melville*. See particularly "Lyon: Battle of Springfield Missouri" (pp. 11–14); "The Cumberland" (pp. 34–35); "Stonewall Jackson: Mortally Wounded at Chancellorsville" (pp. 52–53); "Stonewall Jackson (Ascribed to a Virginian)" (pp. 53–55); "Gettysburg: the Check" (pp. 55–56); "The Battle for the Bay" (pp. 72–76); and several of the "Verses Inscriptive and Memorial" (pp. 107–155).

25. *Ibid.* See particularly "Misgivings" (pp. 3–4); "Apathy and Enthusiasm" (pp. 8–9); "Ball's Bluff: A Reverie" (pp. 14–15); "The Battle for the Mississippi" (pp. 42–44); "Malvern Hill" (pp. 44–45); "The Armies of the Wilderness" (pp. 61–69); "The Released Rebel Prisoner" (pp. 99–100); "Magnanimity Baffled" (pp. 102–103); "On the Slain Collegians" (pp. 103–105).

26. *Ibid.*, p. 40.

3.

A New Kind of War Demands a New Kind of Treatment: The Civil War and the Birth of American Realism

In one of Ambrose Bierce's short stories concerned with the Civil War, "Chickamauga," a young boy who is deaf and mute wanders into a wood to play soldier; frightened by a rabbit, he runs aimlessly until, weary and worn out, he falls asleep. While he sleeps, a battle takes place in the forest, and upon awakening he discovers a host of wounded, mutilated, and dying soldiers all around him. Without comprehending his situation, he hops on the back of one of the crawling figures; the man, his chin blown off in battle, turns violently to knock the boy to the ground. Disturbed, but still not fully aware, he moves in the direction the men are pursuing: away from the battle and toward his home. He finds it aflame and discovers his mother dead:

> There, conspicuous in the light of the conflagration, lay the dead body of a woman—the white face turned upward, the hands thrown out and clutched full of grass, the clothing deranged, the long hair in tangles and full of clotted blood. The greater part of the forehead was torn away, and from the jagged hole the brain protruded, overflowing the temple, a frothy mass of gray, crowned with clusters of crimson bubbles—the work of a shell.[1]

So the boy, whose father was a soldier, and who himself, despite his physical handicaps, had learned enough of the military tradition to play soldier, discovers the horrors of war. As a deaf-mute, he can only gurgle and squawk in an attempt to voice his reaction; but, despite the fact that no communication of his terrible discovery seems possible, the story depicts the war as impersonal and indifferent—a purveyor of death and mutilation for combatants and noncombatants alike. Nothing like this had appeared in Melville's work, and certainly not in Cooper's.

Bierce is not representative of most of the writers of the Civil War, many of whom pour out romantic tales spiced with sectional vituperation.[2] He, on the contrary, with John William De Forest and Stephen Crane, is among a select few who treat war as no Americans had done before. To be sure, not one of them creates, as Melville did, an entire social structure for the purpose of universal political analysis, but they share Melville's interest in the dehumanization of man in the military machine and are much more explicit in detailing the physical and psychological impact of war. In their methods and in the very fact that they present the brutalities of conflict, they seem to be affected as much by the nature of the Civil War itself as by the literary trend toward realism and naturalism.

Opinion among military historians is universal in insisting upon the war either as the first "modern" war, or, at least, as significantly transitional insofar as it introduced most of the elements of total war. The development of new weaponry and new tactical and strategic conceptions changed and extended the areas of conflict from the limited warfare of the Revolution to a total commitment in which opposing economic and social structures attempted to annihilate each other. Walter Millis, while regarding it as more transitional than modern, nevertheless offers an impressive list of innovations that made the Civil War distinctive. They are many, and include the use of the rifle, armored warships without sail, machine guns, rifled field artillery, the marine mine, the torpedo, rudimentary submarines, telegraphy, and railroads and rivers as logistical routes. For the first time, soldiers disappeared into the ground as increased firepower necessitated the use of breastworks and trenches, for the first time factory lines in America became essential to the mass production of the materials of war, and for the first time the United States experienced general conscription.[3]

Bruce Catton, in commenting upon the changed nature of the Civil War, depicts the doom of the kind of horsemanship and heroics that Cooper presented in *The Spy* when he states that increased artillery-fire power finally brought an end to effective use of cavalry except for scouting purposes. But Catton goes on to suggest that the changes in warfare were due less to technical military innovations than to a revolution in attitudes on the part of the governments involved. Neither Washington nor Montgomery erected any barriers that would interfere with the successful prosecution of the war. For the first time, conflict was total—directed against the entire economic and social structure of the enemy with any weaponry and strategy one could devise to accomplish that objective. In an interesting parallel to war in the 1960s, Catton views the Northern use of Sherman's drive to devastate Georgia's productive capacity and Sheridan's destruction of agriculture in the Shenandoah Valley as prefigurements of the modern air strike—aimed, as they were, at denying the enemy the capacity to produce materials necessary for the war effort.[4] Identifying the war as the first distinctly modern conflict, he considers the impact of ideology that permitted total commitment:

> Consider for a moment the logical implications of this attitude. Ultimately, it is nothing less than the road to horror. It obliterates the moralities and restraints which the race has so carefully built up through many generations. If it has any kind of rational base, the rationale is nothing much loftier than a belief that the end justifies the means. It can —and does—put an entire nation at the mercy of its most destructive instincts. What you can do to your enemy comes, at last, to be limited not by any reluctance to inflict pain, misery, and death, and not by any feeling that there are limits to the things which a civilized people may do, but solely by your technical capacity to do harm. Without suffering any pangs of conscience, the group becomes prepared to do things which no single member of the group would for a moment contemplate.[5]

Thus, the industrial revolution, providing mass production of new weapons systems, led to a power morality in which force and techniques of force became the means whereby one government could impose its will upon another. Possession of technical superiority became, in and of itself, justification for its use; certainly, the rules of warfare in which Cooper believed were dying or dead. Millis insists that the ultimate effect of the industrial revolution on war was to reduce the individual soldier to "a lonely and frightened machine-tender." [6] Thus, if it had been possible to transform the Revolution into a pattern of imagined heroics, it became increasingly difficult to do so for the Civil War:

> The American Revolution (also in large part a civil war) had dragged on through seven years in a series of small engagements widely separated in time and place, the forces growing smaller and their impact on the community less as the years went by. The Civil War rose in a steady and terrible crescendo of violence, of shocking casualty lists, of complete commitment of life and fortune; it took but four years to beat the weaker side into an exhaustion and defeat more nearly "total" than even France had suffered in 1814 and 1815.[7]

War had become increasingly complex, increasingly dependent upon industrial production, and increasingly brutal, devastating, and impersonal: so much so, in fact, that a shell could fall from nowhere in the forest at Chickamauga to rip the life from a woman in her own home, leaving her helpless son an orphan. Bierce, De Forest, Crane, and a few others present this new kind of warfare, its impact upon the consciousness of its participants, and, by extension, its impact upon the consciousness of the nation as a whole. Just as the war was revolutionary in technique, so were they.

No major American writer was a combatant in the Civil War. William Dean Howells, as a reward for his campaign biography of Lincoln, received and accepted a diplomatic post in Italy.[8] Mark Twain, after some abortive forays on the Confederate side near his home in Hannibal, went west with his brother to Nevada.[9] Henry James's mysterious back injury seemed prohibitive, and Henry Adams, although occasionally conscience stricken, decided that helping his father with diplomatic chores in a hostile England was more important than becoming another man in a blue uniform. The aging Walt Whitman, in his task as male nurse in Washington, participated more directly than any other major writer. Of those participants who emerged as minor literary figures, John William De Forest and Ambrose Bierce produced the most significant material. De Forest's *Miss Ravenel's Conversion from Secession to Loyalty* appeared earliest and is cited in the *Literary History of the United States* as "the best story of the Civil War."

Carl Van Doren, Arthur Hobson Quinn, Stanley T. Williams, Gordon S. Haight, James F. Light, and Alexander Cowie praise De Forest as an innovator in the use of realism in the American novel. Haight and Quinn go so far as to praise him at Crane's expense, the former seeing Crane as a decadent impressionist and the latter suggesting that Crane was too journalistic. Edmund Wilson, in *Patriotic Gore: Studies in the Literature of the American Civil War,* praises De Forest as "the first of our writers of fiction to deal seriously with the events of the Civil War." [10]

Certainly, more than any other novelist, De Forest

had the kinds of experience enabling him to write knowingly about many areas of the war effort. He recruited a
company of volunteers in New Haven and, during six
and a half years in the army, saw a good deal of action,
including the siege of Port Hudson and Sheridan's Shenandoah campaign; he was mustered out in January 1868
after working in the Freedman's Bureau in Greenville,
South Carolina.[11] As an officer engaged in the manage-
ment of a fighting machine, De Forest might be expected
to reflect the patrician attitudes toward the common
soldier that were evidenced in Cooper. Occasionally De
Forest, in the autobiographical *A Volunteer's Adventures,*
and his fictional alter ego Captain Colburne, in *Miss
Ravenel's Conversion,* do view the men merely as parts
of a military unit.[12] For instance, De Forest is every inch
an officer when he, through Colburne, evaluates a corporal
fleeing battle:

> Every regiment has its two or three cowards, or per-
> haps its half-dozen, weakly-nerved creatures, whom
> nothing can make fight, and who never do fight. One
> abject hound, a corporal with his disgraced stripes
> upon his arm, came by with a ghastly backward
> glare of horror, his face colorless, his eyes projecting,
> and his chin shaking. Colburne cursed him for a
> poltroon, struck him with the flat of his sabre, and
> dragged him into the ranks of his own regiment; but
> the miserable creature was too thoroughly unmanned
> by the great horror of death to be moved to any
> show of resentment or even of courage by the indig-
> nity; he only gave an idiotic stare with outstretched
> neck toward the front, then turned with a nervous
> jerk like that of a scared beast and rushed rearward.
> (pp. 259–260)

More often than not, however, De Forest objectively communicates the horrors of conflict in both books. Colburne feels sick when he watches a man carried by who has had "half his foot torn off by a round shot, the splintered bones projecting clean and white from the ragged raw flesh . . ." (p. 260). He sees other wounds and deaths which De Forest usually describes laconically, reminding one of Crane: "Throwing up both hands he fell backward with an incoherent gurgle, pierced through the lungs by a rifle-ball. Then a little Irish soldier burst out swearing and hastily pulled his trousers to glare at a bullet-hole through the calf of his leg with a comical expression of mingled surprise, alarm, and wrath" (p. 263). In addition, he presents, for the first time in American war fiction, the conditions in which a military hospital operates in the field, and it is not much different from the situation in which Hemingway has Rinaldi express horror at his own butchery in *A Farewell to Arms*.

It [the field hospital] was simply an immense collection of wounded men in every imaginable condition of mutilation, every one stained more or less with his own blood, every one of a ghastly yellowish pallor, all lying in the open air on the bare ground or on their own blankets with no shelter except the friendly foliage of the oaks and beeches. In the centre of this mass of suffering stood several operating tables, each burdened by a grievously wounded man and surrounded by surgeons and their assistants. Underneath were great pools of clotted blood, amidst which lay amputated fingers, hands, arms, feet, and legs. . . . (p. 269)

But, despite the importance of his realistic technique,

De Forest does more than present the dehumanizing and barbaric conditions of war. In his juxtaposition of Captain Colburne and Colonel Carter he contrasts two types of American officer that have traditionally represented military alternatives for the United States—the citizen-soldier and the professional—and he makes judgments concerning the relative merit of the two.

One might apply the same kind of criticism to Colburne as Holden Caulfield applies to Frederick Henry.[13] Colburne takes himself quite seriously and is occasionally inclined to airs of superiority. In addition, he reflects both De Forest's self-consciousness on the race issue and his sense of ethnic superiority.[14] Despite these characteristics, however, he does provide the moral focus of the novel. It is with his reaction to the war that the reader comes to sympathize, and it is his growing disenchantment that provides much of the novel's tone. He goes to war because his moral consciousness forces him, and in a manner similar to Doctor Ravenel's idealism, he regards it as a cause (p. 64). In a sense, he fights for the kind of reason that Americans always like to think they fight for: in this case, to free an oppressed minority, in others to preserve the world for democracy or for the four freedoms, or, most recently and most unconvincingly, to save a "gallant small nation" in Southeast Asia. For the citizen-soldier, winning a war is an onerous task for which he takes time from his normal activities. Despite the fact that he is a part-time soldier, however, Colburne is presented as most effective in military tasks. He adapts himself to the hardships of life in the field in a way that makes his men admire him (pp. 254–255), and he leads by setting an example which his company follows (p. 257). He wishes to be where the great battles are fought in order to contribute more to the cause (p. 97), and when he and his men score a victory, he is not too self-conscious to shout, "We have whipped them. . . . Hurrah for the good old flag' " (p. 312). He may become disenchanted with the boredom and with the injustices he himself experiences and witnesses others experience, but his moral commitment to the overall objectives of the war remains firm. It is important that, in terms of his value as a moral focus, he receives no material benefit from the war—he is not politic enough to gain promotions and he refuses to pillage the conquered land for profit. At the end of hostilities Colburne returns home with nothing to show for his participation except the experience itself and his sense of moral achievement. Although De Forest does not develop fully this aspect of his hero's experience, Colburne is representative of a type that appears frequently in World War I fiction: the unrewarded returned veteran.

Lieutenant Colonel Carter, regular officer and West Point graduate, is at opposite poles from Colburne on almost all issues. While most critics concentrate on his sexual activities with Mrs. Larue as indicative of his immorality, it is more important for the purposes of this study that De Forest presents him as a military figure in sharp opposition to democratic practices. He is the first in a long line of regular officers in the American military novel—among them General Cummings in *The Naked and the Dead* and most recently General Scott *in Seven Days in May* [15]—who embody the totalitarian tendencies of the professional military and are in conflict with the hopes and intentions of American political liberalism.

De Forest never suggests that Carter is inadequate as a leader of men. On the contrary, he is an officer who gets his troops to perform well. His charges may not love him but they greatly respect his capabilities, even to the point where "a word of praise from him was cherished by officer or soldier as a medal of honor" (p. 222). An obsequious underling, Van Zandt, describes him as not " 'one of those plebeian humbugs whom our ridiculous Democracy delights to call nature's gentlemen' " (p. 402). He is, in Van Zandt's words, " 'a gentleman born and bred' " (p. 402), and it is in his sense of traditional aristocracy that Carter initially differs from Colburne. He sets himself up in magnificent settings during the occupation of New Orleans (pp. 175 ff.) and clearly feels that to the victor belong the spoils of prestige and material gain. His extravagant nature leads him eventually to financial dishonesty (pp. 287–390) and his sexual needs lead him into adultery with Mrs. Larue, but, after all, these moral shortcomings are commonplace among men both at war and at peace. Indeed, his financial dishonesty is at least partially caused by his desire to provide his wife with comforts beyond his means, and although he strays into infidelity, he feels a great deal of guilt about it (p. 279). It is rather in his application of an aristocratic politics of élitism that he reveals the essential shortcoming of his character in terms of American political process. He is highhanded in his use of military courts (p. 221), allows little room for differences of opinion among his staff, and seeks generally to manipulate everyone in his command. His position, within the structure, is that of absolute dictator, and he insists on the prerogatives of that position.

De Forest comments that "as commanding officer of a brigade he exhibited his usual energy, practical ability, and beneficent despotism" (p. 216). Of course, one might argue legitimately that despotism within a military structure, if applied to the accomplishment of mission objectives, is often necessary and sometimes beneficial. But it is clear that De Forest wishes to place Carter's despotic tendencies in a larger context. For instance, when the colonel realizes that war is imminent, he goes to the governor of Barataria, a fictional New England state, and offers a plan for mobilization of the population which would lead to a totalitarian state:

> "Now's the chance. We are going to have a long war. I want the State to be prepared and come out strong; it's the grandest chance she'll ever have to make herself famous. I've been to see the Governor. I said to him, 'Governor, now's your chance; now's the chance for Barataria; now's my chance. It's going to be a long war. Don't depend on volunteering—it won't last. Get a militia system ready which will classify the whole population, and bring it into the fight as fast as it's needed. Make the State a Prussia. If you'll allow me, I'll draw up a plan which shall make Barataria a military community, and put her at the head of the Union for moral and physical power. Appoint me your chief of staff, and I'll not only draw up the plan, but put it in force.' "
> (pp. 30–31)

When the governor demurs on the basis that he must be responsive to public opinion and such a course of action would spell disaster at the polls, Carter condescendingly concedes the governor's political practicality, but states that " 'he is a fool by the eternal laws of military reason' " (p. 31). It seems clear that the eternal laws to which Carter alludes are those identified by Samuel Huntington in *The Soldier and the State: The Theory and Politics of Civil-Military Relations* as typical of the military's definition of reality—an essentially conservative definition in which conflict is viewed as inevitable and social amelioration as illusory.[16] Unlike Colburne, Carter is not interested in any moral rationale for the war, and De Forest hints that the colonel regards all attempts at moral justification of the conflict as mere rationalization. As revealed in conversation with Colburne, he could fight on either side with equal commitment: " 'I expected to be a second Cortez. Not that I cared much about their pro-slavery projects and palaverings. I was a soldier of fortune, only anxious for active service, pay and promotion' " (p. 106).

Thus, by his own testament, Carter is the complete opposite of Colburne. The citizen-soldier, regarding war as a disaster to society, will take time out from his usual way of life to fight in a cause which he regards as moral and just; the regular officer, regarding war as a chance for personal advancement and an exercise in professional skill, may also try to change the political structure, amidst the pressures of war, to more closely resemble the totalitarian structure with which he is familiar and in which he wields his power. That De Forest creates two distinct types of American officer in Colburne and Carter is certain; that he admires the citizen-soldier and criticizes the professional is obvious; and it also seems that his condemnation of the professional is greatly influenced by political considerations, notably Carter's tendency toward totalitarianism. Like Melville, De Forest presents a beneficent despot; unlike Melville, he does not surround him with the troublesome universal issue of freedom and authority. One could argue, however, that Carter is more honest than Vere concerning his role as a professional military man. He is a mercenary who wishes to make use of his skill, and he is "anxious for active service, pay and promotion."

De Forest's value, then, to the development of the American novel, while resting solidly on his contribution to early realism, also must include his perceptiveness in presenting different types within the American military and his awareness of the political implications involved in a military definition of reality. It is true that Carter dies as a Brigadier General "in the wild joy of successful battle" (p. 423), but it is also true that, as an embodiment of traditional authoritarianism and as a threat to democratic processes, he has been vividly portrayed. Like Cummings, Scott, and others, he cannot be dismissed as a buffoon. In fact, to the contemporary reader, Carter's admission of self-interest, his sexuality, and his desire for power seem realistic when compared with Colburne's occasional priggishness. He is the first fascinating figure in a long line of soldiers in the American military novel who believe in a conservative and military definition of reality.

Ambrose Bierce, unlike De Forest, is not interested in political issues in his war fiction. As the earlier discussion of "Chickamauga" reveals, he is concerned primarily with the horrors and anomalies of the new kind of warfare that the Civil War produced. Although not a novelist, he creates in a collection of stories, *In the Midst of Life*,[17] a gallery of stark, perhaps surrealistic, pictures of war, which can hardly be surpassed in their portrayal of individual instances of barbarism and brutality. He himself fought at Shiloh, Chickamauga, and Chattanooga, and at Kenesaw Mountain where he suffered a head wound.[18] He performed well in the service, rising from private through the noncommissioned ranks to a battlefield commission and finally a formal commission as an officer.[19] He personally admired his commander, General W. B. Hazen,[20] and one critic suggests that Bierce modeled much of his personality after Hazen's.[21]

Whatever the quality of his performance as a soldier, his stories concerned with the war reveal a bitterness

typical of Bierce.[22] Indeed the war seems a perfect setting
for the portrayal of the pointlessness and absurdity of
man's position in the universe. It is brutal, chaotic, and
unintelligible, and man, engaged in war, becomes the play-
thing of chance and circumstance. Bierce is occasionally
heavy handed in his use of obvious irony, but despite this
shortcoming he forcefully communicates the sense of helplessness and horror that the individual feels when trapped
in the barbaric business of mechanized war. In a passage
resembling Hemingway's "A Natural History of the
Dead," Bierce toys with the conception of traditional
honor:

> Here and there a dead man, his clothing defiled with
> earth, his face covered with a blanket or showing
> yellow and clay-like in the rain, added his dispiriting
> influence to that of the other dismal features of the
> scene and augmented the general discomfort with a
> particular dejection. Very repulsive these wrecks
> looked—not at all heroic, and nobody was accessible
> to the infection of their patriotic example. Dead
> upon the field of honor, yes; but the field of honor
> was so very wet! It makes a difference.[23]

The great conciseness of his insistence upon the
reality of the wet field destroys the imagined heroics of
death for one's country. He goes on to describe how
wounded men left in the field can be mutilated by a herd
of swine, literally eaten alive (pp. 56–57). In contrast to
Cooper, he debunks public heroism and shows it to be
destructive (pp. 29, 44), and, unlike Cooper, who sentimentalizes women, Bierce characterizes one woman as a
snake whose desire for heroics brings a man to his death
(p. 45). This is not a war in which men ride proudly on

the face of the land; it is a war in which they must burrow into the ground for protection (pp. 41, 43). Individual acts of heroism are possible, but Bierce usually shows them to be stupid, egotistical, and inevitably, inconsequential (pp. 29, 44). His is a world in which a general officer, knowingly and maliciously, orders an artillery officer to destroy his own home and family because the man's wife had once insulted the general (pp. 47–53). It is a naturalistic world in which men are constantly described in terms of other animals: rats, bears, swine. It is a world in which death descends impersonally and without meaning. In one instance, Jerome Searing, a Union scout, discovers a line of Confederate soldiers in retreat and decides to shoot into the moving men in order at least to claim one life. Bierce uses the incident to portray the ultimate impersonality of this kind of warfare:

> But it was decreed from the beginning of time that Private Searing was not to murder anybody that bright summer morning, nor was the Confederate retreat to be announced by him. For countless ages events had been so matching themselves together in that wondrous mosaic to some parts of which, dimly discernible, we give the name of history, that the acts which he had in will would have marred the harmony of the pattern. Some twenty-five years previously the Power charged with the execution of the work according to the design had provided against that mischance by causing the birth of a certain male child in a little village at the foot of the Carpathian Mountains, had carefully reared it, supervised its education, directed its desires into a military channel, and in the due time made it an officer of artillery. (p. 32)

This officer, killing time, orders a battery to fire upon a hill on which a group of Union officers seem to be gathered. The shot flies over the target and toward the scout who thought he would claim a life.

> As Jerome Searing drew back the hammer of his rifle and with his eyes upon the distant Confederates considered where he could plant his shot with the best hope of making a widow or an orphan or a childless mother,—perhaps all three, for Private Searing, although he repeatedly refused promotion, was not without a certain kind of ambition,—he heard a rushing sound in the air, like that made by the wings of a great bird swooping down upon its prey. More quickly than he could apprehend the gradation, it increased to a hoarse and horrible roar, as the missile that made it sprang at him out of the sky, striking with a deafening impact one of the posts supporting the confusion of timbers above him, smashing it into matchwood, and bringing down the crazy edifice with a loud clatter, in clouds of blinding dust! (p. 33)

More than any other single incident, this passage sums up Bierce's view of man in the midst of war. He is either ironic in his description of a great "design" ordering these events or he views the traditional Christian God as the great practical joker in the sky. In either case, man is helpless and in the hands of circumstance, and "bravery" is reduced to producing corpses, widows, orphans, and childless mothers. That this "bravery" is absurd Bierce underscores later in the story when he has Union officers mistake the dead Searing for a Confederate

(p. 40). More than either De Forest or Crane, Bierce communicates the unadorned brutality of war as practiced in
the Civil War, and he does so in short, almost imagistic,
pieces that resemble Hemingway's *In Our Time*. Stuart
C. Woodruff, in *The Short Stories of Ambrose Bierce: A
Study in Polarity,* sees the Civil War as the pivotal experi-
etnce in Bierce's life, and entitles a chapter on his war
fiction with a phrase that sums up the change from
Cooper and the Revolution to Bierce and the Civil War:
"War as the Drama of Lost Illusions." [24]

Stephen Crane's treatment of the war contains elements present in both *Miss Ravenel's Conversion* and *In
the Midst of Life*. Like Bierce, he concentrates on the
horrors of war and presents them in a similar way, depicting a chaotic and absurd situation in which a regiment's action, despite widespread death and mutilation,
is inconsequential. Like De Forest's concentration on Colburne, he traces the effects of war on a single figure,
Henry Fleming, whose point of view, like Colburne's,
provides the novel's central focus. The two heroes, however, are dramatically different. Colburne goes to war for
theoretical and moral reasons; as an officer he is responsible for the welfare of others; and he comes away from
the conflict embittered and disappointed. Fleming goes
to war in pursuit of romantic adventure; as a private he
is responsible only for himself, and he finds in the war
the means of attaining social acceptance and, in his own
short-sighted view, maturity and manhood. Crane, like
Melville, considers the enlisted man in detail, but unlike
Melville, he does not make his hero a sympathetic figure.
Each in his own way, White Jacket and Billy Budd
achieve transcendence over the social structure in which
they live. Henry Fleming, the most common of men,
merely desires acceptance within the social structure of

the regiment. Crane, rather than presenting him sympathetically, treats him with merciless detachment, and
Fleming finally emerges as a self-seeking, ignorant boy
who needs, above all else, group acceptance and the praise
of his peers. *The Red Badge of Courage,* in its detailed
concentration on the consciousness of a single enlisted
man caught in circumstances over which he has little
or no control, looks forward to the novels of World War I
more than any other long piece of American nineteenth-
century fiction—but its tone is much different. For instance, Hemingway, possibly because of a close identification with the values Frederick Henry embodies, tends to
sentimentalize his hero. Crane never loses his detachment.
His novel may be an identifiable forerunner of *A Farewell to Arms* and *Three Soldiers,* but Henry Fleming is
not the idealized hero Lieutenant Henry is, and, if he
resembles a figure in Dos Passos' book, it is not John
Andrews, the aesthetic and moral center of the novel,
but rather Fuselli, who craves acceptance and who mistakenly sees in the social structure of the army his means
of attaining prestige and status.

Scholars and critics are divided over the character of
Fleming. Traditionally, *The Red Badge of Courage* has
been regarded as a story in which a boy, withstanding the
pressures of battle, overcomes fear and attains maturity.
Robert W. Schneider recently added a new wrinkle to
this interpretation in *Five Novelists of the Progressive
Era;* he sees Henry Fleming attaining maturity when he
gives up the arrogance of self and becomes "bound up in
the feeling of brotherhood" during the charge with the
regiment the day following his flight.[25] From this admira-
tion of Henry there are shades of descending opinion
through various greys to black. Robert Spiller thinks the
boy achieves self-conquest but does so at the direction of

forces over which he has no control.[26] George Snell sees Henry as "a molecule caught in a vast explosion." [27] Ihab Habib Hassan suggests that the hero is never fully initiated; rather, that the book presents "the subtleties of self-deception, and the vast, brutal anonymity of war, in which the private response and the public demand are so fiercely, so hopelessly, at odds." He thinks that Henry may feel his initiation is complete, but Crane does not.[28] Charles Walcutt, in *American Literary Naturalism,* represents a position opposite to Schneider's, rejecting the notion that Henry achieves social identification and proposing that the primary thing the novel proves is that Henry is absolutely unable to evaluate his own behavior —that the hero's motives are always "vain, selfish, ignorant, and childish." [29] John Berryman, whose interest in Crane seems as extensive as anyone's, appears to agree with Walcutt, suggesting the absurdity of Henry's final view of his own experience and his place in the universe: "In short we are left after all with a *fool,* for Crane knew as well as the next man, and much better, that life consists of very little but struggle." [30]

Robert Wooster Stallman, in a note on the ending of the novel in his *Stephen Crane: An Omnibus,* sees in its romantic tone Crane's hint that Henry has learned nothing, that his personality has undergone no significant change.[31] An examination of Henry's character throughout the book reveals much the same thing.

Almost every conclusion Henry forms during the course of the novel is wrong. He vacillates wildly, constantly changing his position until Crane reveals him as incapable of thought except as a means of rationalizing positions forced upon him by the circumstances of his environment. He is wrong, near the beginning of the novel, in picturing his comrades as possessing immense amounts of courage; he is wrong when he then pictures them all quaking with fear.[32] He is wrong when he thinks that he has been dragged to war by a merciless government (p. 248); in truth, his own gullibility and romantic self-delusion have done the job. He is wrong when he pictures himself as possessing "profound and fine senses" which his lieutenant would never understand (p. 253). He is wrong in his analysis of the military situation after the first Confederate attack is repulsed. It is then that he pictures himself as having passed the supreme test when, just moments before he fleees, he feels he has vanquished the "red, formidable difficulties of war" (p. 265). He is wrong in expecting that his regiment would fold under the pressure of that attack (p. 267). He is wrong when he thinks that all the soldiers he meets can see his guilt (p. 282). He is wrong about the greeting his comrades will give him when he returns to camp (p. 298). He is wrong when he pictures the entire battle as lost to the Confederates (p. 300).

Even after he has discovered real suffering among the column of wounded and dying, he still maintains the capacity to envision himself in an absurdly romantic posture: "Swift pictures of himself, apart, yet in himself, came to him—a blue desperate figure leading lurid charges with one knee forward and a broken blade high— a blue, determined figure standing before a crimson and steel assault, getting calmly killed on a high place before the eyes of all" (p. 294). Even after the discovery of Jim Conklin's death, he can still romanticize about his own: "He thought of the magnificent pathos of his own dead body" (p. 294). Even after his return to camp and the marvelous treatment afforded him by members of the regiment, particularly the loud soldier, Wilson, he fails to comprehend the need for understanding and forgiveness.

In fact, he feels superior to his friend because of the incident in which Wilson, fearing death, had given him the packet of letters: "He now rejoiced in the possession of a small weapon with which he could prostrate his comrade at the first signs of a cross-examination. He was master. It would be he who could laugh and shoot the shafts of derision" (p. 318). He, the man who had run, adopts toward the man who apparently had stayed and fought, "an air of patronizing good humor" (p. 319). He comes to possess a scorn for the others who had run, feeling that he had fled with style while they had not. At last, one must recognize that the single index of behavior that Henry respects is the judgment of the social world in which he functions: "He had performed his mistakes in the dark, so he was still a man" (p. 319). Crane's prose drips with irony when he describes his hero's newly found knowledge: "A man with a full stomach and the respect of his fellows had no business to scold about anything he might think to be wrong in the ways of the universe, or even with the ways of society. Let the unfortunates rail; the others may play marbles" (p. 319).

In short, Henry Fleming learns nothing during his escape from the regiment, the societal representative in the novel, except that he must return to it and have the respect of its members. His wanderings alone, his confrontation with an indifferent universe, his discovery of the reality of pointless death: all are meaningless. In the end, he is as he was at the beginning. Indeed, his feeling at the close of the novel that he has conquered cowardice may be as illusory as his same conviction after the first Confederate attack. He is a hero without any means of evaluating his behavior except through the approval of the social structure he so urgently needs. His delirious heroics during the second day of battle, performed while he "was not a man but a member" (p. 261), ironically provide his only basis for the assumption of his manhood: "He saw that he was good. He recalled with a thrill of joy the respectful comments of his fellows upon his conduct" (p. 366). As long as he has that approval, his thoughts of the day before seem absurd to him: "In his rebellion, he had been very portentous, no doubt, and sincere, and anxious for humanity, but now that he stood safe, with no lack of blood, it was suddenly clear to him that he had been wrong not to kiss the knife and bow to the cudgel" (p. 367).

Thus, it seems clear that one of Crane's central concerns in *The Red Badge of Courage* is the nature of the relationship of the individual soldier to the social unit. In creating a protagonist as ignorant and as unheroic as Henry, he managed to depict the need for conformity, the capability "to kiss the knife and bow to the cudgel," while avoiding the editorialization that seems inevitable when the protagonist is sensitive and aesthetic as, for instance, Noah Ackerman in Irwin Shaw's *The Young Lions.* Despite his hero's shallow motivation and his inability to break through the inadequacies of his own ego, Crane manages, for the first time in the history of the American military novel, to depict the utter helplessness of the individual within the impersonal framework of a social unit engaged in a massive and mechanized war.

The crucial question one must ask when analyzing *The Red Badge of Courage* is whether Henry's reassimilation into the unit is victory or defeat. Certainly, he needs such assimilation. The revelation of his character, as he wanders alone through the forest, discovering death in an impersonal universe, suggests that he is unable to live with the discoveries he makes. Jim Conklin's death suggests what nature has in store for the individual and

Henry fearfully recognizes that he needs the protection of the social unit, that his safety demands depersonalization and group direction.

Although his hero must become a member, Crane is also merciless in his presentation of the social unit in which Henry envisions his personal salvation. Certainly, the imagery the novelist employs to describe the regiment is never complimentary. In an early episode that depicts Henry's larger plight, the young soldier internally rebels against the authoritarian structure that denies his freedom—a structure that can order him to march and fight anywhere it pleases (p. 239)—but, after this brief expression of rebelliousness, he feels "compelled to sink back into his old place as part of a blue demonstration" (p. 238). He is helpless to express himself within a structure that overpowers the individual. When the regiment is on the march, Crane describes it as "one of those moving monsters wending with many feet" (p. 240), and he presents Henry's complete and abject entrapment within the body of this monster: "But he instantly saw that it would be impossible for him to escape the regiment. It enclosed him. And there were iron laws of tradition and law on four sides. He was in a moving box" (p. 248). Individual members within this box may discuss strategy in an effort to decipher where they will march and fight, but they are usually wrong (p. 255).

Crane seems to suggest that it is absurd for them to consider their individual interests because the "moving box" is impersonally packaged by forces and authorities the masses never see. Early in the novel, Henry may resent the feeling that he is merely a member of a mob (p. 248), but after the frightening discoveries of his flight alone, he has no recourse but to return to it. The regiment comes to possess an identity greater than the sum of its individual parts, and Crane continues to describe it as either organic and compelling or as machinelike and enclosing. It bleeds (p. 265), it creaks (p. 267), it punishes (p. 297), it breathes (p. 336), it snorts and blows (p. 339). When an attack begins to wane, it is "a machine run down" (p. 345). Assuredly, it contains all of its members, and, as long as the war continues, it permits death or maiming as the only escapes. The fact that Henry must lie in order to be reaccepted into the social unit (p. 307) suggests that it operates in a world of appearance and illusion, and, when he awakes the morning after his return to the regiment, he thinks that he is in the house of the dead (p. 313). In a sense, he is right; for, if Crane's suggestions are properly interpreted here, he is saying that one must permit the death of his manhood in order to become a member of the social organization—to become not a man but a member in the totalitarian machine of the military.

Thus, the question one must continue to ask involves the issue of when Henry is more a coward: when he runs from battle toward aloneness in the forest or when, discovering the ultimate end of nature's ways—death in the green chapel, the ants eating at the face of a decaying corpse—he begins running back toward the social unit as an agent to protect him from such reality: "Then he began to run in the direction of the battle. He saw that it was an ironical thing for him to be running thus toward that which he had been at such pains to avoid" (p. 276). The young soldier has discovered two horrors, being in a moving box and being alone in nature, and, instinctively and primitively, he chooses the relative protection of the social unit. He will lie to reenter the unit, and out of fear he fights the next day as a member of the blue demonstration: "The men, pitching forward insanely, had burst into cheerings, moblike and barbaric, but tuned in strange keys that can arouse the dullard and the stoic. It made a mad enthusiasm that, it seemed, would be incapable of checking itself before granite and brass. There was the delirium that encounters despair and death, and is heedless and blind to the odds" (p. 339). Thus Henry, in the effort to attain the appreciation of his peers, and particularly the appreciation of the officer who had called Henry's unit "mule drivers" and "mud diggers" (p. 358), performs mindlessly and deliriously— but according to the dictates of the social unit, he performs well. Is this victory or defeat? Crane, it might be argued, leaves the issue open and ambiguous, but he seems to weight the evidence on the side of defeat. First, of course, is the fact that all of Henry's heroics are unconscious:

> It was revealed to him that he had been a barbarian, a beast. He had fought like a pagan who defends his religion. Regarding it, he saw that it was fine, wild, and, in some ways, easy. He had been a tremendous figure, no doubt. By this struggle he had overcome obstacles which he had admitted to be mountains. They had fallen like paper peaks, and he was now what he called a hero. And he had not been aware of the process. He had slept and, awakening, found himself a knight. (p. 331)

Crane is careful to state that Henry regards himself as a hero, but one wonders, with Hassan, if the author agrees. It is important to remember that at no time does Crane present the regiment in imagery connoting approval of its existence or its purposes. Indeed, this monster machine is made up of members who, like Henry,

are usually wrong in their opinions and inevitably mistake appearance for reality. Henry's "wound" is accepted,
mistakenly, as a mark of heroism; and within the structure the ultimate authority figure, a general officer, gains
a victory not because he understands the battle situation
but because his orders are not carried out (p. 271). The
red badge of courage that Henry so values is presented
as no guarantee of manhood and wisdom; one man who
had been wounded on picket duty merely becomes more
pretentious and absurd (p. 256). Finally, at the very
moment that Henry awakes to find himself a knight,
Crane undercuts the idea of any heroics by presenting the
thrashing, screaming, and dying Jimmie Rogers (p. 333).
For the first time in American fiction, a general, watching
a battle before him, can be pictured as "a businessman
whose market is swinging up and down" (p. 271). All is
absurd, chaotic, accidental, and any "heroism" one might
achieve in such a situation may be just as absurd and
certainly as accidental.

Thus, the internal evidence seems to indicate that
Henry achieves no victory, and, when one considers the
dark view of the universe and of society that Crane
creates in many of the poems,[33] in *Maggie: A Girl of the
Streets,* in "George's Mother," and in "The Monster,"
one must agree with the view that Crane is ironic in his
treatment of his hero's closing view of himself and the
universe, in his rejection of those who saw dark land-
scapes, and in his absurd sense of self-importance. Indeed,
a glance at such external evidence as short stories like
"A Mystery of Heroism" and "The Little Regiment" reveals that he substantiates the sense of pointless destruction that he presents in *The Red Badge of Courage.*

"A Mystery of Heroism" particularly resembles *Red
Badge* insofar as it contains an example of pointless cour-

age wherein a young man, pressured by his peers, risks his life for a worthless objective.[34] In addition, in the story "The Veteran" Crane details an act of "heroism" performed by an aged Henry Fleming long after the end of the Civil War. Confronted by a fire on his farm which threatens to destroy much of his livestock, Fleming reacts with what appears to be instinctive courage, running into a burning barn several times to rescue animals. But Crane tells the reader that upon hearing the news of the catastrophe, Henry's "face ceased instantly to be a face; it became a mask, a gray thing, with horror written about the mouth and eyes." He acts instinctively while other men stumble, but in so doing he brings on self-immolation, in order to save two colts. While one is tempted to admire the old man's courage, one must also ask to whom does he owe his primary commitments: to the colts or to the "old woman" who seems to be his wife and to his grandson, Jim.[35]

Crane insists that Fleming's mind is vacant at the moment he races for the colts—just as his mind went blank during his previous acts of "heroism." Thus, "The Veteran" seems almost a *précis* of *Red Badge*. Just as in the novel the youthful Henry leaves his primary obligation to his mother and to his farm in order to pursue a romantic notion of warfare and manhood, so the old man Henry blindly ignores his responsibility to wife and family in a compulsive moment of mindlessness. It would seem that, as Crane suggests near the close of the novel, his hero has learned nothing.

He felt that he was the child of the powers. Through the peace of his heart, he saw the earth to be a garden in which grew no weeds of agony. Or, perhaps, if there did grow a few, it was in obscure corners where no one was obliged to encounter them unless a ridiculous search was made. And, at any rate, they were tiny ones.

He returned to his old belief in the ultimate, astounding success of his life. He, as usual, did not trouble about processes. It was ordained, because he was a fine creation. He saw plainly that he was chosen of some gods. By fearful and wonderful roads he was to be led to a crown. He was, of course, satisfied that he deserved it. (p. 320)

Thus Stephen Crane, in *The Red Badge of Courage,* is the first American novelist to present war as chaotic and absurd, an experience without meaning; he is the first to present the plight of the average man amidst such circumstances; and he is the first to debunk the conception of traditional heroism. Bruce Catton stated that a a war like the Civil War was a road to horror. Crane, Bierce, and De Forest portray that new kind of warfare in a manner that will occur again and again in the fiction that emerges from the two world wars.

Unfortunately, these three writers were the exceptions rather than the rule. Robert A. Lively bemoans the fact "that the mass of Civil War novels flows out in the sluggish stream which has been described as 'subliterary,' " and he describes the typical novel of the war as "the artistic monstrosity of a political pamphlet embedded in fiction. In addition, elements of romance were mixed freely with the politics:

In this costume war when young lovers were not keeping trysts in no-man's land, they were involving themselves as daring spies, brave ladies, loathsome villains, and foursquare heroes in remarkably improbable situations, for the performance of incredible deeds. Their brass buttons and shoulder straps were mounted on costumes, not uniforms; and smoke or blood rarely stained them. Such appropriation of the war scene for fanciful romance appeared very early. . . .[36]

Although this is not the place for detailed analysis of the numerous historical novels that have treated the war, a brief survey of some of the novels that appeared during the nineteenth century might be useful. Also, it would be well to remember that the Civil War recently has interested better writers than those who have dealt with the Revolution. Certainly, Joseph Stanley Pennell's *The History of Rome Hanks* and MacKinlay Kantor's *Long Remember* and *Andersonville* are far more meaningful and truthful novels about war than the efforts of Bruce Lancaster or John Brick discussed in Chapter One.

John Esten Cooke's *Surry of Eagle's Nest: or, the Memoirs of a Staff-Officer Serving in Virginia* fulfills Lively's pessimistic description and is an absurdly romantic novel.[37] The hero is haunted by the face of a girl whose handkerchief he has (pp. 17–18); a distraught woman in white appears out of nowhere (pp. 31–33); a beautiful woman rescues a daring and handsome man (p. 48); an officer wears "his uniform with the air of a man born in it" (p. 95); a dashing woman, naturally not a camp follower, rides with the troops (pp. 121–127); a man dies with a smile on his lips presumably because he knows that he dies in a good cause (p. 177). In short, bathos abounds. At one point, the hero rhetorically asks: "Did you ever lie upon a sofa, my dear reader, while recovering from a gunshot wound, and pass the hours listening to a musical voice reading to you—the voice of the woman

you loved, but who, unfortunately, was engaged to another individual" (p. 143). Most readers, one trusts, answer
"no" with a laugh. At another point, Surry describes a
fellow officer: "I loved and admired him as the pearl of
honor, the flower of chivalry" (p. 203). In short, knights
(one supposes of the variety Henry Fleming wished to be)
and damsels act out parts against the tableau of the war.
Some barbarity appears, but only to show how dastardly
the Union army could be (p. 157); naturally, Southerners
are never so. Finally, Miss Beverley grows to love Surry,
and, despite the fact that her cruel father wishes her to
marry "that hound," Baskerville, she sticks to her guns
and becomes "the queenly rose of 'Eagle's Nest' . . ." (p.
427). Surprisingly, Arthur Hobson Quinn called the book
"one of the best pictures of the Civil War in American
fiction." [38]

While others approach the absurdity of Cooke's
novel, many contain redeeming features. T. C. De Leon,
in *John Holden, Unionist, a Romance of the Days of
Destruction and Reconstruction,* states in his preface that
the intention of the novel is "to place before its readers
a plain picture of the time embraced by it. . . ." Despite
realistic elements in contrast to Cooke's unabashed romanticism, he hardly fulfills his intention. While John Holden
becomes a focus for criticism of the war and of the Confed-
eracy (pp. 28, 29–30), other characters, such as Lieutenant
Beverly Latham and Jen Freeman, are representatives of
the romantic tradition.[39] At one point, in fact, Miss Freeman leads General Forrest in a victorious raid. Thus,
despite his testament that he aims at truth, De Leon is
victimized by romance, and although he is more truthful
than Cooke, he offers no real consideration of the military
either in terms of social structure or political implication.
J. T. Trowbridge's *Cudjo's Cave* is less concerned

with the war and more with the wickedness of slavery. The Negro, particularly Pomp, emerges as nature's nobleman, and is responsible for rescuing the Caucasian hero, Penn, a Quaker who has been sentenced to death by a court-martial that is a mockery of justice. But the criticism of the Confederate army has a sectional ring to it as Southerners in general emerge as evil suppressors. Romantic elements remain as Virginia, the heroine, caught in a "conflagration" and attacked by a bear, is rescued by her beloved Penn and good old Cudjo. Trowbridge moralizes a great deal about love and the novel frequently degenerates into maudlin sentimentality. At the close, one is led to believe that a bright new day is dawning for Negro and Caucasian alike and that tyranny is inevitably self-defeating.[40] One wonders what Trowbridge's reaction would be to racial tension and urban violence in the United States of the 1960s.

Epes Sargent's *Peculiar: a Tale of the Great Transition* also dramatizes the cruelty of the slave system but offers even less in the way of treatment of the war or the military. Joel Chandler Harris, in *Tales of the Home Folks in Peace and War,* is more concerned with the destruction of Southern social structure than with the war itself, but he does envision warfare as the thrust of irrational barbarity through the thin crust of man's civilization.[41] In *On the Plantation: A Story of a Georgia Boy's Adventures During the War,* he presents warfare unheroically.[42] The issue, however, is not central to the novel. Virginius Dabney's *The Story of Don Miff as Told by His Friend John Bouche Whacker: A Symphony of Life,* has a structurally interesting opening in which the author converses with a Chinaman and some Sterne-like irony in depicting romance, but it turns out to be little more than a pro-Confederacy tract in which the antebellum South emerges as a paradise on earth.[43] The title itself is enough to put off most readers, but Dabney's use of a fictional narrator displays good technique for this kind of novel and enables him occasionally to toy with ideas—a development normally missing in the sectional novels of the Civil War.

Joseph Kirkland, Henry Morford, Harold Frederic, and Sidney Lanier, while not of the caliber of De Forest, Bierce, and Crane, are much more significant novelists of the war than those just discussed.

Morford, particularly, breaks new ground. In *The Days of Shoddy: A Novel of the Great Rebellion in 1861*, published in 1863, he anticipates De Forest's concern with corruption produced by the circumstances of war. In fact, Charles Holt is the first war profiteer to appear in American fiction, anticipating Arthur Miller's Joe Keller of *All My Sons* and that ultimate profiteer, Milo Mindenbinder, of Joseph Heller's *Catch-22*. Holt is a totally immoral man, not only profiting from the war but also attempting to seduce Mary Haviland, whose husband, Bartnett, has melodramatically refused a commission in order to fight for right in the enlisted ranks. Therein lies a clue to the basic problem with Morford's fiction as a whole. His penchant for melodrama leads him to present Holt as unequivocally evil, a villain par excellence, and Mary as the heroine in distress. The fact that Morford's intention is serious is revealed in passages in which he condemns war profiteers in general, but he lacks detachment when concretizing his ideas in characters. He is consciously antiromantic concerning war, but his descriptions of battle tend to be generalized and textbookish. Despite the melodramatic tone, however, Morford in *Days of Shoddy* dares to criticize the American businessman and the American middle-class family, detailing some terribly bitter scenes between Holt and his alcoholic wife, Olympia.[44]

In *Shoulder-Straps: A Novel of New York and the Army, 1862,* also published in 1863, Morford again develops a melodramatic plot line in which Colonel Egbert Crawford is slowly poisoning the hero, Richard, in order to take Mary from him. Despite this, however, Morford does speak out against the loss of life caused by military mismanagement, depicts corruption in the army, and presents a Union camp as a den of drunkenness.[45] In *The Coward: A Novel of Society and the Field in 1863,* Morford presents a hero, Carlton Brand, deathly afraid of combat, who finally conquers his fears. As in *Shoddy,* a daring sexual theme is introduced: Doctor Pomeroy's seduction of his ward, Eleanor Hill. Again, however, the tone is melodramatic: the girl succumbs when her heart "had proved traitor to her senses and all the guardian angels of her maidenhood had fled away. . . ." Again Morford attacks war profiteers and the barbarity of warfare.[46]

In the prefaces to *Shoulder-Straps* and *The Coward,* Morford announces that he will not treat the military in any great detail and his lack of experience evidently prohibited him from doing so, but it is clear from his presentation of the war's effects upon the nation that he envisioned the coming of the gilded age:

> . . . a synonym for *miserabe pretence* in *patriotism—* a shadow without a substance. Shoddy coats, shoddy shoes, shoddy blankets, shoddy tents, shoddy horses, shoddy arms, shoddy ammunition, shoddy boats, shoddy beef and bread, shoddy bravery, shoddy liberality, shoddy patriotism, shoddy loyalty, shoddy statesmanship, shoddy personal devotion,—these and

dozens of other ramifications of deception have gone to make up the application of the name. . . .[47]

Frederic's *The Copperhead* is much more truthful in its treatment of the conditions surrounding war than was his novel of the Revolution, *In the Valley*. Although the war is not treated directly, its impact on the lives of a dissenting Northern family is presented in all its brutality. After Jeff Beech goes to war, the family hears nothing of him and must be content with reports of the dead and wounded. He returns, not in glory but without an arm, and in a condition similar to the soldier in Hamlin Garland's "The Return of the Private": "The common soldier of the American volunteer army had returned. His war with the South was over, and his fight, his daily running fight with nature and against the injustice of his fellow men, was begun again." [48] Jeff, too, returns to a community in which the issue of the war had led to a violence that mirrors the violence at the front.

Joseph Kirkland's *The Captain of Company K* traces the disenchantment of Will Fargeon, a citizen-soldier, in a war that Kirkland suggests is absurd in its impersonal killing. He vividly describes the wounded and the dead and is particularly effective in a presentation of battlefield dead being stripped of their valuables.[49] His central narrative, however, is quite romantic, and all ends happily. Fargeon may lose a leg but he gains a bride, Sara, and McClintock and Lydia also marry. De Forest had covered the same ground in *Miss Ravenel's Conversion* and done so much more effectively.

Sidney Lanier deserves special mention. As Garland Greever, one of the editors of the Centennial Edition, suggests, the novel *Tiger-Lilies* "is uniquely non-parti-

san." [50] Although not primarily a war novel it contains
some of the most incisive descriptions of the horrors of
war that have come out of Civil War fiction: ". . . the
blood red flower of war . . . a flower whose freshening
dews are blood and hot tears, whose shadow chills a land,
whose odors strangle a people, whose giant petals drop
downward, and whose roots are in hell." [51] The flower
requires "profuse and perpetual manuring with human
bones" and it grows "in some wet place near a stream of
human blood" (p. 93). In addition, Lanier is the only
Southern writer to approach Crane's and De Forest's
realism in the description of combat and its results (pp.
133-134). Like Crane, he envisions heroism in warfare as
"temporary barbarism" (p. 108), and the condition of
war emerges in *Tiger-Lilies* as absurd and chaotic—a situation in which death is accidental and without meaning:
"for he [John Briggs] was at this moment, in the Jean Paul
sense, promoted. A random bullet entered his mouth . . ."
(p. 135). Also, as in Crane, Lanier presents an impersonal
nature: without heart, without eyes, without ears (p. 139).
Greever sums up Lanier's achievement:

> The novel differs from nearly all rivals in its
> closeness to the actualities of warfare. Though it is
> not fully or consistently realistic, even in Book II, it
> has a preserving salt of realism. It catches the accent
> of soldier talk, the trials of the infantry, the hilarities
> and the hazards of scouting, the scarcity of food and
> clothing in the South in 1864, the loneliness of iso-
> lated civilians, the demoralizing effects of captivity,
> the moods of battle (individual madness in a melee,
> the letdown after the crisis, the composite psychology
> of a military charge), and other aspects of the time
> and the milieu. [52]

Thus, the Civil War gave rise to a great amount of fiction—some of it purely escapist, much of it mediocre, but also including several good novels and one or two approaching greatness. Bierce, Crane, De Forest, Kirkland, and Lanier established a new criterion for judging a writer's performance in regard to his treatment of war: how close does he get to the way it was? Hemingway and others would apply this rule to their writing about World War I, but the novels coming out of that war would often move away from realism in its strictest sense and toward a literature of social and political protest.

Notes

1. *The Collected Writings of Ambrose Bierce,* introduction by Clifton Fadiman, p. 23.
2. See Robert A. Lively, *Fiction Fights the Civil War: An Unfinished Chapter in the Literary History of the American People,* pp. 4, 5, 16–18, 58.
3. Millis, *Arms and Men: A Study in American Military History,* p. 122.
4. Catton, *America Goes to War,* pp. 19; 20–21; 22–23.
5. *Ibid.,* p. 21.
6. Millis, p. 79.
7. *Ibid.,* p. 116.
8. Edwin H. Cady, *The Road to Realism: The Early Years of William Dean Howells,* pp. 79–82.
9. Edgar Marquess Branch, *The Literary Apprenticeship of Mark Twain,* pp. 47–49.
10. Wilson, p. 670.
11. *Ibid.,* pp. 682–683.
12. *A Volunteer's Adventures: A Union Captain's Record of the Civil War;* and *Miss Ravenel's Conversion from Secession to Loyalty,* ed. Gordon S. Haight. (Subsequent references are also to the New York 1957 ed., and are indicated by page numbers in the text.)
13. J. D. Salinger, *The Catcher in the Rye.*
14. James Davidson, *J. W. De Forest and His Contemporaries: The Birth of American Realism,* pp. 20–29, 36, 38–40, 42–43.

15. Norman Mailer, 1948; Fletcher Knebel and Charles W. Bailey, II, 1962.

16. Huntington, p. 63.

17. Included in *The Complete Writings*.

18. See Robert A. Wiggins, *Ambrose Bierce*, p. 10, and Richard O'Connor, *Ambrose Bierce: A Biography*, pp. 22–45.

19. Wiggins, pp. 9–11; Richard O'Connor, p. 31.

20. *The Collected Works of Ambrose Bierce*, I, 283–284.

21. Wiggins, p. 9.

22. Occasionally, in "Bits of Autobiography," Bierce seems to romanticize his war experience (see particularly *Collected Works*, I, 269); he never does so in the fiction.

23. *The Complete Writings*, p. 81. (Because of the limited availability of the *Collected Works*, subsequent references to Bierce's work will be to the former edition and are indicated by page numbers in the text.)

24. Woodruff, p. 54.

25. Schneider, p. 108.

26. Spiller, *The Cycle of American Literature: An Essay in Historical Criticism*, p. 204.

27. Snell, *The Shapers of American Fiction: 1798–1947*, p. 226.

28. Hassan, *Radical Innocence: Studies in the Contemporary American Novel*, pp. 42, 43.

29. Walcutt, *American Literary Naturalism: A Divided Stream*, pp. 76–82.

30. Berryman, "Stephen Crane: *The Red Badge of Courage*," in Wallace Stegner, ed., *The American Novel from James Fenimore Cooper to William Faulkner*, p. 91.

31. P. 370. Stallman's collation of textual variants, while not complete, offers evidence that Crane was more critical of Henry Fleming in the handwritten manuscript than in the first American edition. Although the edition currently being prepared by Fredson Bowers will probably provide a definitive text, Stallman's edition seems currently the best available.

32. Stallman, ed., *Stephen Crane: An Omnibus* (New York, 1958), p. 239. (Subsequent references to *Red Badge* are to this text and are indicated by page numbers in the text.)

33. Wilson Follett, ed., *The Collected Poems of Stephen Crane*. Of particular interest are "Once There Came a Man" (p. 7); "God Fashioned the Ship of the World Carefully" (p. 8); "If There is a Witness to My Little Life" (p. 15); "There Was Crimson Clash of War" (p. 16); "Tell Brave Deeds of War" (p. 17); "There Were Many Who Went in Huddled Procession" (p. 19); "You Say You Are Holy" (p. 54); "War Is Kind" (p. 77); "Once

a Man Clambering to the Housetops" (p. 94); and "A Man Said to the Universe" (p. 101).

34. Thomas A. Gullason, ed., *The Complete Stories and Sketches of Stephen Crane*, pp. 219–226.

35. *Ibid.*, pp. 292–294.

36. Lively, pp. 4, 100, 58.

37. New York, 1894. (Subsequent references are also to this edition, and are indicated by page numbers in the text.)

38. Quinn, p. 129.

39. De Leon, pp. ix; 28, 29–30.

40. Trowbridge, pp. 208, 266, 391–392, 499.

41. Harris, *Tales of the Home Folks*, p. 216.

42. *On the Plantation*, pp. 226–231.

43. Dabney, pp. 17–23, 282–283, 181.

44. Morford, *The Days of Shoddy*, pp. 208; 193; 272; 392–424; 89–94, 318–321.

45. *Shoulder-Straps*, pp. 151–152, 137, 222–231.

46. *The Coward*, pp. 145, 220–222, 460–463.

47. *Days of Shoddy*, p. 174.

48. Garland, p. 129.

49. Kirkland, pp. 120, 213.

50. Garland Greever, Introduction to Sidney Lanier's *Tiger-Lilies and Southern Prose*, p. xxiv.

51. Sidney Lanier, *Tiger-Lilies and Southern Prose*, p. 93. (Subsequent references to *Tiger-Lilies* are also to the Baltimore 1945

52. Greever, p. xxix.

edition, and are indicated by page numbers in the text.)

4.

World War I and the Novel of Cultural Protest

The years following the Civil War brought a sharp decline in influence for the American military community. As Walter Millis suggests, "The Grand Army of the Republic, the finest military machine in existence at that time, made its three-day march down Pennsylvania Avenue —and dissolved." [1] In a short time, the Navy was no longer a viable combat force and the Army, engaged primarily in frontier patrol and Indian fighting, soon consisted of only twenty-five small regiments. [2] Samuel Huntington, quoting an officer of that era, describes the period as one in which military men lived monk-like lives in garrison, almost totally divorced from the mainstream of American life. [3] Perhaps because of such isolation, these years of public eclipse provided a breeding ground for military theoreticians who established the philosophical groundwork for the revolutionary change in the military's role and importance in American social and political life.

Emory Upton, after a world tour inspecting the armed forces of other nations, published in 1878 his extremely influential work, *The Armies of Asia and Europe*.[4] He offered the view that the United States had been haphazard in its reliance upon the citizen-soldier and in its lack of preparation between conflicts. For the future he called for a standing regular establishment capable of meeting any of the military possibilities a growing nation might face. While it may be unfair to compare Upton with De Forest's fictional Colonel Carter, he, like Carter, admired the German Great General Staff, and at least toyed with the idea of instituting in the United States the essential element of the efficient Prussian system: universal peacetime conscription.[5] Captain Alfred Mahan, alarmed at the withering away of U.S. naval capability, created a rationale for a large American military presence at sea both at times of war and peace, encouraging, like Upton, the idea of constant preparedness. In Millis' words, Mahan's theory fulfilled "the thirsting needs of all the new forces—the rising nationalists, the armament manufacturers, the ship and engine builders, military men hoping to enlarge their careers, bankers looking for foreign investment, merchants interested in colonial markets, investors in the 'banana republics'—who might find a big program of naval building and an aggressive foreign policy to their advantage." [6] Certainly, he provided the theoretical substructure for Congress to initiate its shipbuilding spree and aggressive navalism after the blowing up of the U.S.S. *Maine* in Havana Harbor, an event that began in the United States a period described as that of "the new Militarism." [7]

The Spanish-American War ended the years of eclipse, and, under the tutelage of Elihu Root and Leonard Wood, the military began a steady ascent in influence. Wood, like Upton and Mahan, argued that growing world-wide responsibilities of an emerging industrial nation necessitated the establishment of a large military arm. Huntington describes his role as influential: "During the decade prior to American entrance into the World War, Wood was a leading figure in the drive for a positive national policy and the increase in America's armed strength. He played a major role in stimulating the outpouring of preparedness literature which flooded the country." [8] Although Huntington, unlike Millis, does not view the rapid development of military might around the turn of the century with retrospective alarm, he does concede that "the participation of Alfred Mahan and Leonard Wood in the articulation of Neo-Hamiltonian ideas was the first and only time in American history that professional military leaders contributed so directly to the outlook and activities of a political movement." [9] Root added to the clamor for a stronger military establishment, and, as Secretary of War, imposed corporate efficiency upon the department, modeling his overhaul of the structure on the German Great General Staff. Millis concludes that he originated the military managerial revolution in the United States and that "even if Root did not see it, the conscript mass army, available for aggressive action upon a world stage, was the logical end." [10]

Thus, the Spanish-American War provided the incident that enabled the nation to strengthen itself militarily, and, as Richard Preston, Sydney Wise, and Herman Werner suggest in *Men in Arms*, "This war showed that democracies also were not immune from the fever of aggressive war." [11] The small amount of fiction concerned with the war is almost wholly inconsequential. Stephen Crane's *Wounds in the Rain* contains several successful short stories depicting pointless barbarity but nothing beyond his achievement in *The Red Badge of Courage.* Hermann Hagedorn's *The Rough Riders* is little more than romantic escape, and Elswyth Thane's *Ever After,* while an interesting account of life in New York at the turn of the century, contains little material of any interest concerned with the conflict. It is rather the sociological effects of the war that are interesting. Frederick Merk, in *Manifest Destiny and Mission in American History: A Reinterpretation,* identifies the spirit of manifest destiny with the continuing sense of the global mission of the United States and concludes that this spirit led the country into the task of attempting to save Europe for democracy in World War I.[12] In regard to the nation's capability to enter the conflict, Millis concludes: "It would be absurd to suggest that the transformations in our military policy after 1898 were the 'cause' of our entanglement in the European power complex; but it is not so absurd to say that they provided the means without which we could not have become so deeply engaged." [13] Thus, triggered by the conflict in Cuba, the managerial revolution of the American military had taken place and followed the direction indicated by Upton, Mahan, Wood, and Root, providing the basis of force for American commitments abroad.

World War I itself completely fulfilled Catton's suggestion that total war leads to total horror, and most American novelists involved in the war present that horror realistically and in great detail, following the path broken by De Forest, Bierce, and Crane. It seems that they could do little else in dealing with a conflict which amassed such a pile of human corpses for so little tangible accomplishment. The Germans alone lost 500,000 dead at Verdun; General Brusilov's attack on the eastern front, beginning on June 4, 1916, and ending August 17, 1916, cost nearly one million men; the British alone lost 475,000 dead in four and one half months at the Somme and 400,000 in Flanders.[14] The revolution in the development of firepower, begun in the Civil War, continued until, indeed, the individual soldier was reduced to a frightened machine-tender:

> This carefully planned war was within a few weeks of its declaration smashed to pieces by fire-power; fire-power so devastating that as armies could no longer live upon the surface of the battlefield there was no choice but to go under the surface; consequently trenches five hundred miles long were dug, and armies went to earth like foxes. Then in order to secure these trenches from surprise attacks, each side turned itself into an immense spider, and spun hundreds of thousands of miles of steel web around the entrenchments. Thus, after a few weeks of real warfare, the *offensive à outrance,* that high gospel of the pre-war manuals, was reduced to a wallowing defensive among mud holes and barbed wire. Armies, through their own lack of foresight, were reduced to the position of human cattle. They browsed behind their fences and occasionally snorted and bellowed at each other.[15]

Secretary Root, two months after his appointment in 1899, envisioned, in a speech in Chicago, the American soldier as part of a great and complex machine, and dedicated himself to an improvement of its efficiency—by 1916 advocating universal military training.[16] Many of the novelists of World War I, particularly John Dos Passos, Dalton Trumbo, and William E. March Campbell, rebel against a structure that reduces its members to such a condition. In so doing, they follow in a tradition established by Melville in *White Jacket,* and, like *White Jacket,* their books are intended to be corrective exposés, exposing the man-of-war world in all its barbarity in the hope that the possibility of social change might exist.[17] In the light of subsequent events, their hopes seem terribly naïve, but the fact remains that, unlike Crane, many of them intended their novels to be, at least partially, vehicles of cultural criticism. Most directly, they attack the military structure itself, and for obvious reasons. Millis comments:

> Such was the achievement of the scientific soldiers and sailors, the highly trained, studious and devoted men who had taken over the management of arms from the earlier entrepreneurs, swashbucklers and uneducated aristocratic triflers. In taking every military precaution, in ensuring that their nations would be ready for anything, they had managed to create a situation in which their nations were actually ready for nothing save a universal catastrophe. Unintentionally, they had rendered it impossible for the major European powers to fight any war with each other except a war of all-out effort and destruction.[18]

It is evident that, as in Melville, the military structure often serves as a microcosm for western world society as a whole, and these novelists, directly or indirectly, aim their criticism at what Ezra Pound called "a botched civilization." [19] Absurd nationalism, totalitarianism, and hypocritical Christianity all are attacked as the war seemed to some a tumultuous climax, indeed a fulfillment, of misguided cultural goals and ideals. The military historian, J. F. C. Fuller, concurs: "It was because the

Western world was going mad that war was a certainty;
a war which, like a fever, was to debilitate democracy,
to undermine its vitality and to shorten its days." [20] And
Preston, Wise and Werner detail the devastating impact
of this inevitability:

> The World War of 1914–1918 had a most seri-
> ous effect on the society of the whole world. Its
> physical consequences alone were enough to slow the
> onward march of civilization and to destroy that
> general belief in the inevitability of human progress
> which had marked much of the philosophy of the
> nineteenth century. The material cost of the war,
> including property damage, has been estimated at
> twenty-eight billion dollars, and the number of killed
> and permanently disabled, military and civilian, at
> twenty millions.[21]

Thus, the "great catastrophe of militarism which had
been building up for over a hundred years" occurred.[22]
Masses of Americans became directly involved and more
than in any previous war they wrote about it. As a group,
their novels emerge as a protest against the culture which
had led them, so innocent, to the slaughter. Few were
politically sophisticated enough to offer alternatives to
the economic-political structure they criticized, but an
untested Communism often looms as a possible panacea.
In any case, for the first time since Melville, American
novelists dealt critically with an entire social structure
through a consideration of a military situation, and, by
and large, they wrote in the mood of the young Melville
of *White Jacket*. Only William Faulkner, in *A Fable*, approximates the elegiac tone of *Billy Budd*.

After establishing the idea that most of the World

War I novelists are at least somewhat political, it may seem peculiar to begin discussion of them with a consideration of the early work of Ernest Hemingway. On the surface, at least, he seems the least political of any of them, but his subject matter is representative, his style best captures the tone of war-weary disillusionment, and, beneath the surface, political and cultural criticism exists in the work. In a purely literary context, Carlos Baker emphasizes the novelist's admitted debt to Crane, and Earl Rovit discovers parallels between him and Bierce.[23] Compared to the direct impact of the war, however, literary influences seem less significant. In the most perceptive treatment of Hemingway's attitude toward war in general, John Atkins, in *Ernest Hemingway: His Work and Personality,* argues convincingly that for Hemingway war was somehow the most truthful condition of man's existence—a condition that best exemplified the general postwar disenchantment with western world culture. "War, or more exactly battle, gave Hemingway his real chance to exhibit a world which consisted entirely of things. Millions of things, most of them broken, most of them useless, and filling the spectator with a sense of despair and desolation. . . ." [24] While Atkins admits that Hemingway, as a novelist, may have regarded the war as just another useful landscape or milieu,[25] it seems clear that this particular landscape, with its death, mutilation, destruction, and despair, was the particular one which summed up the author's sense of postwar western world culture. Most things are shattered, broken, and the totality of the conflict had reduced man to minuscule dimensions, dwarfed by the mechanism of his own creation.

Although Hemingway resembles Crane in his description of the war, his intention in the creation of Frederick Henry and Nick Adams is radically different from Crane's intention for Henry Fleming. Crane never permits his protagonist to become fully self-reflective concerning his insignificance within the total structure of the war and the universe, and he never serves as a reliable spokesman for the author's attitudes toward the conflict and the culture that produced it. He is, in the last analysis, a little man in search of social adjustment. In contrast, the Hemingway hero, like his creator, becomes aware of the cultural significance of the war and seeks escape from the absurd conflict in order to attempt a formulation of a meaningful rationale for his existence. In this pattern of involvement, revelation, and escape, he sets a pattern that a number of protagonists of World War I novels follow. Atkins suggests that "Hemingway did more to set the tone for writing about war than any other modern writer," [26] and if one wishes to understand the American novelist's reaction to this first global conflict, one should first consider the tone and the subject matter of *In Our Time, A Farewell to Arms,* and *The Sun Also Rises.*

In the interchapter pieces and in several of the stories of *In Our Time,*[27] Hemingway imagistically presents a number of broken lives and broken things—natural objects sufficient in their totality to suggest a shattered culture: a world, in Fuller's words, gone mad. It is an environment in which a column of drunken soldiers, the officer and authority figure drunkest of all and placed anachronistically on horseback, march toward engagement (p. 13); a world in which a procession of displaced persons, seemingly without end and without beginning, move through rain and mud to nowhere (p. 23), reminiscent of Bierce's products of war: widows and childless mothers and husbandless wives; a world in which men take pride in building perfect barricades of destruction (p. 43) and in properly killing the men who happen to be the enemy

(p. 33); a world of brutal and apparently pointless executions both in Europe and in the United States (pp. 63,
193–194); a world in which, back in the heartland of
America, two cops, Drevitts and Boyle, kill two Hun-
garians Boyle mistakes for "wops" in a personal expression
of the grander scale nationalistic and bigoted behavior of
the European countries (p. 103). It is a world in which
traditional political and social values have lost meaning
and so one seeks one's separate peace (p. 81).

Although Hemingway is normally considered to be
decidedly apolitical and his one "political" novel, *To
Have and Have Not,* an artistic failure, there are subtle
political implications in *In Our Time.* For instance, the
sympathetically drawn communist in "The Revolutionist"
is in marked contrast to Drevitts and Boyle whose interchapter piece precedes the story. But although he may
offer a social theory in opposition to the capitalist world
of the munitions manufacturers, Hemingway holds no
hope for his success, having his narrator report that "the
last I heard of him the Swiss had him in jail near Sion"
(p. 106).

Also, in the closing piece of the original *in our time,*
"L'Envoi," Hemingway drops a hint that all revolution-
aries eventually sell out and that belief in political amelioration is illusion. In that brief story, the revolutionary
committee is keeping the king in good whiskey and the
queen in roses (p. 213), and one gets the feeling that these
nobles will keep themselves alive and that, finally, there
must be change in order that things remain the same. It
is true that Hemingway does not make a political "statement," if by that one means propagandistic oversimplification in the name of a cause, but, like Melville's concern
for the defeat of the forces of innovation, so Hemingway
implies similar concern for his revolutionist and the

ideals he embodies. Hemingway, then, is concerned with politics primarily because man is, at least partially, a political animal. In a much later story, "The Gambler, the Nun, and the Radio," he has his *persona*, Mr. Fraser, include political beliefs among all the other illusions that man creates to make life bearable:

> Religion is the opium of the people. He believed that, that dyspeptic little joint-keeper. Yes, and music is the opium of the people. Old mount-to-the-head hadn't thought of that. And now economics is the opium of the people; along with patriotism the opium of the people in Italy and Germany. What about sexual intercourse; was that an opium of the people? Of some of the people. Of some of the best of the people. But drink was a sovereign opium of the people, oh, an excellent opium. Although some prefer the radio, another opium of the people, a cheap one he had just been using. Along with these went gambling, an opium of the people if there ever was one, one of the oldest. Ambition was another, an opium of the people, along with a belief in any new form of government.[28]

Mr. Fraser has discovered what most Hemingway heroes discover: the essential "nothingness" at the heart of experience, or at least at the heart of western world values. The old waiter, in "A Clean, Well-Lighted Place," most concisely sums it up: "It was a nothing and a man was nothing too. It was only that and light was all it needed and a certain cleanness and order." [29] In short stories specifically concerned with the war, such as "In Another Country," "Now I Lay Me," and "A Way You'll Never Be," Hemingway deals with disheartening physical and psychological maiming in which the wounded are trying to learn to live with what has happened to them; and, in "A Natural History of the Dead," he is self-consciously hard-boiled in detailing the various horrors of death—as if he too must write it out of his system in order to get used to it.[30] In any case, a statement in *Green Hills of Africa* reveals how much he valued the war experience: "It was one of the major subjects and certainly one of the hardest to write truly of and those writers who had not seen it were always very jealous and tried to make it seem unimportant, or a disease as a subject, while, really, it was just something quite irreplaceable that they had missed." [31]

In his single major novel directly concerned with the war experience, Hemingway traces Frederick Henry's awakening to this sense of "nothingness," and the World War I world of broken things is the environment in which he makes his discoveries. John W. Aldridge, in *After the Lost Generation: A Critical Study of the Writers of Two Wars,* sees Henry's withdrawal from the retreat after Caporetto as a withdrawal from an absurd political and social structure—from a system no longer defensible.[32] Philip Young identifies Henry as an American culture-hero whose pattern of "complicity, bitterness, escape" approximates the nation's involvement in the European war.[33] Both seem correct, and, as the reevaluation of Hemingway's work continues, it is interesting to note that the validity of the novel is increasingly identified with its depiction of war and not with the love relationship between Catherine Barkley and Henry. George Snell depicts that relationship as outrageously sentimental but respects the treatment of the war.[34] Two critics most favorably inclined toward *A Farewell to Arms,* Malcolm Cowley and Carlos Baker, also seem to judge Hemingway's handling of the war more favorably than his handling of the love relationship. Cowley concludes that "only *The Red Badge of Courage* and a few short pieces by Ambrose Bierce can be compared with it," [35] and Baker, after somewhat overextendedly describing Frederick as Romeo and Catherine as Juliet, makes good sense in viewing Miss Barkley's death in a larger social context, "associated and interwoven with the whole tragic pattern of fatigue and suffering, loneliness, defeat and doom, of which the war is itself the broad social manifestation." [36] Leslie Fiedler, while the most critical of the novel's sentimental element, also has respect for the war material: "Hemingway's *A Farewell to Arms* in its earlier chapters captures the sense of disorganization and loss of identity typical of modern war, particularly at a moment of retreat, but quite soon becomes a love story, which is to say, an erotic dream of escape and pure sensuality, so haunted by unconfused guilts that it can only end in death and eternal separation." [37]

So, in the last analysis, it would seem that *A Farewell to Arms* is of particular value insofar as it portrays the war, the individual American's reaction to it, and, by implication, his reaction to the culture that produced the war. In a single pronouncement, Frederick Henry sums up the essential tone of many of the novelists' reactions.

I was always embarrassed by the words sacred, glorious, and sacrifice and the expression in vain. We had heard them, sometimes standing in the rain almost out of earshot, so that only the shouted words came through, and had read them, on proclamations that were slapped up by billposters over other proclamations, now for a long time, and I had seen nothing sacred, and the things that were glorious had no glory and the sacrifices were like the stockyards at Chicago if nothing was done with the meat except to bury it. There were many words that you could not stand to hear and finally only the names of places had dignity. Certain numbers were the same way and certain dates and these with the names of places were all you could say and have them mean anything. Abstract words such as glory, honor, courage, or hallow were obscene beside the concrete names of villages, the numbers of roads, the names of rivers, the numbers of regiments and the dates.[38]

Implied is the individual's disgust with absurd patriotism, chauvinistic politicians, and a culture that could permit the massive killing in the name of national interest that Henry must become toughened to: "At the start of the winter came the permanent rain and with the rain came the cholera. But it was checked and in the end only seven thousand died of it in the army" (p. 4). Frederick and Catherine may be, in Mr. Fraser's words, "some of the best of the people" insofar as they pursue sexual love as their escape, but, like their prototypes in the earlier "A Very Short Story," they are doomed to be additions to the landscape of broken things and shattered illusions. In Pound's words, the best among them died for "battered books" and "broken statues." They died for that "old bitch gone in the teeth"—yes, that "botched civilization." [39]

Frederick Henry, like most Hemingway heroes, begins a retreat from traditional Christianity and other western world values toward a tough-skinned individuality which protects him from the illusions of that shamful world.[40] When the heroes emerge from this cocoon of personal protection, as Robert Jordan does in *For Whom the Bell Tolls* and Harry Morgan somewhat belatedly does in *To Have and Have Not,* they are, like the revolutionist, inevitably aligned with the forces of innovation and change and in opposition to totalitarianism and capitalism. Just as inevitably, they are destroyed. In *A Farewell to Arms* Henry discovers the troublesome sense of "nothingness" at the center of western world values; Jake Barnes, crippled by the war, lives with it in *The Sun Also Rises.*

Barnes lives his life according to the forms, however, and is hard working, technically religious, and genuinely romantic. As a traditional figure, he provides the moral focus of the novel, but in a meaningful ironic ploy, Hemingway presents him as emasculated—one might suspect as emasculated as the values he represents. Like them, he has been ruined by the war that ravaged the continent, and Hemingway hints that the real representative of the culture is not Jake Barnes but the composite of homosexuality, nymphomania, and drunkenness that surrounds him and that he abhors. He is a kind of caretaker for Lady Brett Ashley, who, while not gone in the teeth, does suggest a botched civilization. Frederick Hoffman views *The Sun Also Rises* as Hemingway's best war novel,[41] and his insight helps clarify the novelist's intention in creating Adams, Henry, and Barnes. Unlike Crane, whose interest lay in depicting the plight of an average boy under the stresses of war, Hemingway attempts in all three characters the creation of culture-heroes who embody both the sense of western world disenchantment and the emptiness of western world values during and after World War I. However subtly, he criticizes those forces he thinks particularly responsible for that slaughterhouse in Europe: totalitarianism, absurd patriotism, and technically ritualistic but morally ineffectual Christianity. In the military structure of *A Farewell to Arms,* Henry comes in contact with representatives of those forces. The Carabinieri, who would kill him, are the blind and unthinking agents of a blind and unthinking totalitarianism, patriotically doing their duty, and the simple priest, who, like Frederick and Catherine, belongs in an Eden-like simplicity of the Abruzzi, is almost totally ineffectual in the real Europe at war.

Although perhaps the best, Hemingway is not the first American novelist to write of World War I. In fact, John Dos Passos, Thomas Boyd, Willa Cather, E. E. Cummings, Elliot Paul, William Faulkner, Leonard H. Nason, and Laurence Stallings all have works preceding the 1929 publication of *A Farewell to Arms.* Almost all write in the same mood of disenchantment, but most are more overt in their cultural and political criticism. Although Cummings' *The Enormous Room* is one of the most forceful antiwar novels ever written and an indictment of tyranny in any form, it does not deal directly with an American military unit or with the war itself. Alfred Kazin defines Cummings' attitude toward war as "compounded equally of resignation, hatred for all authority, and an almost abstract cynicism," [42] and Norman Friedman correctly describes the thematic center of the work: "What Cummings is really after is implied by the emotional tone of the book, the joy he feels when the individual triumphs over the system which has done its best to destroy him." [43] Much of the poetry suggests a similar theme; inevitably, "I Sing of Olaf Glad and Big" comes to mind. [44]

Although Cummings captures the essential thematic thread that binds most of the World War I novels together and although Hemingway's style best encompasses the tone of disenchantment that results from the war, John Dos Passos, in *Three Soldiers* and *First Encounter,* breaks new ground, and, in effect, establishes the form that most of the novels occasioned by World War II and the Korean War would take. In fact, his concentration on an American unit, representative of various ethnic groups and social strata within United States culture at large, becomes standard for an avalanche of novels out of the two wars.

Joseph Warren Beach may exaggerate its value when he suggests: "*Three Soldiers* was the first important American novel, and one of the first in any language, to treat the War in the tone of realism and disillusion. It made a deep impression, and may be counted the beginning of strictly contemporary fiction in the United States." [45] Certainly the novel had terrific impact and presented the American war effort in a way that shocked the folks back home.[46] While Crane, in the last analysis, may be more ironic than any of the World War I writers, he presents, on the surface, a traditional tale of a young man's initiation and his acceptance of the rite; Dos Passos, and many who follow him, present protagonists who reject the usual initiation in war, and, in so doing, voice protests about the culture as a whole. John H. Wrenn, while pointing out Dos Passos' great debt to Crane, suggests an important difference in regard to their attitudes toward maturation: "Like Crane, he [Dos Passos] considers the problem of courage of central importance in war as in life. But to Dos Passos the courage that each man must attain is a courage to face life, not death; for life is the ultimate reality." [47] For Dos Passos in *Three Soldiers,* the commitment to life means commitment to personal freedom in the face of the monstrous machine of law and tradition that encloses the individual in the military structure. His protagonist, John Andrews, unlike Henry Fleming, runs from the machine, acts defiantly, and is destroyed. If

Elihu Root, as early as 1899, had envisioned the American soldier as a cog in a vast machine, Dos Passos, in 1921, began a campaign in fiction to combat such dehumanization and denial of personal liberty.

Three Soldiers, among other things, is a novel of social statement, and Dos Passos, encompassing little of the complexity of Melville's world, is occasionally guilty of painful oversimplification. He strikes out at the vast machine by detailing the fates of three individuals caught in it: Fuselli, Chrisfield, and John Andrews. Dos Passos emphasizes the thrust of his criticism by meaningfully entitling sections of the book: "Making the Mould," "The Metal Cools," "Machines," and "Rust." All three characters, products of the army, are destroyed by it. The Italian-American, Fuselli, sees the service as providing him with social mobility: " '. . . this war's a lucky thing for me. I might have been in the R. C. Vicker Company's store for five years an' never got a raise. An' here in the army I got a chance to do almost anything.' " [48] He hungers for promotion (pp. 16–17), hoping for a sick corporal's death in order that he may attain his position (p. 37). In order not to "get in wrong," he accepts what he regards as slavery (pp. 62–63) and avoids those enlisted men of whom the officers are suspicious (pp. 89, 94). Fuselli, like the soldier in Hemingway's "A Very Short Story," ends up with venereal disease, and, in addition, the rewards of constant kitchen duty in a labor battalion. He never makes corporal (pp. 301–303). Thus, the ignorant immigrant is defeated in his efforts to enter the social structure and reap its rewards of status and personal advancement.

Chrisfield, a somewhat dim-witted boy from Indiana, kills an officer who had earlier arranged for his court-martial. After feeling a "warm joy" upon hurling the grenade that kills the man (p. 188), he discovers the remedy for guilt. "He did not feel lonely any more now that he was marching in ranks again. His feet beat the ground in time with the other feet. He would not have to think whether to go to the right or to the left. He would do as the others did" (p. 190). This loss of individuality and morality, for Dos Passos, seems the system's ultimate achievement: the reduction of the human being to the role of automaton in a machine of death. Chrisfield is perhaps the most brutalized. Mechanically, he seeks sexual release (p. 167) and the enjoyment of killing (p. 185); through most of his appearances later in the novel he seems hardly conscious. Fuselli remains self-reflective enough to occasionally feel lost in the machine (pp. 63, 71), but the artist, John Andrews, is most aware of the debilitating effects of army life and so becomes the moral center of the novel, the focus of Dos Passos' antiwar and antimilitary statements.

"Andrews thought suddenly of all the tingling bodies constrained into the rigid attitudes of automatons in uniforms like this one: of all the hideous force of making men into machines" (p. 331). He sees himself as a slave in a brutal system (pp. 199, 243, 269) and would risk death to escape that degradation (p. 211). Throughout, he pictures the men as automatons (pp. 216, 243) and sums up his feelings by suggesting that the Army made "the warm sentient bodies into coarse automatons who must be kept busy, lest they grow restive, till killing time began again" (p. 256). As a composer, he wishes to present in music the "thwarted lives" and "the miserable dullness of industrialized slaughter" (p. 269), and there can be little doubt that Dos Passos dedicated his novel to the same task. Like Hemingway, however, he maintains little aesthetic distance between himself and his hero, and Andrews often seems altogether too romantically conceived and unduly naïve. Wilbur Frohock sees him as paranoid in his attitude toward the Army, insofar as Andrews views it as "one vast conspiracy to take away his liberty." [49] At times, his naïveté seems unbelievable, and he becomes somewhat histrionic in his refusal to contact the authorities after his encounter with the brutal military police (pp. 352–357), and his escape in the river (pp. 372–375) to an idyllic respite with Genevieve Rod. This pattern of action directly parallels Frederick Henry's escape to Catherine, and, like Hemingway, Dos Passos seems more interested in his hero as a symbolic culture-hero than as an individual character. Just as Thoreau bathed in Walden Pond as a religious exercise,[50] both Andrews and Henry undergo baptisms into new identities through their plunges into rivers. They emerge confirmed in their individualism and in their opposition to the culture.

Frederick Hoffman points out that the army in *Three Soldiers* is "a machine for which traditional values no longer had a meaning." [51] Andrews, in fleeing the microcosm of the military unit, like Frederick Henry, flees western world values in general. Early in the novel, Dos Passos indicates that Andrews, in entering the army, wished to submerge his personality in the mass, and is racing from an American society for which he has great distaste and in which he is unable to find happiness (p. 26). Of course, he finds in the army a reflection of the culture he flees, and Dos Passos characterizes that culture as brutal, prejudiced, and hypocritically Christian. Violence and anti-Italian and anti-Jewish feelings are frequent, but Dos Passos concentrates most on what he and his protagonist regard as the moral bankruptcy of Christianity. The representatives of the religion, the YMCA men, are, without exception, stupid, absurd, or downright malevolent. One of them remarks that he has discovered the essence of America in the army and reminds Andrews that the war is a Christian undertaking (p. 157). In a hospital talk, the Reverend Mr. Skinner announces that the allies should have crushed Germany completely without the least thought that Germany is also a "Christian" country (p. 218). Andrews asks a "Y" man why he so totally hates the Huns: " 'Because they are barbarians, enemies of civilization. You must have enough education to know that,' said the 'Y' man, raising his voice angrily. 'What Church do you belong to?' " (p. 210). After this particular revelation, Andrews thinks: "So was civilization nothing but a vast edifice of sham, and the war, instead of its crumbling, was its fullest and most ultimate expression" (p. 210). Christianity, thus, becomes a part of a decadent tradition, devoid of meaning, and servant to nationalistic unleashings of power. In a conversation with Genevieve Rod, Andrews dismisses the whole tradition in a manner similar to Frederick Henry's: " 'Oh, those long Roman words, what millstones they are about men's necks!' " (p. 421). Thus, he implies, it is in the wartime army that one discovers the truth about the culture, and what he discovers is organized brutality, sanctioned by Christianity, within a system of autocratic control, supported by arbitrary laws and brutal police. Andrews foresees the crumbling of the system (p. 400), and his heroics at the end are symbolic of the honest individual's desire to avoid complicity in a culture he sees as morally corrupt.

Just as *Three Soldiers* resembles *A Farewell to Arms,* Dos Passos' earlier novel, *First Encounter,* resembles the war stories of *In Our Time,* containing vignettes of war and men at war and concentrating upon the cruelty and absurdity of the conflict itself. The hero, Martin Howe, parallels Nick Adams, and Tom Randolph serves the same purposes as the companion who frequently accompanies Nick. Howe, who epitomizes American political innocence, early in the novel envisions the crumbling of all the evils in the world; [52] the rest of the novel deals primarily with the crumbling of the illusions held by these young men from the provinces of the new world. After seeing wounded men for the first time, Howe exclaims, " 'God, it's so hideously stupid!' " (p. 43); his companion, upon seeing a man with his sexual organs shot away, concurs: " 'Oh, God, it's too damned absurd! An arrangement for mutual suicide and no damned other thing . . .' " (p. 44). After discovering that the allies are guilty of as much atrocity as the "Huns" (p. 67), they, and others they meet, begin to see the war as solemnly inane (p. 65), viciously stupid (p. 65), and idiotic (p. 114). Soon, they stop thinking of it as an engagement among nations representing different moral points of view; rather, it becomes the ultimate expression of a corrupt civilization, engineered somehow by a conspiracy of interests:

> "Think, man, think of all the oceans of lies through all the ages that must have been necessary to make this possible! Think of this new particular vintage of lies that has been so industriously pumped out of the press and the pulpit. Doesn't it stagger you?"
> Martin nodded. (p. 30)

There is a sense of national tragedy when, in a conversation among Howe, Randolph, and some Frenchmen, Dos Passos suggests that the United States has become involved in the conspiracy:

"In exchange for all the quiet and the civilization and the beauty of ordered lives that Europeans
gave up in going to the new world we gave them
opportunity to earn luxury, and, infinitely more
important, freedom from the past, that gangrened
ghost of the past that is killing Europe to-day with
its infection of hate and greed and murder."

"America has turned traitor to all that, you see;
that's the way we look at it. Now we're a military
nation, an organized pirate like France and England
and Germany." (p. 142)

After discussing the loss of individual freedom
within the context of an organized conspiracy concocted
by industrial and political interest groups, they offer the
toast, " 'To Revolution, to Anarchy, to the Socialist
state . . .' " (p. 154). But, just as Hemingway has his
revolutionist in the hands of the Swiss police and his
Greek king living on in the garden of roses, so, too, Dos
Passos offers little hope for change. All of the young men,
who, somewhat drunkenly, discussed social amelioration
and drank to change, end up destroyed or disenchanted.

In summing up Dos Passos' contribution to the tradition of the American military novel, it must be stated
that he was the first novelist since Melville to use the
military novel as a vehicle for social analysis and political
statement. *First Encounter* and *Three Soldiers* may lack
the sober objectivity of *Billy Budd,* but the conclusions
Dos Passos draws are remarkably similar to Melville's.
John Andrews and Billy meet similar fates at the hands
of an organized society whose representative is the military structure. One killed, the other imprisoned, both
are victims of a man-of-war world in which neither is
able to live. Both are sympathetically drawn and their

pathetic fates are reflections of lost illusions and ends to
innocence. In his preface to the 1945 reissue of *First
Encounter,* Dos Passos indirectly reveals that in Andrews
and Howe he had projected the whole sense of shattered
American ideals and naïveté. An older man, his own
political views radically changed, he comments on the
political discussions of the last pages of *First Encounter*:

> Reading it over I find the chapter scrappy and un-
> satisfactory, but I am letting it stand because it still
> expresses, in the language of the time, some of the
> enthusiasms and some of the hopes of young men
> already marked for slaughter in that year of enthusi-
> asms and hopes beyond other years, the year of the
> October Revolution.
>
> It was this sanguine feeling that the future was
> a blank page to write on, focusing first about the
> speeches of Woodrow Wilson and then about the
> figure of Lenin, that made the end of the last war so
> different from the period we are now entering. Per-
> haps the disillusionments of the last quarter of a
> century have taught us that there are no short cuts
> to a decent ordering of human affairs, that the climb
> back out of the pit of savagery to a society of even
> approximate justice and freedom must necessarily
> be hard and slow. (pp. 9–10)

Thomas Boyd's *Through the Wheat,*[53] published two
years after *Three Soldiers,* is inferior to its predecessor in
almost all respects.[53] Boyd takes some petulant pop-shots
at the YMCA men (pp. 43, 75, 218) but fails to create the
sense that they are representative of a whole religious
tradition. His hero, William Hicks, moves from the pas-
toral setting of a northern Michigan farmhouse (p. 22)

through one horrifying experience after another until, finally, his soul numb, he walks with his platoon to probable death (p. 266). He functions as a representative of all those who underwent the same process. Boyd does not develop him fully, however, and he is two-dimensional, flat, and conventional—like all other characters in the novel. For instance, little is revealed concerning his relationships with home, with women, or even with the other men in his unit. Near the end of the novel, Boyd has his hero comment on American involvement in Europe, and, in so doing, suggests that it spells an end to American innocence: " 'The point is, the French hate the English and the English hate the Americans and the Americans hate the Germans, and where the hell is it all goin' to end?' " (p. 216). That statement is about as profound as Boyd ever gets, and, all in all, the novel is not particularly distinguished. Leonard H. Nason's *Chevrons* is even less so, merely offering detailed depictions of some of the difficulties of army life in an effort to prove that war is not a very pleasant experience.

A number of American women wrote of the war with varying degrees of success. All are outside the mainstream of the World War I novel, primarily because of their general lack of intimate knowledge of the conflict. Edith Wharton's *A Son at the Front* is more concerned with psychological relations between father and son and with life in Paris than with the war itself, and Willa Cather's *One of Ours,* while more explicit on the subject of conflict, is really more concerned with the moral and cultural desolation of the American midwest. Mary Lee's *It's a Great War!* is a hodgepodge of experiences that detail the difficulties and joys of being an American nurse in Europe, but, except for the presentation of some of the brutally wounded, is hardly concerned with

the war.[54] Perhaps Mary Raymond Shipman Andrews
epitomizes the worst of Warld War I writing, filling her
novels with bathos and sentimentality.[55]

In one of the stories of *In Our Time,* "Soldier's
Home," Hemingway deals with the problems of the returned veteran's difficulty in readjusting to a value system that now seems out of step with his experience. The
returned veterans of William Gilmore Simms [56] and
Hamlin Garland [57] faced, primarily, problems of economic adjustment. Hemingway's protagonist, Krebs, who
"went to the war from a Methodist college in Kansas,"
simply cannot readjust to the simple Christianity of the
provincial midwest. In the war and the European experience he has discovered that he needs nothing that his
former environment has to offer him: not marriage with
one of the nice girls (p. 147) nor his father's bribe of the
car (p. 149) nor his mother's sentimental love (pp. 151–
152) nor traditional Christian values (p. 151).[58] It is clear
that he regards the beliefs of the culture as shams.

Laurence Stallings' *Plumes,* an excellent minor novel
of social protest, also deals with the returned veteran but
in a more traditional manner than Hemingway did.
Richard Plume, wounded seven times, returns to his
family filled with antagonism for the stupidity of war.
His first words to his wife are, " 'God forgive me for my
folly,' " and he attacks even those he loves when they
romanticize war.[59] His problems are at least partially economic, returning home to outrageous rents, high prices,
corrupt politics, and to a religion that ignores social justice. In short, he returns to a corrupt society enjoying a
prosperity based on the war itself, a depiction of the
American economic system common today among those
concerned with the power of the Pentagon. *Plumes* is an
unpretentious novel that expresses, in terms of a troubled

and despairing returned American, an indictment of war and of American society. William Faulkner also deals with the situation of the returned veteran in an early and generally unappreciated work, *Soldier's Pay.*

Filled with echoes from Pater, Wilde and others,[60] Faulkner's novel is as pretentious as Stalling's is not, but both indict a nation unappreciative of a soldier's sacrifice. While differing sharply concerning the book's artistic merit, Richard Chase, Joseph Warren Beach, and Alfred Kazin view it as a lost-generation novel, and William Van O'Connor states one of its important themes as an expression of that generation: "Patriotism, the title implies, is meaningless in a world of selfishness and inevitable defeat." [61] Donald Mahon, the returned veteran, has suffered such nearly total physical destruction that he is hardly more than a vegetable. Chase sees him as the first of Faulkner's doomed young men, but thinks that he is not fully created: ". . . he is so mortally wounded and so vaguely understood by the author that he is hardly more than an inanimate object." [62] But it seems Faulkner's intention to present him, not as a character, but as the symbolic center of the novel—the symbol of a whole generation of American young men destroyed by the war.

As Hemingway so often does, Faulkner splits the novel's characters into two groups: those who have been touched by the war and violence and so understand the significance of Mahon, and those who have not had such experience and so lack understanding. Those who understand are Joe Gilligan, Margaret Powers, Emmy, and the Negro woman, Callie. Olga Vickery, in *The Novels of William Faulkner: A Critical Interpretation,* suggests that only those characters with direct experience of the war understand Mahon.[63] Emmy is one of the exceptions to that rule. In fact, it is in her appreciation of his loss that Faulkner best emphasizes the theme of American innocence shattered by the war. She remembers her former lover as vital, innocent, guiltless, faun-like: " 'He wouldn't never have a hat or a coat, and his face was like—it was like he ought to live in the woods.' " [64] Also, her recollection of their love making reveals it as natural, uninhibited—full of youth, spontaneity, and life (pp. 126–128). Contrasted with Emmy is Mahon's fiancée, Cecily Saunders, who, as a type more fully realized in Temple Drake in *Sanctuary,* is superficial, incapable of compassion, and finally, as her elopement with George Farr indicates, interested only in her own sexual gratification. Cecily is Mahon's principal betrayer, but there are others. He has, of course, been betrayed by the whole cultural illusion that the United States entered the war to save the world for democracy; his father, a minister, betrays him in not recognizing his implied responsibility for his son's condition; and the townspeople betray him insofar as he merely becomes an amusement for them, the subject of their gossip.

As so frequently happens in Faulkner's work, a Dilsey-like Negro woman, existing outside the white man's Christian culture and a victim of it, sums up the central experience of the novel: " 'Donald, baby, look at me. Don't you know who dis is? Dis yo' Callie whut use ter put you ter bed, honey. Look here at me. Lawd, de white folks done ruint you, but nummine, yo' mammy gwine look after her baby' " (p. 170). "De white folks," with their European heritage, had made a war, and the destruction of Mahon, as a symbol of American youth and vitality, was the natural outcome of American involvement.

What Hemingway had accomplished in his psychological portrait of Krebs, Faulkner suggests in the symbolic destruction of Mahon. Mrs. Powers comments on its tragic significance: " 'That man that was wounded is dead and there is another person, a grown child. It's his apathy, his detachment, that's so terrible. He doesn't seem to care where he is nor what he does' " (p. 118). Whereas Hemingway left his story open-ended, however, Faulkner wishes to portray Mahon's complete defeat, and he does so, near the end of the novel, in Januarius Jones' seduction of Emmy. Faulkner somewhat romantically suggests that the gallant Mahon is dying and portrays in the Snopes-like Jones the ultimate victory of the patient and the cunning. The taps played for Mahon at the moment of the seduction seem to commemorate not only his personal death but also the death of a nation's youthful dreams.

> Emmy's sobbing died away: she knew no sensation save that of warmth and langorous contentment, emptiness, even when Jones raised her face and kissed her. "Come, Emmy," he said, raising her by the armpits. She rose obediently, leaning against him warm and empty, and he led her through the house and up the stairs to her room. Outside the window, afternoon became abruptly rain, without warning, with no flapping of pennons nor sound of trumpet to herald it.
>
> (The sun had gone, had been recalled as quickly as a usurer's note and the doves fell silent or went away. The Baptist dervish's Boy Scout lipped in his bugle, sounding taps.) (pp. 297–298)

This sense of pointless and unredeemed destruction is also present in several of Faulkner's short stories. "Crevasse," "Victory," and "Ad Astra" [65] conjure up reminiscences of Eliot's *The Waste Land* and Hemingway's *The Sun Also Rises,* particularly in their presentation of the dessicated landscape of war and war's effects upon the consciousness of those involved. In addition, the Subadar in "Ad Astra" seems to be in a line of disenchanted observers that runs from Hemingway's Count Mippipopolous to the old man in the brothel in *Catch-22.* In "All the Dead Pilots," Faulkner has a narrator maimed by the war relate the events surrounding a death as pointless as Mahon's: the death of John Sartoris—the death that precipitates the action of the first Yoknapatawpha novel, *Sartoris.*[66] It is in the story "Turnabout," however, that Faulkner seems to voice his most pointed antagonism concerning the war.[67] After hearing of the death of a brave and youthful English officer, the American Captain Bogard wishes while on a bombing run that he could kill all those responsible for the war. "Then his hand dropped and he zoomed, and he held the aeroplane so, in its wild snarl, his lips parted, his breath hissing, thinking: 'God! God! If they were all there—all the generals, the admirals, the presidents and the kings—theirs, ours —all of them.' " [68] This antagonism toward a structure regarded as responsible for the war will be further developed in Faulkner's final presentation of the conflict in the allegory of *A Fable.*

The hero of Dalton Trumbo's *Johnny Got His Gun* never makes it home, but Joe Bonham, left by the war faceless, limbless, without identity, emerges, like Mahon, as the ultimate product of war: the ruined innocent youth. Enclosed in bandages, capable only of conversations with himself, he attacks the same abstract words that Frederick Henry and John Andrews attacked, making a more forceful statement for pacifism than either of his predecessors had accomplished.[69] One realizes how far one is from Cooper's romanticism when Trumbo has his hero speak about dying for a cause:

> There's nothing noble in death. What's noble about lying in the ground and rotting? What's noble about having your legs and arms blown off? What's noble about being an idiot? What's noble about being blind and deaf and dumb? What's noble about being dead? Because when you're dead mister it's all over. It's the end. You're less than a dog less than a rat less than a bee or an ant less than a white maggot crawling around on a dungheap. You're dead mister and you died for nothing.[70]

In addition to its pacifism, *Johnny Got His Gun* is also the most class conscious of the World War I novels. Joe Bonham thinks of himself as one of "the little guys" who, throughout history, are victimized by those who control the economies and the politics of nations. He specifically links the United States to the Mediterranean past when he compares the American soldier with the slaves rowing on that sea, the slaves of Carthage and Rome, and the slaves who built the pyramids,[71] and concludes that the only hope for social amelioration lies in class warfare and not in warfare among nations. He envisions himself as the perfect picture of the future and he hopes to serve as a warning to those who follow him, to prevent the powerful few from again causing war.

> To fight that war they would need men and if men saw the future they wouldn't fight. So they were masking the future they were keeping the future a soft quiet deadly secret. They knew that if all the little people all the little guys saw the future they

would begin to ask questions. They would ask questions and they would find answers and they would say to the guys who wanted them to fight they would say you lying thieving sons-of-bitches we won't fight we won't be dead we will live we are the world we are the future and we will not let you butcher us no matter what you say no matter what speeches you make no matter what slogans you write. Remember it well we we we are the world we are what makes it go round we make bread and cloth and guns we are the hub of the wheel and the spokes and the wheel itself without us you would be hungry naked worms and we will not die.[72]

Johnny Got His Gun is not the best of the World War I novels, and Trumbo is frequently guilty of artistic and political oversimplification; yet, it deals forthrightly with those political considerations hinted at by Hemingway, dealt with generally by Dos Passos, and touched upon by Boyd, Faulkner, and Stallings: that an end to the constant of warfare in the western world lay in resistance to traditional economic and political structure.

John Dos Passos, in *Three Soldiers,* had partially initiated the tradition in American war novels of analyzing in detail various members of a single military unit. Two novelists in the thirties, William E. March Campbell and Hervey Allen, imitate that technique. Allen's *It Was Like This: Two Stories of the Great War* is the less successful of the two, containing a shocking scene or two of Americans enjoying the killing of Germans [73] and a rather heavy-handed initiation of an American innocent named William Henry Virgin.

Campbell's *Company K* is an infinitely better novel, supplying an adequate array of points of view and capturing in vivid detail an entire unit's disenchantment with the war and its country's involvement in it. Contained in it is criticism of Christianity more profound than the petulance of Boyd and Allen. At one point, a captain orders his men to slaughter German prisoners, and, shortly thereafter, orders them to attend church services.[74] In a comic aside, his YMCA representatives supply woman-impersonators rather than have American boys mix with French women (pp. 106–107). As in Heller's *Catch-22,* Campbell's men are at the mercy of experimenting doctors (pp. 31–32, 35–36), and, like Melville, he presents military justice as cruel and expedient (p. 110). Like Crane, he seems to conclude that all soldiers are prisoners, controlled by inhuman laws and absurd traditions (p. 69). The more educated members of the company see the war as "brutal and degrading" and common soldiers as "pawns shoved about to serve the interests of others" (p. 51). Campbell's Unknown Soldier is unknown because, lying on barbed wire with his entrails dripping out (p. 96), he destroys his dog-tags, letters, and everything else that might identify him in order that his body would not be returned to the States and be fawned over by hypocrites (pp. 96–97). Those members of Company K who live through the war and return home meet defeat in one form or another, and Campbell makes clear that the war experience is ultimately responsible (pp. 113–131).

Thus, Campbell, like Hemingway, Dos Passos, Trumbo, and Stallings, uses a novel about the war as a vehicle of protest—a protest not directed at a specific political party or theory, but a protest against the hypocrisy of an entire culture, with particular emphasis upon Christian religious hypocrisy as underpinning all the others. Private Yancey, in *Company K,* conjectures that, "If the common soldiers of each army could get together by a river bank and talk things over calmly, no war could possibly last as long as a week" (p. 48).

Novelists were not alone in this naïve hope, but World War II waited in the wings to dispel it. From the vantage point of the post-World-War-II world, William Faulkner published in 1954 a retrospective novel, *A Fable,* imposing a Christ myth on the World War I experience, and, in effect, showing Campbell's Private Yancey what would happen should the common soldiers of opposing sides attempt to call an end to war. While the main thrust of the social criticism contained in the World War I novels was aimed at economic and religious traditions, particularly the hypocrisies of institutionalized Christianity, *A Fable,* like *Billy Budd,* suggests the ultimate victory of authority and tradition over innovation —in this case the innovation of trying to apply the pacifist social teachings of primitive Christianity. The obvious allegory of the corporal as Christ is often annoying, but, in its summing up of postwar disenchantment, the novel is often profound. The corporal's relationship with his father, the General, resembles Billy's relationship with Vere, and he is rejected for much the same reason as Vere rejects Billy.

Irving Malin comments: "The General admires the courage of his son, and he sympathizes with his desire to help people. But he feels that most people need the strength of authority to direct their actions. Like Mr. Compson, the General sees the folly and weakness of men, their motivation for wanting to be led. Thus he firmly believes that he is actually helping humanity, and he refuses to accept his son's philosophy." [75] Peter Swiggart compares Vere and the Marshall, and in commenting on Faulkner's attitude toward the French military figure perhaps offers a parallel to Melville's attitude toward his Englishman:

> In complementary opposition to the idealistic Christ-figure is the French commander of the Allied armies, who understands and appreciates the Corporal's humanistic message, but nevertheless feels compelled to crucify him. Like Captain Vere in Melville's "Billy Budd," the old Marshall is saddened by his awareness of incompatibility between personal human values and a corrupt human society. However, Faulkner's character acts not out of a sense of duty but out of his author's paradoxical conviction that the two forces are only superficially opposed, that the Corporal's crucifixion is the best way of causing his martyrdom and thus confirming the value of his mission.[76]

Faulkner seems to say that, like Christ and Billy Budd, the Corporal achieves religious transcendence but has little effect upon the actions of men and nations. "A secret conference is arranged between the Allied and German generals, which decides that ordinary soldiers must never be allowed, in violation of all the rules, to end a war at their will." [77] The powerful representative of authoritarianism and tradition, the Marshall, inevitably triumphs over the figure of change and innovation, the Corporal. Dos Passos, Trumbo, Campbell, and others, even in presenting the most destructive effects of war, offered their novels as testaments of horror, and, in so doing, expressed some hope for change. One feels that Faulkner would value them as representatives of the Corporal's message, but *A Fable* is testament that such hope is doomed to failure. In *Soldier's Pay* Faulkner dramatized Mahon as war's ultimate product, but by 1954 he knew that World War II and the small wars in its aftermath had produced a multitude of Mahons, and the United States was inextricably involved in the traditional alignments and realignments of European diplomacy and militarism. The novelists of World War II would not react to the country's participation with such naïveté, and would treat the war as, more or less, a normal expression of the culture.

Notes

1. Millis, *Arms and Men: A Study in American Military History*, p. 132.
2. *Ibid.*, pp. 132, 133.
3. Huntington, *The Soldier and the State: The Theory and Politics of Civil-Military Relations*, pp. 227–228.
4. See also Upton's, *The Military Policy of the United States*.
5. Millis analyzes Upton's intention in *Arms and Men*, p. 140.
6. *Ibid.*, p. 161.
7. *Ibid.*, pp. 172–173.
8. Huntington, p. 280.
9. *Ibid.*, p. 273.
10. Millis, pp. 176–180.
11. *Men in Arms: A History of Warfare and Its Interrelationships with Western Society*, p. 256.
12. Merk, pp. 262–264.
13. Millis, p. 168.
14. J. F. C. Fuller, *War and Western Civilization*, pp. 209, 210, 216.
15. *Ibid.*, pp. 227–228.
16. Millis, p. 175.
17. Dos Passos, Trumbo, and Campbell, while probably the most effective, are not alone in this intention. Other novelists who pursued the same objective include: Theodore Fredenburgh, *Soldiers March!* Charles Yale Harrison, *Generals Die in Bed* and Elliot Paul, *Impromptu*.
18. Millis, pp. 208–209.
19. Pound, *Personae: The Collected Poems of Ezra Pound*, p. 191.
20. Fuller, p. 224.

21. Preston, Wise, and Werner, p. 273.
22. Millis, p. 210.
23. Baker, *Hemingway: The Writer as Artist,* pp. 27, 179; Rovit, *Ernest Hemingway,* p. 35.
24. Atkins, p. 6.
25. *Ibid.,* p. 119.
26. *Ibid.,* p. xvii.
27. (Subsequent references to *In Our Time* are to the New York 1958 Scribner Library edition, and are indicated by page numbers in the text.)
28. *The Short Stories of Ernest Hemingway,* pp. 485–486.
29. *Ibid.,* p. 383.
30. *Ibid.,* pp. 267–272; 363–371; 402–414; 440–449.
31. *Green Hills of Africa,* p. 70.
32. Aldridge, p. 9.
33. Young, *Ernest Hemingway,* p. 62.
34. Snell, *The Shapers of American Fiction: 1798–1947,* p. 164.
35. Cowley, *Exile's Return: A Literary Odyssey of the 1920's,* p. 45.
36. Baker, p. 99.
37. Fiedler, *Love and Death in the American Novel,* pp. 454–455.
38. New York, 1929, pp. 184–185. (Subsequent references are to this edition, and are indicated by page numbers in the text.)
39. Pound, p. 191.
40. See Stanley Cooperman, *World War I and the American Novel,* for a more detailed analysis of the World War I novelists' reactions to Christianity.
41. Hoffman, *The Twenties: American Writing in the Post-War Decade,* p. 80.
42. Kazin, *On Native Grounds: An Interpretation of Modern American Prose Literature,* p. 324.
43. Friedman, *E. E. Cummings: The Growth of a Writer,* p. 28.
44. E. E. Cummings, *Poems: 1923–1954,* p. 244.
45. Beach, *American Fiction, 1920–1940,* p. 34.
46. See Consingsby Dawson, "Insulting the Army," *New York Times Book Review* (October 2, 1921), pp. 16–17.
47. Wrenn, *John Dos Passos,* pp. 107, 113.
48. New York, 1921, p. 43. (Subsequent references are to this edition, and are indicated by pages numbers in the text.)
49. Frohock, *The Novel of Violence in America,* pp. 32, 33.
50. Henry David Thoreau, *Walden.* Variorum edition, ed. Walter Harding, p, 87.
51. Hoffman, *The Twenties,* p. 60.
52. New York, 1945, p. 14. Originally published in England as *One Man's Initiation.* (Subsequent references are to the New

York 1945 edition, and are indicated by page numbers in the text.)

53. New York, 1923. (Subsequent references are to this edition, and are indicated by page numbers in the text.)

54. Lee, pp. 192–198, 212–213.

55. See *His Soul Goes Marching On; Her Country; Joy in the Morning; Old Glory;* and *The Three Things.*

56. Simms, *Woodcraft,* p. 96. Interestingly, Joseph V. Ridgely, in *William Gilmore Simms,* entitles his section on *Woodcraft,* "Soldier's Pay."

57. Garland, *Main-Travelled Roads,* pp. 112–129.

58. *In Our Time.* See note 27.

59. Stallings, pp. 67, 82.

60. See Frederick J. Hoffman, *The Modern Novel in America,* p. 154.

61. Chase, *The American Novel and Its Tradition,* p. 222; Beach, p. 126; Kazin, *On Native Grounds,* p. 453; O'Connor, *The Tangled Fire of William Faulkner,* p. 27.

62. Chase, p. 222.

63. Vickery, p. 243.

64. *Soldier's Pay* (New York, 1926), p. 125. (Subsequent references are to this edition and are indicated by page numbers in the text.)

65. *Collected Stories of William Faulkner,* pp. 465–474; 431–464; 407–429.

66. *Ibid.,* pp. 511–531.

67. *Ibid.,* pp. 475–509.

68. *Ibid.,* p. 509.

69. Trumbo, p. 72.

70. *Ibid.,* p. 74.

71. *Ibid.,* pp. 112–114.

72. *Ibid.,* pp. 148–149.

73. Allen, pp. 129–130; 147–148.

74. New York, 1958. (Subsequent references are to the New York 1958 edition, which is more accessible than the original 1933 edition, and are indicated by page numbers in the text).

75. Irving Malin, *William Faulkner: An Introduction,* pp. 29–30.

76. Swiggart, *The Art of Faulkner's Novels,* p. 184.

77. Irving Howe, *William Faulkner: A Critical Study,* p. 270.

5.

The World War II Novel:
A Divided Stream

In *Creating the Modern American Novel,* published in 1935, Harlan Hatcher, looking back to World War I, voiced the not uncommon hope of the years between the wars:

A society may make soldiers of its plowboys and escape as it has through the centuries. This War was singular. Men of understanding witnessed and fought it. When it set E. E. Cummings to polishing the car of a dolt who happened to be an officer, when it sent Ernest Hemingway to haul back the wounded and dying from the Italian front, when it amputated the leg of Laurence Stallings and threw him back into the peace, the results were different. They have made it less easy for the next coterie of interested chauvinists to send young men to the slaughter pens, and in so doing they have added a worthy chapter to the creation of the American novel.[1]

In fact, however, the protest novel of World War I had little or no effect upon policy making either in the United States or in Europe. Leslie Fiedler, in considering the novels of both wars, suggests that Senators and Commissars seldom listen to protesting artists, and states further: "The anti-war novel did not end war, but it memorialized the end of something almost as deeply rooted in the culture of the West: the concept of honor." [2] Indeed, just previous to the outbreak of World War II, one of Hatcher's "protesters," Ernest Hemingway, edited *Men at War: the Best War Stories of All Time,* a book at least partially intended to prepare American youth for participation in the conflict.[3] In addition, Hervey Allen published *It Was Like This* in order to answer some of the questions American young men were asking: " 'What will it be like when I am in the army? What is the American army like? What is war like? Not war over the radio, or in the headlines, but real war, fighting? How would I, and how do American soldiers, act and react in modern battles?' " [4]

John Dos Passos, the originator of both the tone and form of so much of American war literature in the twentieth century, surveyed the attitudes of the American fighting man in the forties and found him quite different from his earlier counterpart. For his generation World War I had seemed a horrible interruption in man's march toward a better life. The next generation was more disenchanted.

> The boys who are fighting these present wars got their first ideas of the world during the depression years. From the time they first read the newspapers they drank in the brutalities of European politics with their breakfast coffee.

War and oppression in the early years of this century appeared to us like stinking slums in a city that was otherwise beautiful and good to live in, blemishes that skill and courage would remove. To the young men of today these things are inherent deformities of mankind. If you have your club foot you learn to live with your club foot. That doesn't mean they like the dust and the mud and the fatigue and the agony of war or the oppression of man by man any better than we did. But the ideas of these things are more familiar.[5]

So, too, the literature produced by the war is quite different from the literature of World War I. First of all, there is much more of it, and, second, it is much more diversified both in terms of content and tone. Of course, whole new areas opened up for the writer as a result of technological and scientific developments. The deployment of air power and the use of the tank provided both more destructive firepower and increased mobility,[6] the former involving massive civilian deaths in strategic conflict and the latter providing the means of breaking the kind of defensive stalemate and attrition typical of World War I.[7] Also, American novelists, for the first time in large numbers, explored the Far East as a result of the war in the Pacific; and, finally, many United States soldiers remained as occupation troops and a good number of novels deal with the problem of military men in positions of governmental control over civilians.

When one considers that the World War I novel dealt almost exclusively with the horrible conditions of a bogged-down infantry amassing dead bodies, the subject matter of the second World War seems quite varied. In addition, the tone of the earlier novels was remarkably uniform, expressing shock at the physical facts of war, horror at the brutality of the totalitarian military structure, and disenchantment with western world diplomacy, politics, and Christianity. The World War II novel is not at all uniform in tone and attitudes. Besides those works that use the war almost exclusively as a setting for adventure,[8] it splits into three general groups whose lines of demarcation occasionally overlap and frequently blur: the novels that follow in the World War I tradition; those that present warfare as a brutal but normal human experience; and those that, while much less doctrinaire than their forerunners of the previous war, offer specific criticism of aspects of American society.[9]

Robert Lowry's *Casualty*, published in 1946, was the first to follow in the tradition of the World War I novel. The hero, Private Joe Hammond, much like the enlisted-men heroes of Dos Passos or Stallings or Campbell, thinks of military training as a means of deforming the individual,[10] feels caught in a totalitarian trap, and, very much like John Andrews, is "intense, essentially a private person, unhappy in the gray immoral leveling of the army system . . ." (p. 55). He describes the army as "this rotten lie that men had built up as a machine for poor-spirited bastards to glorify themselves in" (p. 75). He feels betrayed by an America that produces officers like Colonel Polaski, who, during occupation duty, lives in the same luxurious home the leading fascist had occupied (pp. 23–24), drinks the same good wine (p. 90), and is more cruel to his Italian subjects than the fascist had been. Naturally, Polaski is anti-Jewish (p. 103), and, if one needs visual clues, his villainy is confirmed when Lowry describes him as closely resembling Herbert Hoover (p. 27). Like so many of the officers in the World War I novel, Polaski is a caricature—a useful caricature in a protest against authoritarianism. The hero, Hammond, considers himself quite ironic when he states that "some innocent American boys had even arrived at the startling conclusion, why the army is a Fascist institution itself . . ." (pp. 143–144).

After all, one could deal with Lowry's novel in the same ironic tone. If the central theme of *Casualty,* as it seems to be, is the revelation that a democratic nation fields a totalitarian army and that Americans are not immune from cruelty, greed, and a desire for power, then he offers nothing new, and the novel itself, while not badly written, becomes an exercise in the repetition of the shock and disenchantment felt and established by an earlier generation. David Davidson's *The Steeper Cliff* is thematically similar to *Casualty,* expressing dismay at American totalitarianism and brutality during the occupation, and identifying the American Jew as the man of nonviolence in a warlike Christian culture.[11] Although the Jew appeared frequently in the novels of World War I as a sensitive and suffering figure, not until Hitler began his "final solution" did Jewish characters in the American novel become almost universally symbols of a persecuted minority.[12] Martha Gelhorn's *The Wine of Astonishment* is very much a part of this trend, presenting a Jewish-American protagonist, Jacob Levy, who, disfigured by the war, is almost as pathetic a product of conflict as Dalton Trumbo's Johnny. Indeed, Noah Ackerman's brutalization and death in Irwin Shaw's far better novel, *The Young Lions,* is indicative of the continuation of a rejection of the totalitarian military social structure and the bigoted Christians whom it comprises.

Among novels concerned with the problems of returned veterans, Merle Miller's *That Winter* most closely resembles the last sections of Campbell's *Company K* and

Stallings' novel, *Plumes*. Miller presents his returned Americans almost exclusively as disenchanted innocents. The narrator, Peter, who went to the war from a small town in Iowa, writes a novel whose outline resembles the opening sentence of Hemingway's "Soldier's Home": "It was the story of a midwestern boy, a sensitive boy, I liked to think, who had gone almost directly from a peaceful college campus into the Army and into the war." [13] Peter, himself, returns to Iowa when his father dies only to find himself a displaced person, still longing for an innocence he knows now to be illusory. Ted, another veteran, haunted by nightmares of the war, commits suicide (pp. 12, 92–93), and a minor figure, reared in a strait-laced Southern Baptist tradition, returns an alcoholic (pp. 1–2). Everyone meets defeat in a novel that contains most of the ingredients of the antiwar formula: hatred of authoritarian officers (p. 53), criticism of representatives of the Christian tradition (p. 244), dismay at American anti-Semitism (p. 108), and the depiction of the army as destructive of individuality and self-respect (p. 48).

While Miller is sometimes obvious and self-consciously sophisticated, *That Winter* is often an engaging novel; however, like Lowry's *Casualty,* it is repetitive and imitative. Similarly, another novel in the protest tradition that suffers from self-conscious hypersophistication is Vance Bourjaily's *The End of My Life,* which, in its detailed depiction of the shattering of personality under the avalanche of the war experience and in its glimmerings of real talent, reminds one of Faulkner's *Soldier's Pay.*

Joe David Brown's *Kings Go Forth* emphasizes the physical horrors of war (pp. 36, 16–40, 54) and ends with one of its important characters, Loggins, physically and psychologically ruined in a conflict that has come to seem pointless (p. 255).[14] Brown deals with the problem of American racism, a parallel to anti-Semitism in the novels, when he has Sergeant Butt reject the French girl, Monique, because she is part Negro.[15] The race issue is central in John Cobb's *The Gesture*, as the sensitive, music-loving, liberal Major Harris, brings about disaster and finally his own death in attempting to integrate his unit. Here ruthless bigotry grows out of the masses themselves, and Cobb seems to suggest that Harris' gesture of democratic idealism and its defeat prove that the ideals for which the war was waged were doomed to failure.

In an interesting offshoot of the protesting military novel, a Black writer, John Oliver Killens, in 1963, uses the form as a vehicle for Black protest. In *And Then We Heard the Thunder* the persecuted Jew is replaced by the persecuted black man, but the ingredients of protest remain essentially the same. The officer corps, representing a white power structure, is almost universally corrupt —bigoted, fascistic, and often homosexual; and the Black hero, torn between commitments to his race and to his country, finally sees himself as a member of the exploited masses and announces the message of pacifism: " 'There'll be wars and rumors of wars just like he said the Bible said, as long as fools like me go out and kill each other and never know the reasons why. I'm also saying how in hell are you going to fight a democratic war with a racist Army?' " [16] Despite some obvious propaganda and oversimplification, in which it seems that most Blacks are good and almost all whites are part of a gigantic lynching party, *And Then We Heard the Thunder* is an effective novel of protest, which, after a Negro-Caucasian bloodbath, ends on an optimistic note with white and Black soldiers sitting together in the street.[17]

In his discussion of Irwin Shaw's *The Young Lions*,

Willard Thorp sees the novel as "a carry-over from the social-crusading, proletarian thirties." [18] Frederick Hoffman concurs that the book is "a deeply sincere, almost literal acceptance of the ideological moralities of the 1930's. . . ." [19] Actually, *The Young Lions*, along with all the novels just discussed, is in a tradition begun a decade before the thirties in the novels of World War I. As late as 1964, the tradition continues in the form of Alfred Slote's *Strangers and Comrades*. Slote presents dishonest generals,[20] an inept company commander known among the men as "Captain Horseshit," and a hero named Aaron Geller who comes to some of the usual conclusions concerning the military world: "It suddenly occurred to Aaron that he didn't like the Army, and as that thought occurred to him a second soon followed. He couldn't leave. He had suddenly lost freedom of action. He could walk out on a job at Rutter's, he could walk out on his family. But he couldn't leave here. A wave of self-pity flowed through him. This was not Army; this was prison." [21] Thus, nineteen years after the end of the war, in a novel in which General MacArthur has begun to have some of the mythic mysteriousness Washington had in Cooper's *The Spy*,[22] the tradition of protest continues.

Of all the works within this tradition, perhaps James Jones' *From Here to Eternity* is most typical. Malcolm Cowley, in *The Literary Situation*, remarks that Jones is the only writer to sympathetically treat a dedicated thirty-year Regular Army soldier as hero.[23] But this fact, after all, is incidental. Prewitt, as fully as any of the citizen-soldiers, is victimized by the system. Hassan seems near the truth when he suggests: "In the unequal conflict between individual and society, Prewitt stands as an emblem of antipower. Recalcitrance is the badge of his heroism—and his victimization." [24] Like so many others,

he is the figure who stands up to the social structure and
is destroyed. David L. Stevenson, in "James Jones and
Jack Kerouac: Novelists of Distinction," comments that
Jones captures "a Neanderthal culture" in *From Here to
Eternity*.[25]

Certainly, it is a simple one. Not since Trumbo's
Johnny Got His Gun has there been more simple black
and white demarcation between the good and the evil,
and in Jones' book the good are the persecuted masses of
enlisted men and the bad are the officers who exploit
them. The morality is occasionally a little silly as when
Jones, on the one hand, glorifies the enlisted man's pursuit of pleasure at the New Congress Hotel, but, on the
other, casts an officer's bacchanal in a sinister tone of condemnation.[26] In one obvious portrait, he presents the evil
organization man, Captain Holmes, as a pyramid-climbing sharpie who uses his men's athletic capabilities as a
means of gaining his promotions. His sympathetically
drawn first Sergeant, Warden, who eventually has an
affair with the Captain's wife, Karen, sums him up:
" 'Holmes is the CO, but he is like the rest of the officer
class: a dumb bastard that signs papers an rides horses
an wears spurs an gets stinking drunk up at the stinking
Officers' Club' " (p. 49). Karen, who naturally prefers
Warden to Holmes, serves as a voice of condemnation,
explaining that she had to have a hysterectomy because
her husband infected her with gonorrhea (pp. 333–335).
She, with Warden, feels outside the upper-middle-class
world of her husband, and so can criticize it:

> "Loves like ours have always suffered," Karen
> said brighteyedly ardently. "We both knew that
> when we went into it. Loves like ours have always
> been hated," she said, looking at him with the half-

parted mouth and warm-shining eyes of a Joan of Arc that made him suddenly want terribly to take her to bed. "Society does everything it can to prevent love like ours and what it cant prevent it destroys. Securely married American men dont like to think their wives have the right to leave them—not for love, which has never bought anything yet. And securely married American women, who have been talked into believing it, know they've been duped, thats why they hate that kind of love worst of all because they have all had to sacrifice it for security and hate themselves for doing it so much they dont want anybody else to have a chance at it." (p. 621)

As noted in Chapter Four, the love relationship in *A Farewell to Arms* has begun to seem overly sentimental; certainly, Jones, in his glorification of the self-consciously rebellious relationship between Karen Holmes and Milt Warden, is guilty of the same thing. Whores and deserters, in Jones' book, are almost all sensitive and persecuted people; officers and other members of the middle class are the villains. Warden sums up that class in a passage that seems to reflect the novelist's point of view by claiming that it is responsible for every political wrong in creation—even declaring that Communism is a middle-class plot to keep the peasants in their place (pp. 621–622). After this curious interpretation of political reality, he then tells Karen, who like Yossarian's Nurse Duckett in *Catch-22*, loves everything about her man and therefore wants to change him: " 'And now I'm supposed to go on and become an Officer, the symbol of every goddam thing I've always stood up against, and not feel anything about it. I'm supposed to do that for you' " (p. 622). Earlier in the novel, Jones had announced: "Warden had a theory about officers: Being an officer would make a son of a bitch out of Christ himself. And they had you by the nuts. You couldn't do a thing. That was why they were such ones" (p. 47). Indeed, perhaps the most sympathetically drawn figure in the novel, Jack Malloy, further reflects Jones' sentimentality and over-simplification. Like Steinbeck's Jim Casey in *The Grapes of Wrath,* Malloy is a kind of Christ figure, representative of a new morality based upon social justice. The reader knows he is one of Jones' good guys because he reads Whitman's *Leaves of Grass* and Veblen's *Theory of the Leisure Class,* knows Joe Hill's songs, is a member of the IWW, has an "unembarrassed dreamer's eyes," and likes to make love to prostitutes (pp. 639–641). He is in opposition to the power moralists like General Slater and Captain Holmes and so he is in jail.

In his sentimentalization of the common man and in his damnation of all officers as villains, in his depiction of corrupt military justice (pp. 522–523) and brutal military prisons (pp. 648–657), Jones is like the most doctrinaire of the novelists of World War I. As revealed in Slote's *Strangers and Comrades,* it is a continuing tradition, but in no one more self-consciously than in Jones, who in reality is an apostle although declaring himself the prophet of the military novel as a force for protest. When he describes Prewitt's playing of taps it is clear that he describes his own work:

This is the true song, the song of the ruck, not of battle heroes; the song of the Stockade prisoners itchily stinking sweating under coats of grey rock dust; the song of the mucky KP's, of the men without women who collect the bloody menstrual rags of the officers' wives, who come to scour the Officers' Club —after the parties are over. This is the song of the scum, the Aqua-Velva drinkers, the shameless ones who greedily drain the half-filled glasses, some of them lipsticksmeared, that the party-ers can afford to leave unfinished.

This is the song of the men who have no place, played by a man who has never had a place, and can therefore play it. Listen to it. You know the song, remember? This is the song you close your ears to every night, so you can sleep. This is the song you drink five martinis every evening not to hear. This is the song of the Great Loneliness, that creeps in like the desert wind and dehydrates the soul. This is the song you'll listen to on the day you die. When you lay there in the bed and sweat it out, and know that all the doctors and nurses and weeping friends dont mean a thing and cant help you any, cant save you the small bitter taste of it, because you are the one thats dying and not them; when you wait for it to come and know that sleep will not evade it and martinis will not help you to escape it; then you will hear this song and, remembering, recognize it. This song is Reality. Remember? Surely you remember? (pp. 218–219)

Had Jones been announcing this challenge in 1921 he would have been a prophet—an initiator of a tradition. As it is, *From Here to Eternity* is little more than a grab-bag of clichés in a protest that had long since grown familiar.

His two other works dealing with the war, *The Pistol* and *The Thin Red Line,* while not in a tradition of protest, offer nothing new. The former is a clumsy novelette filled with two-dimensional figures who dramatize man's worshipping of power; the latter, a repetitive and monstrously long novel, merely concentrates on a naturalistic depiction of men at war. As he seems unoriginal in terms of ideas in *From Here to Eternity,* in *The Thin Red Line* he is just as unoriginal in terms of style. The book is little more than a host of clichés including descriptions of battle that may have been new for Bierce or Crane but which seem in 1962 stale and repetitive. Stevenson is partially correct when he suggests that in *The Thin Red Line* Jones's "authentic observations often seem about to be drowned in a sea of words." [27] In addition, these "authentic observations" all too often seem echoes of other writers. The story of Fife's initiation follows the same pattern as Henry Fleming's. In fact, Fife views a dying young soldier who very much resembles Crane's Jim Conklin,[28] but, unlike Crane, Jones does not offer the possibility that the young man's victory may be a shallow one. Rather, he seems to rejoice with Fife in the discovery: " 'I can kill, too! I can! Just like everybody! I can kill, too!' " (p. 438). In presenting what it is like to be wounded, Jones sounds like Crane filtered through Hemingway: "They had crossed a strange line; they had become wounded men; and everybody realized, including themselves, dimly, that they were now different" (p. 44). The primary reason for the book's gargantuan length is revealed when a short time later Jones merely repeats himself: "These men had crossed a line, and it was useless to try to reach them. These had experienced something that they themselves had not experienced, and devoutly hoped they would never experience, but until they did experience it they could no longer communicate with them" (p. 45). As to the ideas contained in the novel, just as Jones was pretentious in *From Here to Eternity* concerning his social protest, so in *The Thin Red Line* he is pretentious about his naturalistic view of the human experience—again, a view that may have shocked the readers of Crane or Dreiser but which, in 1962, is hardly exciting. Sergeant Bell, the intellectual center of the novel, voices its naturalistic message, but, certainly, he is no harbinger of a new belief:

> They thought they were men. They all thought they were real people. They really did. How funny. They thought they made decisions and ran their own lives, and proudly called themselves free human beings. The truth was they were here, and they were gonna stay here, until the state through some other automaton told them to go someplace else, and then they'd go. But they'd go freely, of their own free choice and will, because they were free individual human beings. Well, well. (p. 267)

Well, well indeed. Devoid of perceptiveness or ideas, *The Thin Red Line* emerges as a long and boring book, filled with the leavings of other books that had dealt less pretentiously with the same subjects.

With reference to Jones's development as a thinker, it is interesting that between 1951 and 1962 he dropped the war novel as a vehicle for social protest. In fact, at one point Welsh, the tough First Sergeant in *The Thin Red Line*, admits: "The truth was he liked all this shit. He liked being shot at, liked being frightened, liked lying in holes scared to death and digging his fingernails into the ground, liked shooting at strangers and seeing them fall hurt, liked his stickywet feet in his stickywet socks. Part of him did" (p. 410). Most of the characters in this novel, unlike the sergeant, may not like the war, but they bear out Dos Passos' observation that Americans in World War II accepted the realities of conflict and the realities of military life much more readily than did the previous generation.

Much earlier than Jones's *The Thin Red Line* and in contrast to works like *Casualty, That Winter,* and *From Here to Eternity,* many of the novels of the forties and fifties diverge from the tone of shock, dismay, and disenchantment. For many participants who wrote about it, the war experience was not a shock—nor, in a sense, should it have been. The preceding generation had written enough to prepare American youth for the brutal reality. Chester E. Eisinger, in *Fiction of the Forties,* reaches a conclusion similar to Dos Passos'. He suggests that the American soldier regarded World War I as a noble cause but was not idealistic about World War II and so experienced little disenchantment.[29] Basing his conclusions in part on *Studies in Social Psychology in World War II,*[30] Eisinger suggests that most of the men involved in the conflict regarded it "as a defensive or national necessity" and felt little commitment to the war as a cause.[31] Frederick Hoffman, in *The Modern Novel in America,* discovering less sense of purpose and less disenchantment in the World War II novels, concludes: "The persistent impression given by these novelists is of a dirty and inconvenient break in the rhythm of the prewar life. Only occasionally does the rhetoric of purpose intervene."[32] To be sure, for most of these writers the war remains brutal, stark, and destructive, but, as in the case of a club foot, one must adjust to it.

Harry Brown's *A Walk in the Sun* is the earliest and one of the best novels to deal with the conflict as a brutal fact of life and not in protest. It is important to note at the outset that he does not romanticize or glamorize war. In fact, he presents it in much the same way as the earlier writers. He sees it as "incoherent" and "unreasonable" and "full of paradoxes." [33] His enlisted man still feels dwarfed and insignificant and must cultivate patience if he is to survive (p. 34). Death still descends with the same lack of logic. But, the central figure in the novel, Tyne, who takes command of the platoon after the lieutenant is killed and Sergeant Porter goes to pieces, is not the culture-hero that Frederick Henry or Jake Barnes or John Andrews was. He is simply an average American who feels the pressures of conflict and the pressures of responsibility as he devises the tactics and then directs the seizure of a farmhouse held by German soldiers. He is, in no sense, representative of the exploited masses; nor, in a larger context, is there any sense of class conflict between enlisted men and officers. In fact, Brown seems to think of officers only in terms of their capacity to realize mission objectives: "In the Army the word 'good' is a superlative. A good officer is the Merriwell type. He always gets where he wants to go, and he keeps his casualties down. He knows when to be hard and when to relax. He will bear down on his men in barracks, but when he's out in the field he will call them Joe and Charlie and swear at them and pat them on the back as though he were the coach of a football team" (p. 15). Tyne fulfills these requirements in the process of taking the house, and, as he runs toward it, he comments simply on the obstacles he has overcome: " 'It is so terribly easy' " (p. 187).

Hoffman, in examining the tone of *A Walk in the Sun,* suggests: "The novel lacks the kind of interpretation which Lieutenant Henry had given the Caporetto retreat in *A Farewell to Arms.* There are no outbursts of violated dignity in Brown's representation, only a rather quiet explanation of immediate emotions and strate-

gies." [34] It is an attitude similar to the hero's attitude in
James E. Ross's *The Dead Are Mine* when he states that
he isn't interested in ideological issues—just killing Germans;[35] and it resembles the hero's sentiment in Robert
M. Coates's *The Bitter Season* which suggests that, regardless of the reasons for the war, the United States,
once involved, must win it: "That, of course, is the pragmatic approach, and it's one of the traps that history is
always laying for us; but it is the only possible practical
view of the situation, nevertheless." [36]

On scales much larger than Brown's *A Walk in the
Sun,* Ned Calmer's *The Strange Land,* Tom T. Chamales' *Never So Few,* Anton Myrer's *The Big War,* Leon
M. Uris' *Battle Cry,* Ward Taylor's *Roll Back the Sky,*
and Theodore H. White's *The Mountain Road* all express, in varying degrees, the horrible facts of war, but
also accept these facts as inevitable phenomena. Indeed,
Chamales, in his novel of guerrilla activity against the
Japanese in Burma, seems to take pleasure in showing
how brutal his hero, Con Reynolds, can be. In presenting
a conversation between Reynolds and the group's doctor,
he seems to delight in his hero's argument for expedient
torturing:

> "You don't look like no all-American boy any-
> more," Con said.
> "I'm a pig. We're all pigs," the Doctor said dis-
> gustedly. "Dirty murdering pigs."
> "You'll get on my nerves if you keep talking like
> that."
> "Your nerves were insensitive a long time ago."
> "Insensitive shit. Adjusted. That's all. Adjusted."
> "You like this life, don't you. You and Ringa
> both."

"Come off it," Con said. "Remember that Jap Ringa tortured outside Myitkyina. Near the river."

"I remember. When he put the bamboo splinter up his penis and lit it."

"All right, if that's the way you want to put it. But that goddamn stupid piece of information just happened to have saved the lives of over six hundred Americans and two thousand Chinese. And every Chinese that can fight takes some of it off our guys." [37]

Thus, Chamales has Reynolds win the argument, and, within the context of the war situation, seem quite reasonable. His hard-nosed viciousness is a sharp departure from the World War I novel; and, as in *A Walk in the Sun,* questions of morality have been replaced by questions of tactics and maneuvers. Interestingly, none of the tension between officers and enlisted men, so frequent in the protest tradition, exists in *Never So Few.* As in *A Walk in the Sun,* the men have little sense of class structure. They merely work together to accomplish a series of tactical objectives. The novel is not without ideas, but they tend to be political rather than moral and are frequently quite objective about United States intentions. Gone is any notion of saving the world for democracy. Rather, Chamales has a local priest comment on the plight of the small nations of Southeast Asia: " 'What would be the use of the Kachins liberating themselves of Japanese domination only to have the rape and pillage and crooked rule of the Chinese? Or even the Americans. It was a tragic predicament that small nations would always face.' " [38]

Anton Myrer, in *The Big War,* is content to present the horror and pointlessness of war, and, even though his most sympathetically drawn characters, Amory Newcombe and Danny Kantaylis, are killed, there is little protest in the novel. Neither is there in Calmer's *The Strange Land*. A hard-boiled and ruthless general, Mallon, appears, but he is counterbalanced by the humane General Hennessey. Naturally, Calmer presents the horrors of war, but there is no sense of class conflict, and Captain Crosby, Lieutenant Keith, and Sergeant Vorak all attain some degree of heroism.

Leon Uris, in *Battle Cry*, deviates most from the World War I novels, announcing in the preface: " 'My pride in serving with the Marines is obvious to anyone reading *Battle Cry*. I admired and respected the officers of my battalion." [39] Indeed, despite wholesale bloodshed and savagery, the novel presents a military unit that functions well in terms of its mission objectives, and that concern seems to be the basis upon which Uris makes his judgments. There is brutality in boot camp but it is viewed as necessary in order to turn out trained killers (pp. 35 ff.). The sense of social structure so obvious on troop ships, officers above and enlisted men below, that had so enraged some of the World War I heroes, is accepted by the men as quite natural (p. 193). The narrator of the novel, a professional soldier, is sympathetically drawn and his acceptance of military life pervades the entire novel. The officer-in-charge, Lieutenant Colonel Huxley, is an excellent and understanding leader who can say, " 'The happiness of every one of my boys concerns me . . .' " (p. 337). When he orders an almost impossible forced march in order to outdo another unit, his men understand and appreciate his interest in their pride (pp. 358–372). When he fights to get them an initial assault position for a beachhead landing in which three hundred will probably be killed, they understand and wish to follow him (pp. 477–480). In death, he achieves an ultimate victory: "Huxley's Whores rose to the heights of their dead captain. They no longer resembled human beings. Savage beyond all savagery, murderous beyond murder, they shrieked, 'Blood!' " (p. 498). In Dos Passos, such a statement would mean defeat and dehumanization; in Uris, it means the success of a system in training men to defend their country. Poles apart from *From Here to Eternity, Battle Cry* is as simple as Jones's novel in its view of military structure.

Neither Ward Taylor nor Theodore H. White goes as far as Uris, but their novels also testify to an American acceptance of the war. When the United States Air Force began its strategic bombing in Europe, it orginally placed great faith in pinpoint daylight bombing attacks,[40] and, only after some shocking losses, did it come, like the Royal Air Force, to favor nighttime saturation attacks. In so doing, there was the obvious recognition of the impossibility of limiting targets to military and strategic industrial sites.[41] So, with some moral misgivings, the decision was made to make air strikes a means of terrorizing the civilian population. In *Roll Back the Sky*, Ward Taylor expresses acceptance of, not opposition to, nighttime saturation bombing of Tokyo with incendiaries. At one point, Withers tells the hero, Captain Richardson: " 'I talked to one of the photo pilots right after he landed this afternoon. Said the wind was blowing the smoke away enough so they got a fair look, and about half the town at least is burning.' " To which, Richardson replies " 'I'll take the fire bombs ten to one, in preference to a day formation strike.' "[42] In White's *Mountain Road*, the American hero, Major Baldwin, identifies with destruction: "It *was* a good outfit; now it was his to use, these men had probably destroyed more in the last two days' work than the value of a good engineer's lifetime of building. If you figured back to the whole summer's operation the outfit had probably destroyed more than *any* engineer had ever built in any lifetime. And only eight of them. The feel of their power rose in Baldwin." [43] Unlike John Hersey, in *The War Lover,* White does not probe the psychological possibility of sexual maladjustment as the root cause of his protagonist's attitudes. In fact, Baldwin is a rather grim reminder of D. H. Lawrence's warnings concerning the inevitability of American destructiveness.[44]

Michael Millgate, in *American Social Fiction: James to Cozzens,* suggests that Herman Wouk is one of the World War II novelists who accepted expedient fascism in order to win the war.[45] Certainly, Wouk is diametrically in opposition to the writers of World War I. Like Uris and others just considered, he accepts warfare as a national prerogative, accepts the methods of the military during wartime as necessary, and offers neither protest nor critical analysis of the military itself or the military as a microcosm of American society. Frederick Ives Carpenter compares Wouk with Melville, and concludes that *The Caine Mutiny,* like *Billy Budd,* "begins with the dream of individual liberty" and "ends with the affirmation of traditional authority." [46] This may be true but, certainly, the two novelists differ in their attitudes toward the process. Willy Keith, unlike Billy, does not end in death; rather, he accepts organizational authority and, finally, seems to direct his total rebellion at his mother, whose wishes he will disappoint when he marries Mae Wynne. There is little sense of tragedy in that. Millgate seems closer to the mark than Carpenter when he says in criticism of Wouk that ". . . he does not draw the political conclusions which his 'message' implies, and that he thus obscures the deadly irony involved in fighting Fascism with a military instrument which, perhaps necessarily, but none the less actually, is itself fascistic both in its organization and its demands for loyalty and obedience." [47]

It is clear that Wouk has in mind the tradition of military novels of protest when he has Greenwald criticize Keefer's work as dishonest and Keefer himself as both opportunistic and intellectually naïve. Greenwald describes Keefer's manuscript: " 'I'm sure that it exposes this war in all its grim futility and waste, and shows up the military men for the stupid, Fascist-minded sadists they are. Bitching up all the campaigns and throwing away the lives of fatalistic, humorous, lovable citizen-soldiers." He continues: " 'I like novels where the author proves how terrible military guys are, and how superior sensitive civilians are. I know they're true to life because I'm a sensitive civilian myself." [48] In effect, Wouk shows the liberal intellectual, Keefer, theoretically so committed to social justice, to be as cowardly and self-seeking as Queeg. Both are shallow and opportunistic. Queeg may prove his cowardice when during engagements he stays close to the ship's side away from incoming shells, but Keefer matches him at the trial when he avoids the issue of his complicity in the mutiny and leaves Maryk, the simple American, at the court's mercy. Queeg may be a poor officer, but Keefer is little more than a slick young man with intellectual pretensions.

With neither one does Wouk wish his readers to sympathize. Rather, it is the consciousness of Willy Keith and his apparent growth in maturity that he wishes to emphasize. But he is not at all ironic in his treatment of Willy and therein lies one of the faults in the work that prevent it from attaining the greatness of *Billy Budd* or *The Red Badge of Courage*. Wouk asks the reader to place faith in the judgment of a young man, who, throughout the novel, exhibits almost incredible short-sightedness and naïveté. From his quick and wrongheaded appraisal of Captain De Vriess (pp. 120 ff.) to his fantasies concerning the heroes' welcomes he thinks the Navy will accord its mutineers (p. 417) to his shock at discovering that Queeg is still an active officer (p. 550), Willy reveals, at best, an often imperceptive mind. Yet, it is his conclusion, in a letter to Mae, that Wouk seems to present as truth: "The idea is, once you get an incompetent ass of a skipper—and it's a chance of war—there's nothing to do but serve him as though he were the wisest and the best, cover his mistakes, keep the ship going, and bear up. So I have gone all the way around Robin Hood's barn to arrive at the old platitudes, which I guess is the process of growing up" (p. 542).

Willy goes on to reveal that his mentor is Greenwald, a Jewish fighter-pilot lawyer, who felt from the outset that the mutineers should be punished (pp. 406–407) and who concludes in the famous speech at the victory celebration: " 'Queeg deserved better at my hands. I owed him a favor, don't you see? He stopped Hermann Goering from washing his fat behind with my mother' " (p. 517). So, in the context of this outburst, it would seem that Wouk does not advocate the chauvinism of "my country, right or wrong," but rather believes that the genocide in Europe induces a moral basis for action that overrides any objections to the temporary totalitarianism to which the American must subject himself in order to achieve the defeat of Nazi Germany and the other Axis powers. Millgate seems right, however, in accusing Wouk of political and philosophical oversimplification, for in the bipolar environment of constant conflict that the world has endured since World War II, Willy's conclusion that, during times of crisis, one must follow one's leader becomes little more than "my country, right or wrong." If Americans were to follow such a course, Harold D. Lasswell warns in *National Security and Individual Freedom,* then inevitably the results would be a loss of freedom and the growth of a police state [49]—exactly the kind of political order that would permit a Goering to turn anybody's mother into soap. "Our aim," Lasswell states, "is to prevent successful aggression by a totalitarian dictatorship without becoming transformed in the process into a garrison prison." [50]

Wouk, at least in *The Caine Mutiny,* seems too shortsighted to appreciate the possible ultimate results of his political oversimplification. Thus in the final analysis, the differences between Wouk's and Melville's attitudes toward authoritarianism are manifest. Melville, recognizing it as a terrible necessity and possible inevitability, presents Billy Budd's experience in a tragic or at least pathetic dimension; Wouk reaches no such dimension and seems almost in active pursuit of a means to debunk the liberal tradition. Instead of the depths of complexity to which Melville dives, he seems content to wade in the waters of political simplicity and offers in *The Caine Mutiny* an entertaining but intellectually naïve novel. Wouk's performance is even more shallow insofar as he frequently makes use of the very devices he has Greenwald condemn in his scathing evaluation of Keefer's manuscript.

Three other novels, William Wister Haines' *Command Decision,* John Marquand's *Melville Goodwin, USA,* and, especially, James Gould Cozzens' *Guard of Honor,* are examples of works which accept warfare as a normal human experience and are much more intensive than Wouk's in their analysis of military structure and various types of professional American soldiers. They will be considered together with Morris Janowitz's sociological work, *The Professional Soldier,* in Chapter Six.

Lasswell, in 1950, wrote his study of the effects of constant crisis upon American democracy in order to warn of the diminishing of individual freedom in the name of national security, and, in general, seemed fearful of the growth of the power of the executive toward quasi-totalitarian rule. A number of World War II novels, both before and after Lasswell's book, warn of similar problems. Unlike those that follow in the tradition established by Dos Passos, Hemingway, and others, these works do not voice a general cultural condemnation; rather, they offer some analysis of American totalitarianism as expressed in the military structure, and, as a group, seem to warn of a general drift in the United States away from democratic practices toward increased authoritarianism. Walter Millis warns that the facts of war inevitably force democratic nations to adopt measures that severely limit the freedoms of thought, information, and dissent. He states that, "It was not only in Russia and Germany but in Britain and the United States that war proved again the great forcing-bed of the unitary state." [51] In addition, according to Millis, "A degree of regimentation and centralization which was never possible during the Civil War, which was still at least strange and disquieting after 1917, had by 1941 become no more than a normal and patently necessary order of affairs." [53] World War II only strengthened this flow of events, and a number of novelists, perceptive enough to perceive its drift, warned of the process and its possible outcome.

Most pointedly, a group of novels concerned with the occupation of Europe warn of American totalitarianism by depicting the ways in which United States military leaders rule and govern. Stefan Heym's *The*

Crusaders, filled with clichés and possibly the least successful of the group, condemns. American occupation
practices as brutal and neofascist and presents the commanding general, Farrish, as boyish, dangerously simple,
and disdainful of objections to his keeping Nazis in
power.[53] He is not a dark and devious figure, but, like
De Forest's Colonel Carter, he would carry into the gov-
erning of civilians the same rigid patterns of totalitarian
thought with which he directs his military structure.
Alfred Hayes, in the Hemingwayesque *The Girl on the
Via Flaminia,* is most concerned with the debilitating
effects upon the Italian population of United States military rule, particularly symbolized in the pathetic Antonio,
and the novel in its totality is permeated by a sense of a
restrictive and threatening totalitarianism.

Lionel Shapiro, more romantic about the war in his
Sixth of June, limits himself to the problems of military
government in *The Sealed Verdict.* Major Lashley, the
moral focus in the latter novel, is shocked by American
behavior in Europe and is the American innocent through
whose eyes Shapiro views the professional officer: "Experience had made him suspicious of men whose processes of
thought had been molded at West Point, Fort Riley, and
an army post in the Philippines. He had known too many
younger career men whose training had blunted the sharp
edge of their concern, who thought less about individuals
and more about armies, less about pilots and more about
air power, less about the feel of tragedy and more about
the grasp of victory." [54] General Marriner, as such a man,
embodies a military definition of reality. Although the
novelist is sensitive to the difficulties faced by a ruler of
occupied territory (pp. 98–99), he does not condone Marriner's violation of normal legal practices in turning
Themis Delisle over to the French (p. 134), his speeding

up of executions for questionable reasons (p. 150), his hints to lower ranking officers serving in a court-martial that he needs a speedy conviction (p. 168), or his willingness to circumvent justice in order to avoid public scandal (p. 178). Shapiro is not, however, without sympathy for the general. It is clear from the outset that Marriner is a competent, even outstanding, military leader, and, through his own words, he makes clear that his role as governor is one for which he is not prepared and one which he does not covet:

> "I'm a soldier, Lashley. My father was a soldier. I was brought up and trained to fight for my country. That's the tradition of soldiering. You fight for your country and you don't ask many questions beyond that. Matters of humanity and a new world— things like that you leave to the men in the cutaway coats. That's soldiering.
> "Well, it's changing now. I can feel it. The old style of soldiering is slipping away from me. Now problems are coming up—problems we were never trained to solve. We come up against questions we can't find answered in the manual of tactics." (p. 267)

In contrast to Shapiro, John Hersey has no such understanding for Marriner's counterpart, General Marvin, in *A Bell for Adano*. He is a destructive, bigoted, and ruthless governor who hates Italians and demands complete subservience from them and from his underling officers and men.[55] In short, Marvin is a gross and prejudiced American, who, like Colonel Polaski in Lowry's *Casualty*, is more ruthlessly totalitarian than the fascists from whose rule the Italians have just been liberated. Major Joppola, Marvin's antagonist and the book's hero, is representative of a liberal political tradition. He likes his role as judge because "he liked to see the happy effect of real justice on the people of Adano. . . ." [46] Almost inevitably, like almost all representatives of the liberal tradition in the American military novel, Joppola is defeated. Hersey is not particularly dramatic in depicting the Major's defeat—Joppola is not killed and he does not face a long prison term—but just as he manages to secure the bell for Adano he is reassigned by Marvin. Hersey does not project the old sense of shock and dismay at Joppola's fate; rather, it seems that both he and the reader, accustomed to the exigencies of the military novel as a reflection of military life, have been quietly anticipating it. One finds oneself rooting for Joppola in the face of the authoritarian structure, but one recognizes, almost from the outset, that he is headed for the inevitable and increasingly quiet and low-keyed defeat.

This same sense of inevitable doom for the liberal tradition is present in one of Norman Mailer's best novels, *The Naked and the Dead*. Willard Thorp, in *American Writing in the Twentieth Century*, cites the novel as "the most class-conscious work of fiction written since the thirties." [57] While this may be so in terms of subject matter, Mailer's tone in presenting class antagonisms is much different from the attitudes of Dos Passos or Trumbo or Campbell. John W. Aldridge [58] and Diana Trilling [59] recognize in *The Naked and the Dead* debts to the protest novel of World War I, but both doubt Mailer's faith in the efficacy of the liberal tradition. Mrs. Trilling views the novel as essentially political testament but thinks Mailer much more disillusioned than Dos Passos;[60] Aldridge thinks the novel ineffectual as protest because the moral questions are diffused when both Hearn and Cummings meet defeat.[61] Almost all the critics identify the American general, Cummings, and his noncommissioned imitator, Croft, as the forces of evil, and identify Lieutenant Hearn and Red Valsen as the forces of good, at least insofar as they guard their individuality and are representative of the liberal tradition. Beyond this general agreement, however, controversy rages over Mailer's tone and thematic intention.

"Mailer's intentions are perfectly clear," says Norman Podhoretz. "Cummings and Croft exemplify the army's ruthlessness and cruelty, its fierce purposefulness and its irresistible will to power, while Hearn and Valsen together make up a picture of the rebellious individual who, for all *his* determination and courage, is finally defeated in an unequal contest." [62] On another track, Jack Ludwig cites Cummings as heroic.[63] Sidney Walter Finklestein, in *Existentialism and Alienation in American Literature,* insists that Mailer believes that democratic traditions are impotent and doomed.[64] Walter Rideout insists on quite the opposite—suggesting that the mass will triumphs over the power moralist.[65] Frederick Hoffman stakes out a position midway between Finklestein and Rideout. According to him, Mailer imposes no value judgment at all; rather, he presents both liberal and authoritarian traditions objectively.[66]

Clearly, the critics are almost as divided concerning Mailer's attitude toward Hearn and Cummings as they are over Melville's attitude toward Billy and Vere. The parallel seems not to be limited only to disagreement among the critics. In both works a strong-willed and intellectual military authority figure, logical, calculating, and with a view that man is inherently corrupt and in need of control, comes in contact with a younger man, who, either instinctually or intellectually, possesses the view that man is inherently good or at least capable of improvement. Both of the older men are attracted to the younger, but when the latters' innocence seems to threaten the social order over which the authority figures rule, the young men's deaths are arranged. In both cases, the death sentence is carried out by willing tools of the social system, Claggart and Croft. Billy, at least, takes the master-of-arms with him. The completely ineffectual Hearn cannot deal with Croft at all. The sergeant arranges for the lieutenant's death on the patrol toward Mount Anaka,[67] and, as Millgate suggests, Hearn "realizes before he dies how devastatingly accurate is the analysis on which Cummings's ideas are based and how strong the American potential for fascism actually is." [68]

In *The Naked and the Dead*, as in *Billy Budd*, the military structure, as an embodiment of a totalitarian society, appears as a dark inevitability to an author whose hope may be in political liberalism but who has come to accept regretfully a cultural drift toward authoritarianism. Indeed, Mailer's representative of liberalism, Hearn, is a particularly hapless figure. Completely incapable of dealing with Cummings intellectually, he is reduced to grinding a cigarette into the floor of the general's tent as an act of rebellion (p. 314); and, when on the abortive patrol, he instinctively waits for Croft to lead (p. 511). He thinks he can take over the leadership of the platoon by causing the men to like him, but Mailer seems to view this as absurd or weak or both: "His approach would end by confusing and annoying them. Croft they would obey, for Croft satisfied their desires for hatred, encouraged it, was superior to it, and in turn exacted obedience" (p. 506). Hoffman describes Hearn as a product of the liberalism of the thirties;[69] Mailer describes him as emerging from an "addled womb" (p. 328). His death, arranged by Croft, is quick and anticlimactic, and

Mailer, unlike Dos Passos, does not seem to expect too much sympathy for his liberal hero.

Nor does Mailer expect any for General Cummings. Unlike Jones' overly simple and overly sinister authoritarian theorist, General Slater,[70] Cummings emerges as a character of great intellectual capability and an even greater will to power. Early in the novel, Hearn, however reluctantly, admires him (p. 83), and, at one point, thinks him a great man (p. 77). Mailer calls the general in his time machine portrait of him "a peculiarly American statement" (p. 403), and implies that, given the cloistered training of West Point (p. 408) and a puritanical and unsatisfying sex life (pp. 411, 416, 417), Cummings is truly representative of the culture: resourceful, courageous, cunning, and in a search of massive power. Unlike the officer-caricatures that so often appear in antimilitary fiction, Cummings is an intelligent, self-aware spokesman for the radical right. Despite the fact that Aldridge and Rideout see him as defeated by the mass will or by circumstance, Cummings has situated himself in a position of power and has the capacity to control the mass of men most of the time. Throughout the novel he calls upon Hearn to face the apparent lack of logic in liberalism, its amorphousness, and, according to him, its childish definition of human nature. Using the army as his guide, he envisions the most efficient society as one in which fear and hate provide motivation and every member of the society fits into a "ladder of fear" (p. 176). An admirer of the tactics of both Hitler (p. 420) and Stalin (p. 427), he sees the United States as the perfect environment in which to incubate competent totalitarianism. In fact, he argues that World War II will transform the American potential for fascism into a vital reality, contending that the only reason Hitler failed lay in the fact that Germany was too small a country. He predicts that the United States will march out of World War II a nation conditioned to accept lock-step authoritarianism and ready to emerge as the major imperialist power (pp. 321–322).

He warns Hearn that the country will be less self-consciously liberal (p. 322), cites man's overriding goal as the attainment of godhood or omnipotence (p. 323), and concludes that the only morality in the American future will be a power morality. When Hearn argues that "We're not in the future yet," Cummings replies "You can consider the Army, Robert, as a preview of the future" (pp. 323–324).

Thus, in the last analysis, Cummings emerges as a kind of demonic organization man who is riding slipshod over a weak liberalism toward ultimate power in America. Thorp implies that Hearn's defeat at Cummings' hands is inevitable because Hearn is "the liberal who has never known how to put his vague liberalism to work." [71] In an extension of this idea, Hassan suggests that the liberal's idealism is weak and transitory, and, as such, is representative of "the eternal betrayals of the American dream." [72]

A war novel that deals with these same betrayals is John Horne Burns's *The Gallery*. More clearly a protest novel than most of the World War II works, *The Gallery* in large measure turns the protest around from the direction taken by the World War I novelists and their followers. In general, the typical protest novel followed a pattern in which innocent Americans discover horror and guilt when drawn to a war in another country for idealistic reasons. Burns, more than any other previous American novelist, sees Americans in Europe not as innocents but as corrupters—members of a conquering army that rapes and pillages and ruins.

There are obvious debts to the earlier protest novel. For instance, the enlisted men live like "pigs in the hold" of a troop ship while the officers above deck dally with the nurses—a situation reminiscent of Dos Passos.[73] There is the same criticism of the Red Cross representatives as once was directed at the YMCA men. One woman representative, Louella, convinces herself that officers are more lonely than enlisted men, and, therefore, need her more (pp. 26–27). At times she seems almost a prototype for Terry Southern's Candy Christian as she constantly wants to give of herself in order to "stop one heart from breaking" (p. 27). In order to rationalize her sleeping with an Air Force pilot she imagines his wife in numerous affairs with officer candidates back home. That evening, for a nightcap, she has a phenobarbital capsule in vermouth (p. 44). Officers, besides some sympathetically drawn company grade men, are almost always stupid and unfeeling. For example, one marches his battalion in formation along the beach at Salerno with the result that the entire outfit is decimated (p. 20). Burns sums up the officer corps through the eyes of an enlisted man:

> I know my army officers pretty well, having observed them for years from the perspective of a pebble looking up and squinting at the white bellies of the fish nosing above it. Americans usually go mad when by direction of the president of the United States they put a piece of metal on their collars. They don't know whether they're the Lone Ranger, Jesus Christ, or Ivanhoe. Few Americans I ever knew could sustain the masquerade of an officer. Their grease paint kept peeling in unexpected places. I heard that in combat the good officers simply knew their men well and did them one better in daring.

But to be a good officer out of combat demands a sort
of shadowboxing between truth and posing. Europeans know the secret but few Americans can play
the nobleman without condescension or chicken.
(p. 122)

Burns goes into most detail in depicting an officer
when he deals with Major Motes, and Motes, perhaps
more than any other figure in the novel, suggests for him
the epitome of what is wrong with the American male.
His relationship with his wife, sexually and emotionally
vacuous, reminds one of the relationship between Hemingway's title characters in "Mr. and Mrs. Elliot." In
their prewar days, Mrs. Motes sublimates her sexual needs
in her poetry and Mr. Motes gets himself a reserve commission (p. 160). He feels the imminence of war and wishes
to have a position of some respect when it begins: "He
knew that soon, all over America, young men would be
saluting him on every street in every town. He'd got in
early. Soon he'd be Major Motes, and then Lieutenant
Colonel Motes and then . . ." (p. 164). A southerner, he
hates Negroes, and, ironically, is given command of a
Black outfit. "Their venereal rate was the highest in
camp. He tried court-martialing for every case of venereal
disease until the commanding officer heard of it. Finally
he no longer dealt with his men personally. From his
orderly room, himself unseen, came a vise of control and
discipline. On Sunday afternoons he had his men, wear-
ing full field packs, out washing their barracks windows"
(p. 166). Since America is at war, he thinks that all
Americans, particularly his Black troops, should be
machine-like automatons in service to the state. He fails
miserably as the commander of a combat outfit and is re-
lieved of command. In his second position as "The father

of censorship in North Africa" (p. 185) he fails again but is promoted for his failure. Because of this promotion, Motes dreams of other things—notably the extension of his censorship to all United States civilians (p. 205).

In his absurd racial and national pride, Major Motes thinks that all Europeans are obscene—like the "Negras" (p. 202). Burns indicates throughout the novel that the Major's attitude is not unique among Americans, whom he is at great pains to present as bigoted and corrupt. In *The Gallery* United States troops are not led astray by more knowledgeable European women; rather, quite the opposite occurs:

> The Spanish wives of the cork magnates are especially luscious and cordial. One of them loves one of us, and he uses her love for her benedictine and fruitcakes. She looks like Dolores Del Rio. He hasn't told her that he's married and has a kid. After all, that was back in Charleston. She waits for him on evenings when her husband is away in Rabat, leaves her patio gate open for him, and sits hushed and cool in her silken wrapper. She's an accomplished mistress, he tells me. But he enjoyed more seducing her daughter, to whom he taught the secrets that her mother taught him, and which are not dispensed at the convent school in Casablanca. At midnight sometimes (he says) mother and daughter sit up with him while he chews chicken and swills Chablis. Mother and daughter look at one another slyly, conspirators with one another against Papa. They don't know that they are against one another. He takes all that they give. After all, he's on vacation from Charleston, South Carolina. They are foreigners, aren't they, and who conquered this desert oasis of Fedhala? (pp. 52–53)

From this presentation of a single American, Burns extends his criticism to the culture as a whole.

> I remember that my heart finally broke in Naples. Not over a girl or a thing, but over an idea. When I was little, they'd told me I should be proud to be an American. And I suppose I was, though I saw no reason I should applaud every time I saw the flag in a newsreel. But I did believe that the American way of life was an idea holy in itself, an idea of freedom bestowed by intelligent citizens on one another. Yet after a little while in Naples I found out that America was a country just like any other, except that she had more material wealth and more advanced plumbing. (p. 259)

In another context, an intellectual captain sums up the reasons for United States participation in the war:

> Truth is always treasonous, the captain said, clicking his glass with a soft ferocity on the bar. And now these poor dears are involved in a war. This war is simply the largest mass murder in history. Theirs is the only country that has enough food and gasoline and raw materials. So they're expending these like mad to wipe out the others in the world who'd like a cut of their riches. In order to preserve their standard of living for a few more years, they've dreamed up ideologies. Or their big business has. So they're at war with nearly everybody else in the world. The rest of the world hates Americans because they're crude and stupid and unimaginative. . . . They will win this war. They'll reduce Europe to a state of fifteen hundred years ago. Then their busi-

nessmen and their alphabetical bureaucracies will go
into the shambles of Milan, Berlin, and Tokyo and
open up new plants. . . . International carpetbaggers.
. . . Millions of human beings will be dead forever.
. . . Hurray for our side. . . . We're destroying all the
new ideas and all the little men of the world to make
way for our mass production and our mass thinking
and our mass entertainment. Then we can go back
to our United States, that green little island in the
midst of a smoking world. Then we can kill all the
Negroes and the Jews. Then we'll start on Russia.
(p. 76)

In the last analysis, Burns suggests, the American,
unlike the Italian, is incapable of love or any strong
emotion; in *The Gallery* the representative citizen of the
United States emerges as a cold, calculating organization
man—an emotional neuter who seems to revel in destruction. Like Mailer and some of the novelists who dealt
with the occupation, Burns warns of the problems raised
in Lasswell's study. Unlike them, he goes on to condemn
American society in its totality. It is true that Mailer in
his "Portraits" approaches Burns' vehemence, but not
until Joseph Heller's *Catch-22* would there appear another American war novel with such a destructive view of
life in the United States.

A number of bittersweet comic novels emerge from
the World War II experience but offer little that is new
in analysis of either the military structure or that structure as a microcosm of American society. Thomas Heggen's *Mister Roberts* is the earliest and perhaps the best.
The main character, Roberts, is memorable primarily because he is representative of American idealism in a
structured world ruled by an incompetent dictator.

William Brinkley's *Don't Go Near the Water* gently satirizes the public relations mentality of a civilian soldier as much as the military itself, and Donald Morris' *Warm Bodies* is little more than a long joke depicting the process through which a daring young bachelor becomes a married "brown-bagger." Viewing the comic novel of World War II from *Mr. Roberts* in 1946 to *Warm Bodies* in 1957, one is tempted to suggest that it exhibits a marked descent in both its comedy and in its serious intention. An exception to that formula, however, is Leo Rosten's *Captain Newman, M.D.*, a novel which deals with some of the amusing and not so amusing problems in an army clinic for disturbed soldiers.

In concluding this consideration of the World War II novel, one finds it revealing to contrast the works of the only major American writer to deal with both this conflict and with World War I—Ernest Hemingway. Although Colonel Cantwell, the hero of *Across the River and into the Trees*, seems quite different from Jake Barnes and Frederick Henry, like them, he is a representative of a culture. In effect, just as Henry and Barnes embodied the American experience of an earlier time, Cantwell is Hemingway's American in Europe in the late 1940s. Older, more disenchanted, a reluctant organization man, and a purveyor of violence, he is the product of a culture that has created massive organized power.

Cantwell never declared his "separate peace." He has been a professional American soldier for much of his adult life, and, in almost every conceivable way, Hemingway presents him as an embodiment of the military mind and of the military definition of reality. He sees almost everything in terms of conflict. Referring to his own experience when lost in contemplating Renata's face, he thinks: "I'll get killed sometime that way. . . . On the other hand it is a form of concentration, I suppose. But it is damned careless." [74] He likes to sit at a corner table in bars and restaurants in order that he can cover both flanks (p. 115). His eyes are like "the hoodmuzzle of the gun of a tank" (p. 143), and, when he discovers two Italian youths trailing him in the street, it is clear that he would like to turn into a tank—a formidable and destructive force: "It is true they only saw my back and ass and legs and boots. But you'd think they might have told from the way they must move. Maybe they don't anymore. But when I had a chance to look at them and think, Take the two of them out and hang them, I believe they understood. They understood quite clearly" (p. 188). When someone interferes with his duck shooting, he thinks: "I wish that son of a bitch that is lousing up the duck shooting had a rifle and I had a rifle. We would find out pretty soon who could figure things out. Even in a lousy barrel in a marsh where you can't maneuver. He'd have to come to get me" (p. 291). In almost every instance, the Colonel's answer to a problem is the use of violence.

It seems clear that Hemingway intends Cantwell's affair with Renata to be the purifying love relationship in a life of violence. Like Henry's escape to Switzerland with Catherine, Cantwell escapes from his business of dispensing death (p. 188) to this respite in Venice. But even in the love relationship the imagery of warfare remains. While making love in a gondola, she asks him to switch sides in order that he might run his hurt hand through her hair. He answers: " 'Good. That is a sensible order couched in simple language and easily understood' " (p. 152). He tells her what her love means to him: " 'I feel as though I were out on some bare-assed hill where it was too rocky to dig, and the rocks all solid, but with

nothing jutting, and no bulges, and all of a sudden instead of being there naked, I was armoured. Armoured
and the eighty-eights not there'" (pp. 128–129). In addition, the topography of the battlefield is the imagery in
which they describe their love making. She tells him,
"'Just hold me very tight and hold the high ground,
too'" (p. 153). And later:

> "You are making the discovery. I am only the
> unknown country."
> "Not too unknown," the Colonel said.
> "Please don't be rude," the girl said. "And
> please attack gently and with the same attack as
> before."
> "It's no attack," the Colonel said. "It is some-
> thing else." (p. 155)

What else is not specified, but the imagery of warfare
remains a constant throughout the novel. Later, in one
of the less fortuitous references, Cantwell reacts to the
bathroom in his hotel room: "This bathroom had been
cut, arbitrarily, from a corner of the room and it was a
defensive, rather than an attacking bathroom. . . ." (p.
111). With death approaching, he writes his will on an
order blank, giving to Renata his most personal posses-
sions—two shotguns (p. 308).

Like other Hemingway heroes, Cantwell prefers the
company of men who have shared the war experience,
particularly those who have been wounded.

> I wish he did not have to have that glass eye, the
> Colonel thought. He only loved people, he thought,
> who had fought or been mutilated.

Other people were fine and you liked them and were good friends; but you only felt true tenderness and love for those who had been there and had received the castigation that every one receives who goes there long enough.

So I'm a sucker for crips, he thought, drinking the unwanted drink. And any son of a bitch who has been hit solidly, as every man will if he stays, then I love him. (p. 71)

Unlike the other heroes, however, he is the only one to remain in the military service and attain some power within its structure. As a career officer, he thinks in terms of taking people out to be hanged or shot, particularly if they disagree with him (pp. 162, 188). Announcing that his greatest sorrow is other people's orders (p. 210), he tells Renata: "'I know how to fight forwards and how to fight backwards and what else?'" (p. 211). In conversation with her, he describes his army experience:

"In our army you obey like a dog," the Colonel explained. "You always hope you get a good master."
"What kind of masters do you get?"
"I've only had two good ones so far. After I reached a certain level of command, many nice people, but only two good masters." (p. 234)

He has no illusions whatever concerning his own servitude in the system. Although he says he likes the Russians and they are the people most like Americans, as a soldier he is prepared to fight them (p. 70). He sums up his sense of moral responsibility in the following way: "'Christ, I am opposed to the excessive butcher-bill,' he thought. 'But you get the orders, and you have to carry them out' " (p. 188). That the butcher bill will be higher in the next war he admits, and, if there is a next war, he has no doubt that the United States will use every weapon in its arsenal:

> "We have the most terrific military secrets that one General's wife ever told another. Energy crackers is the least of it. Next time we will give all Venice botulism from 56,000 feet. There's nothing to it," the Colonel explained. "They give you anthrax, and you give them botulism."
> "But it will be horrible."
> "It will be worse than that," the Colonel assured him. "This thing isn't classified. It's all been published. And while it goes on you can hear Margaret, if you tune in right, singing the Star Spangled Banner on the radio. I think that could be arranged." (pp. 197–198)

There is in Cantwell's attitude toward history an ultimate disenchantment, an end to innocence. He seems to say that the history of the western world is a history of warfare, and Hemingway seems to indicate that the Colonel is the culture's representative—now specifically an American because the United States possesses the preponderance of power. He has neither religious nor political hope. Like Mr. Fraser in "The Gambler, the Nun, and the Radio," Cantwell regards these as opiates, and like the old waiter in "A Clean, Well-lighted Place," he has attained acceptance of the "nothingness" at the center of the culture and at the center of existence. He is the professional soldier who has come to terms with life by fitting into a system and doing his job well. In terms of ultimate knowledge, he gives his truths to another generation:

> Death is a lot of shit, he thought. It comes to you in small fragments that hardly show where it has entered. It comes, sometimes, atrociously. It can come from unboiled water; an un-pulled-up mosquito boot, or it can come with the great, white-hot, clanging roar we have lived with. It comes in small crackling whispers that precede the noise of the automatic weapon. It can come with the smoke-emitting arc of the grenade, or the sharp, cracking drop of the mortar.
>
> I have seen it come, loosening itself from the bomb rack, and falling with that strange curve. It comes in the metallic rending crash of a vehicle, or the simple lack of traction on a slippery road.
>
> It comes in bed to most people. I know, like love's opposite number. I have lived with it nearly all my life and the dispensing of it has been my trade. But what can I tell this girl now on this cold, windy morning in the Gritti Palace Hotel?
>
> "What would you like to know, Daughter?" he asked her.
>
> "Everything."
>
> "All right," the Colonel said. "Here goes." (pp. 219–220)

As it turns out, "everything" has quite a lot to do with combat, with nations at war, and with the results of warfare. Cantwell's definition of reality, seemingly presented by Hemingway as the truth, closely resembles Samuel Huntington's depiction of the military view. (See Chapter Seven.) Indeed, the colonel is the embodiment of Huntington's description of what the professional soldier should be—disciplined, hard, and, in the final analysis, uninterested in moral issues. Cantwell says: " 'I only give orders and obey orders. I don't mind' " (p. 277). To him, the Christian tradition is little more than a joke. He refers to those issues taken so seriously by the World War I novelists in an offhand and jocular tone. Christians are like shrimp, he says, always in retreat (p. 193).

John Killinger, in *Hemingway and the Dead Gods: A Study in Existentialism,* sees a connection between Cantwell and that earlier soldier who declared his separate peace.[75] In the twenties, Hemingway wrote of a young American, Nick Adams or Frederick Henry, on a pilgrimage of discovery. Henry, in *A Farewell to Arms,* flees the pointless and absurdly destructive social structure of the army and seeks a personal and idyllic relationship with Catherine. His tragic discovery is that existence itself is a biological trap. Jake Barnes, the hardworking and technically religious American, impotent and ruined, caters to some of those people broken by the war, particularly Lady Brett Ashley. Both Henry, the quester for truth, and Barnes, the priest-psychiatrist of a world shattered by conflict, emerge as sympathetically drawn representatives of American culture. In *Across the River and into the Trees,* it seems that Hemingway again creates in Colonel Cantwell a hero he feels to be representative of that culture. He is no innocent in search of a theory of existence; he possesses one. He does not cater to the representatives of European culture; rather, he insists that they cater to him. As he possesses Renata, so, too, through conquest, he has come to possess Europe. However unwillingly, he is an organization man in the business of war, and, like General Cummings, he is the representative of a power morality. He, according to Hemingway, is the new American—disenchanted with past ideals and content to follow orders in a vast and impersonal military structure which is the basis of his nation's influence and strength.

Although many of the novels that grow out of the World War II experience are not great fiction, certainly *The Naked and the Dead, The Gallery, Guard of Honor,* and *Catch-22* are excellent. Too many critics have lumped the novels of both world wars into one big and bland pile of mediocrity. As late as 1960, Leslie Fiedler could write: "If the novels written after World War I seem to become clichés even as they are committed to print, the novels of World War II are echoes of those clichés, products of minds so conditioned by the stereotypes of the earlier works that they seem never to have lived through the events of 1939–1945 at all." [76] The diversity of style and tone between *From Here to Eternity* on the one hand and of *The Caine Mutiny* on the other belies such simplicity, and a comparison of *A Farewell to Arms* with *Across the River and into the Trees* reveals striking differences within the work of a single writer. Indeed, the American novelists of World War II created a divided stream that represents opposed political ideologies and opposed definitions of man and his experience. One liberal and the other conservative, the divergent views are most fully represented in two of the best novels occasioned by the war, Joseph Heller's *Catch-22* and James Gould Cozzens' *Guard of Honor.*

Notes

1. Hatcher, p. 233.
2. Fiedler, *Waiting for the End*, pp. 29–30.
3. Hemingway, ed., *Men at War*, p. xxiii.
4. Allen, p. 4.
5. Dos Passos, *First Encounter*, pp. 7–8.

6. See Walter Millis, *Arms and Men: A Study in American Military History*, pp. 283–296; and Richard A. Preston, Sydney F. Wise, and Herman O. Werner, *Men in Arms: A History of Warfare and Its Interrelationships with Western Society*, pp. 298–313.

7. Millis, p. 283.

8. Adventure novels concerned with the war are numerous and often resemble the historical novels dealt with in Chapter One. Some of them are: Commander Edward L. Beach, USN, *Run Silent, Run Deep;* Kenneth Dodson, *Away All Boats;* Hugh Fosburgh, *View from the Air;* Dean Brelis, *The Mission;* Richard Powell, *The Soldier;* Leon Statham, *Welcome, Darkness;* and David Westheimer, *Von Ryan's Express.*

9. Although the novels considered in this chapter constitute more than a sampling, some selectivity has been necessary. For instance, summarily excluded are works that deal with the war but do not directly consider the American military. Among them are: Albert Maltz, *The Cross and the Arrow;* John Steinbeck, *The Moon Is Down;* and William Woods, *The Edge of Darkness.* Also, essentially espionage novels like H. L. Humes' *The Underground City* are not included.

   While the risk exists that one or two outstanding works may be overlooked, the number of World War II novels considered here seems sufficient to establish a sense of the genre both in its uniqueness and in its internal diversity.

10. New York, 1946, p. 14. (Subsequent references are indicated by page numbers in the text.)

11. Davidson, p. 278.

12. Among the World War I novels, sympathetically drawn Jewish characters appear in Thomas Boyd's *Through the Wheat,* John Dos Passos' *Three Soldiers,* and Laurence Stallings' *Plumes.*

13. New York, 1948, p. 6. (Subsequent references are indicated by page numbers in the text.)

14. New York, 1956, pp. 36, 16–40, 54, 255.

15. *Ibid.,* pp. 145–146.

16. Killens, p. 333.

17. *Ibid.,* p. 485.

18. Thorp, *American Writing in the Twentieth Century,* p. 135.

19. Hoffman, *Modern Novel in America,* p. 173.

20. Slote, pp. 223–224, 412.

21. *Ibid.,* p. 100.

22. *Ibid.,* p. 398.

23. Cowley, p. 26.

24. Ihab Habib Hassan, *Radical Innocence: Studies in the Contemporary American Novel,* p. 86.

25. In *The Creative Present: Notes on Contemporary American Fiction,* eds., Nora Balakian and Charles Simmons, p. 203.

26. *From Here to Eternity* (New York, 1951), pp. 223, 338. (Subsequent references are indicated by page numbers in the text.)

27. Balakian and Simmons, p. 206.

28. *The Thin Red Line* (New York, 1962), p. 346. (Subsequent references are indicated by page numbers in the text.)

29. Eisinger, pp. 23–24.

30. Samuel A. Stouffer, *et al.,* 4 vols. (Princeton, 1949–1950).

31. Eisinger, p. 24.

32. Hoffman, p. 173.

33. Harry Brown, *A Walk in the Sun,* Philadelphia, 1944, p. 33. (Subsequent references are indicated by page numbers in the text.)

34. Hoffman, *Modern Novel in America,* pp. 175–176.

35. Ross, p. 175.

36. Coates, pp. 63–64.

37. Chamales, p. 307.

38. *Ibid.,* pp. 75–76.

39. Uris, p. 1. (Subsequent references are indicated by page numbers in the text.)

40. See Millis, p. 290; and Preston, Wise, and Werner, pp. 312–313.

41. Millis, pp. 252–253.

42. Taylor, p. 61.

43. White, p. 74.

44. Lawrence, *Studies in Classic American Literature,* p. 93.

45. Millgate, p. 147.

46. Carpenter, *American Literature and the Dream,* p. 205.

47. Millgate, p. 147.

48. *The Caine Mutiny,* p. 413. (Subsequent references are to the New York 1964 edition, which is more accessible than the original 1951 edition, and are indicated by page numbers in the text.)

49. Lasswell, pp. 1, 47–49.

50. *Ibid.,* p. 49.

51. Millis, p. 298.

52. *Ibid.,* p. 302.

53. Heym, pp. 234 ff.; 14–15, 18; 627; 628.

54. *The Sealed Verdict,* pp. 49, 97. (Subsequent references are indicated by page numbers in the text.)

55. Hersey, *A Bell for Adono,* pp. 112; 114, 222; 237.

56. *Ibid.,* p. 175.

57. Thorp, p. 136.

58. Aldridge, *After the Lost Generation: A Critical Study of the Writers of Two Wars*, p. 139.

59. Trilling, "The Radical Moralism of Norman Mailer," in *The Creative Present*, eds., Balakian and Simmons, p. 152.

60. *Ibid.*, pp. 152–154.

61. Aldridge, p. 139.

62. Podhoretz, *Doings and Undoings: The Fifties and After in American Writing*, p. 183.

63. Ludwig, *Recent American Novelists*, p. 25.

64. Finklestein, pp. 270–271.

65. Rideout, *The Radical Novel in the United States, 1900–1954: Some Interpretations of Literature and Society*, p. 272.

66. Hoffman, *Modern Novel in America*, pp. 177–178.

67. Mailer, pp. 599–602. (Subsequent references are indicated by page numbers in the text.)

68. Millgate, p. 149.

69. Hoffman, *Modern Novel in America*, p. 177.

70. Jones, *From Here to Eternity*, pp. 338–345.

71. Thorp, p. 136.

72. Hassan, p. 143.

73. Burns, pp. 18–19. (Subsequent references are indicated by page numbers in the text.)

74. *Across the River and into the Trees* (New York, 1950), p. 100. (Subsequent references are indicated by page numbers in the text.)

75. Killinger, p. 81.

76. Fiedler, *Love and Death in the American Novel*, p. 455.

6.

Haines, Marquand, and Cozzens: The Analysis and Acceptance of the Military Elite

In 1951, the same year in which *From Here to Eternity* and *The Caine Mutiny* appeared, John P. Marquand published *Melville Goodwin, U.S.A.*, a novel which quietly presented the portrait of a typical American general. Compared to the other two, the book generated little controversy or interest. It contained no wholesale indictments of the middle class, no sinister plots of a military *coup d'état*, no brutal élite oppressing the masses. There were no indictments of the self-interested and liberal Christian, no emotional courtroom scenes, no satirizing of the anti-war tradition. There was no violence and very little sex. In short, the novel contained nothing designed to titillate the reading public, which, it is clear, had grown accustomed to military novels containing a good bit of violence, at least a smattering of sex, and an exposé of one thing or another—works like *From Here to Eternity* or *The Caine Mutiny.*

A statement by Michael Millgate suggests the uniqueness of Marquand's novel within the military tradition: "Even a novel like *Melville Goodwin, U.S.A.* (1951), which begins with all the marks of an *exposé,* ends by being nothing of the kind: we learn that however stultifying the army may be, we must respect rather than judge it. Marquand does not so much satirize or expose as explain: we learn, above all, that this is the way things are." [1] Marquand, with little or no political intention, creates in the character, General Melville Goodwin, a portrait of the professional soldier in the United States. With neither malice nor adulation, he records the background, the characteristics, and the attitudes he regards as determining a distinctly American military type. Since the publication of Morris Janowitz's definitive sociological study, *The Professional Soldier: A Social and Political Portrait,* his success cannot be denied. With a cool objectivity approximating the social scientist's, Marquand, nine years before the publication of Janowitz's findings, reaches most of the same conclusions in an evocative and sympathetic rendering of Goodwin.

The Professional Soldier, filled with statistics, reveals a number of characteristics which the majority of American officers possess. Native-born, they are from rural, noncosmopolitan backgrounds and can frequently trace an American lineage of several generations.[2] Overwhelmingly Protestant (p. 97), most want their sons to be soldiers and many of the sons comply (p. 100). Many view themselves as isolated from civilian society and feel morally superior to the business ethic (pp. 252–253), regarding their profession as a special vocation similar to a minister's or priest's (pp. 104, 107, 115). In summing up his findings,

Janowitz suggests that "The military élite has been drawn from an old-family, Anglo-Saxon, Protestant, rural, upper middle-class professional background" (p. 100). The young men emerging from this background receive their educaton at one of the military academies where, in effect, they are inducted into a fraternity and trained to regard themselves as uniquely dedicated to selfless service to their country (p. 130). After graduation, they enter a closed society in which family life and dedication to honor and loyalty are emphasized. Generally, they are neither intellectual nor artistic, and they do not consider ultimate philosophical or political questions. They take their place in an established social structure and dedicate themselves to success within its defined limits.

Marquand, in his single portrait, almost duplicates the composite Janowitz develops. Goodwin, a Protestant, is from a small town background, the son of a middle-class professional man, a pharmacist, and he can trace a family lineage back to the French and Indian War.[3] He attends the United States Military Academy at West Point where he accepts the simple virtues of honesty and loyalty as his moral guideposts (pp. 233 ff.). He marries a woman who understands military life and helps his career, and he thinks of American civilian life as lavish and lax (p. 114). His sons follow in his footsteps, one already an officer and one preparing to enter the Point (p. 86). In reminiscing about his education there, he suggests: "West Point's primary function was to turn out leaders who could win wars for their country. It was not intended to turn out philosophers or artists. West Point was neither a boys' school nor a university. It was a professional institution for professionals" (p. 252). There he learned to fit into a mold in preparation for a life within the corporate structure of the military establishment

(p. 233). As the general states, "The army was a closed corporation, and you had to learn its amenities and how to
get on with difficult superiors and how not to stick your
neck out" (p. 330). Not as reluctant an organization man
as Colonel Cantwell, neither is he as ambivalent about
warfare:

> "War is hell, and war is a hell of a profession, but
> looking at it from a professional point of view, it's
> pretty tough on professionals when a war stops and
> we're not wanted any more. Now old Clausewitz
> would understand me and so would Julius Caesar.
> War's an art. We professionals start getting good and
> just when everything gets cracking right the war's
> over. Look at the old Silver Leaf. That was a sweet
> division, a coordinated, battle-wise division, and
> where is it now? Can you blame me if losing some-
> thing like that hurts me artistically? You can call it
> fascist if you like. I haven't had much time to study
> ideology." (p. 136)

A statement such as this, in an antiwar novel, would
serve as a condemnation; clearly, Marquand regards it as
the normal reaction of a professional soldier. His *persona*
in the novel, the sophisticated and literate narrator,
Sidney Skelton, observes, "The way he spoke of himself
aroused my sympathy but obviously it was impossible to
maintain a continual state of war to give him happiness"
(p. 161). Skelton serves as a skeptical eye. Yet, from the
first, he is attracted to the general, and, in the final
analysis, regards him in a favorable light:

> I was still thinking of the Horatio Alger success story
> I had been following—young Mel Goodwin, the

hundred-per-cent American boy. The fresh-faced shavetail who had prematurely left West Point, young Goodwin at the front, knocking out those machine guns, the serious Goodwin at Cannes, recovering from his wounds—all combined to make a juvenile hero; but there was something more. There was character behind those exploits, but then again was it character or simply a lack of imagination, or had he done these things simply because he was not familiar with other choices? No outsider could ever understand the drives of the armed services, any more than he could comprehend those of a dedicated monastic priest. (p. 299)

Throughout, Marquand presents Gilbert Frary, a sleazy and unscrupulous business manager, as Goodwin's antithesis. Whereas the general believes himself dedicated to a cause, Frary is motivated solely by self-interest; and whereas the general believes in honor and loyalty, those concepts the World War I writers came to regard with contempt, Frary believes in nothing but himself and material wealth. The sensitive Skelton, with Goodwin's aid, finally rejects the agent, and sounds a little like Nick Carraway praising Gatsby when he characterizes the general: "There was something behind all that Melville Goodwin had said that was dedicated and magnificent and undemanding of justification. Perhaps a psychiatrist would call it immaturity, but whatever the attribute was, it had its own splendor" (p. 354). If Gatsby's essential characteristic was his colossal innocence, so is Goodwin's. But, unlike Gatsby, whose platonic sense of self can never be fulfilled, Goodwin, at the close of the novel, gets everything he wants. He has had his fling with Dottie Peale, and, without realizing that she has grown tired of him, feels magnanimous in giving her up and returning to complete fidelity to his wife (p. 595). He rejoices when his assignment to a desk job in the Pentagon is canceled and he receives instead a combat command in Japan:

> "Boy," he said, "I'm still slap-happy. I still can't believe I'd get anything like this. Boy, the only thing we need now is a war out there, and things don't look so good in China, do they? I've got a hunch it might happen in Korea."
>
> He was never as dumb as you thought he was going to be. He knew his terrain and he had the prescience. It was the first time I had ever heard a serious mention of Korea. (p. 590)

Regardless of how one is tempted to condemn his wish for war, Goodwin emerges as the innocent American who, without comprehending the complex world that surrounds him, manages to achieve his objectives. More important in the history of the American military novel, Marquand's study reveals the military élite in a manner neither critical nor adulatory. In fact, Goodwin is just another portrait in Marquand's gallery of upper-middle-class Americans. Neither villain nor hero, he performs a function within the social structure which he feels is meaningful and for which that structure rewards him with respect and prestige. Marquand accepts the necessity of a military establishment, views it as neither moral nor immoral, and sets himself the task of discovering what its ultimate product is like. In creating General Melville Goodwin he succeeds admirably.

Since the close of World War II, interest in the American military élite has grown as its importance and its power have grown. C. Wright Mills, alarmed by the trend in terms of its effects upon democratic practices, warns: "The military order, once a slim establishment in a context of distrust fed by state militia, has become the largest and most expensive feature of government, and, although well versed in smiling public relations, now has all the grim efficiency of a sprawling bureaucratic domain." [4] He also warns of the dependence of American industry upon defense spending (pp. 202, 212–215), and of the natural psychological dependence upon the military during times of national crisis (p. 172). The nineteenth century, to Mills, was a brief period of civilian domination in the western world. World War I prepared the way for military ascendance and the United States has not been immune to the process: "And in America, too, into the political vacuum the warlords have marched. Alongside the corporate executives and the politicians, the generals and admirals—those uneasy cousins within the American élite—have gained and have been given increased power to make and to influence decisions of the gravest consequence" (p. 171). While Mills fears the military élite's effects on policy making, he respects their capabilities as much as Mailer respects General Cummings': "Whatever the case may be with individuals, as a coherent group of men the military is probably the most competent now concerned with national policy; no other group has had the continuous experience in the making of decisions; no other group has such steady access to world-wide information" (p. 199).

Interestingly, Mills cites *Melville Goodwin, U.S.A.* as a novel that captures the sense of organizational conformity that career in service breeds, but, unlike Marquand, he makes a moral judgment—regarding it as dangerous and destructive (pp. 194–196). Among others, Fred J. Cook and Tristram Coffin share Mills' concerns and fears, and Millis, while less doctrinaire than the others, warns too of the possible political consequences of the military's growth.[5] Only Janowitz among the political scientists and social scientists comes close to being completely apolitical. In so doing, he resembles those novelists who have set themselves the task of just "recording" the characteristics of the military mind and of the military élite in action. He resembles Marquand and also two of Marquand's predecessors in this effort—William Wister Haines and James Gould Cozzens.

Haines's *Command Decision* is one of the few World War II novels to deal exclusively with the military élite —high ranking officers engaged in corporate decision-making and structural infighting. Like Marquand, Haines introduces a sophisticated and articulate character who views the military hierarchy with a critical eye. Elmer Brockhurst, a war correspondent, initially despises the book's protagonist, Brigadier General K. C. Dennis. However, after realizing the difficulties Dennis faces, both in the life-and-death decisions he makes and in working for a self-seeking and image-conscious commander, Brockhurst comes to have a grudging respect for him. In fact, both for Brockhurst and for Haines, Dennis seems to embody the tragic predicament of man in an imperfect world. In a conversation that begins with the correspondent's baiting Dennis about his weak commander, General Kane, a sense of Dennis' importance emerges.

"I'm paid to serve General Kane; others are paid to judge him."

"You have faith they're better at the top?"

"We have chaplains for questions of faith, Mr. Brockhurst."

"You keep everything; you've got it all taped,

haven't you? Your own chaplains, judge advocates, food, pay, promotion, decoration, and unlimited free coffins . . . you've made a separate world out of it with everything a man . . ."

"Everything but freedom"—Dennis smiled wryly now—"but I've read, in your press, that we're fighting for that."

"And your personal part in this . . ."

"Is very simple. Life without freedom is. I am responsible for making this command inflict maximum injury on the enemy, within orders."

"And when the orders are deliberately ambiguous?"

"Your superior may be receiving the same kind."

Brockhurst nodded wearily. "Okay, General, you get a hundred on the rules. But don't ask me to think you believe in them against everything in reason . . ."

"That's what war is, Mr. Brockhurst. If we win, reason may get another chance." [6]

Thus, General Dennis exists in a situation similar to Captain Vere's. Possessing a conservative view of the human condition, he takes his place within the military structure and performs according to its dictates. He suggests to Brockhurst that reason may have a chance, but does not seem to believe that the history of mankind offers much hope for such an occurrence. Unlike Vere, however, he has no illusions concerning freedom within the structure, admitting that he will do what he is told. Brockhurst finally sees Dennis as embodying the tragedy of human existence: "The darker tragedy hid behind the form of Dennis, behind the army itself. The army was only the projected form of a deeper malignance. It had been created as a shield against a more highly developed tyranny than its own; it would survive by a superior ferocity" (p. 219). He comes to see the very existence of armies as proclamations of "the tragedy of mankind," but has little hope for change (p. 219). The courageous and knowledgeable man, without belief in any radical amelioration of the human condition, finds in service to the existing order the greatest possible good.

Haines raises several issues concerning the activities of the military élite that Janowitz also identifies as critically important. These include interservice rivalry, problems of dealing with Congress about appropriations, and an overriding concern with public relations. General Dennis, like Goodwin, embodies most of the characteristics that Janowitz identifies as typical. A graduate of West Point (p. 7) and the son of a doctor (p. 107), he is from a rural, midwestern background. From an early age he felt an obligation to serve his country and steadfastly pursued that objective (p. 108). Like General Cummings, he is "a peculiarly American product," and he possesses what Mills and Huntington call a military definition of reality. Unlike Cummings, however, he does not wish to use conflict for his own personal aggrandizement; rather, he views it with a sense of sadness and foreboding, wishing it were otherwise: "It had all been done before and would be done again. The battle cries differed; the end was homicide. Dennis judged, on past performance, that they would continue it, intermittently, until the race had achieved its only ineferable [sic] purpose in extinction. The evidence seemed plain that of all the purposes men had, the most certain and recurrent was homicide" (p. 159).

Thus, like Melville, Haines holds out little hope for man in a world of violence, conflict, and the inevitable reliance upon authority.

James Gould Cozzens is not so explicit concerning an ultimate world view, but his analysis of members of the military hierarchy in *Guard of Honor* is perhaps the most studied and objective in the history of the American military novel. It is significant that Janowitz, the sociologist, dismisses most military novels as somewhat peevish protests but has nothing but praise for Cozzens' work. He particularly appreciates what he regards as the novelist's truthful treatment of the personal relationships in the officer corps at the higher levels of command.[7] Frederick Bracher, in *The Novels of James Gould Cozzens,* reports that "*Guard of Honor* was submitted in manuscript to an Air Force general in order to eliminate errors of fact, and he is said to have found none." [8] Thorough, calm, and impersonal, Cozzens is the best representative of what Millgate calls "the recording novelist" to deal with the military structure.[9] Bracher describes him as possessing a "high degree of sensitivity to the institutional side of life" and of displaying a "profound respect for the responsible citizens who actually make our civilization work." [10] While depicting the novelist as non-ideological, Bracher does see in Cozzens the conservative trait of abhorring the simplistic thought of either the right or left; unlike many military novelists, he never "resolves social complexity into the elementary stereotypes around which liberal and revolutionary enthusiasms concentrate." [11] Finally, in an excellent analysis, Bracher sums up Cozzens' attitudes:

> Though full of ideas, the novels present no ideology. At a time when violent social conflicts might seem to force a writer to consider the dynamics and direction of American society and to take a firm stand on one side or another, Cozzens has remained a spectator rather than a partisan. Moreover, his analysis of society . . . is not based on the coherent framework

of organized abstract doctrine, general and inclusive, that distinguishes ideology and the political novel.[12]

In short, Cozzens offers "a scrupulously honest report of American society as seen by a detached, highly perceptive observer." [13]

In *Guard of Honor,* this detached and perceptive observer brings all his powers of analysis to the American military establishment, and he does not see it through rose-colored glasses. Much of the absurdity and the cruelty that appear in the antiwar novel also appear in *Guard of Honor.* For instance, a number of paratroopers are pointlessly killed during an exercise arranged by Colonel "Pop" Mowbray to celebrate the birthday of the commander of Ocanara, General Beal. In a situation that could easily be treated as totally absurd, Mowbray suggests a funeral service for the soldiers:

Brightening again, Colonel Mowbray said: "Well, don't you think we ought to do a little more than just nail them up and ship them off by express —I mean, supposing their people want a home burial. Would you like me to work out some kind of little ceremony, service, out by the lake? Tomorrow's Sunday; we could have something religious. Just a short thing. Parade a couple of squadrons—maybe use Johnny Sears's men, so they'd look good. Have a firing party; sound Taps. We could have the chaplains —I suggest Captain Appleton and Captain Doyle each read something appropriate. Better have Lieutenant Meyer, too; in case one of them was Jewish. I could check on that, of course. But anyway, it makes it more non-denominational. Might bring a plane over at the same time and drop a wreath on the water—" [14]

Thus, it seems clear that no satirist is more aware than Cozzens of the existence of stupid and bigoted men within the military structure. Mowbray, for instance, rages at integration and almost despairs at the idea that Negroes can be pilots (pp. 250–252). Although he arranged the "party" in which the paratroopers died and although his officer failed to provide proper rescue equipment, Mowbray merely falls back upon military symbols to muddle through the crisis. In order to show everyone that "this is a serious thing," he straps a pistol around his waist and puts on heavy GI shoes and leggings. Beal, after a moment of looking at this pathetic little man who had flown with the Wright Brothers, advises him to sit down and have a drink (pp. 613–614). While it is evident that Cozzens regards Mowbray as a fool, he also insists that the colonel is not a fool just because he is a military man. Rather, the novelist seems to suggest that in any organization or in any large group of people fools will be found, and, naturally, they exist in the military. In fact, Cozzens presents a number of them among the population of Ocanara. Besides Mowbray, there is Lieutenant Colonel Benny Carricker, the intensely individualistic and asocial pilot ace, whose answer to every problem is the use of violence. There is Lieutenant Colonel Howden, the Counterintelligence Officer, who seems a spokesman for the radical right. Suspicious and excitable, he sees disaffection and disloyalty in any action that deviates from his conception of the normal, and wishes, for instance, to arrest those who favor integration (pp. 460–462). There are Lieutenants Edsell and Phillips, two rather shrill liberals, whose only means of expressing themselves within the pyramid structure of the officer hierarchy is to shout moral judgments from the bottom toward the top.

Colonel Ross, a judge in civilian life and the central consciousness within the novel, evaluates the character of the people who surround him:

"I think Colonel Mowbray is a good man, and he is the biggest fool I know. We are having a little trouble with some Negro officers. They feel they are unjustly treated. I think in many ways they are; but there are insurmountable difficulties in doing them justice. The only people who stood up for them were two offensive young fellows, I think principally interested in showing off, in making themselves felt. I really saw nobody all day who was not in one way or another odious." (p. 285)

Ross, like Cozzens, is apolitical. Cool, reserved, and practical, he is, in Bracher's words, one of those people who make our society run. Like Sidney Skelton and Elmer Brockhurst, he is a critical eye, but, unlike them, he is also a part of the structure—a citizen-soldier who anxiously sought an active role in the army when the United States entered the war. The novel covers a three-day period during which, among other things, Ross has to deal with a conflict between Caucasian and Negro officers, the pressures of the press to get the story, the suicide of Colonel "Woody" Woodman, the complaints of a group of WAC's that they are peeped at and molested at the base hospital, the marital problems of General and Mrs. Beal, the choosing of personnel to fill sensitive positions, the deaths of the paratroopers and the resulting clamor of the press, the visit of General Nichols from Washington on a mission designed to evaluate General Beal, and the constant infighting within the structure between the liberals and the conservatives. Clearly, *Guard of Honor* is not a vehicle for the simplicities of ideology. Those simplicities exist within the structure and are embodied in various characters, but they are merely part of a complex organism which Colonel Ross must handle. Bracher sees Ross as the epitome of Cozzens' heroes: a disciplined man of reason who "exercises in a position of authority and responsibility the virtues of good taste, self-control, and rational judgment." [15] Wilbur Frohock may oversimplify when he views war novels previous to *Guard of Honor* as all simple protestations by ex-privates, but his comment on Cozzens' creation is a good one: "What the War Novel needed was a good colonel." [16]

One must always remember that Ross is not a professional. He is a citizen-soldier interrupting his normal activities in order to involve himself in the war effort. As such, he is a critical eye within the system, making the reasoned and rational judgments that are obviously Cozzens'. For instance, the novelist describes the colonel's reaction to the military mentality:

> Colonel Ross did not mean to say that they were complete fools—not even Pop. In some ways Pop was astute. It was the habit of all of them to look straight, and not very far, ahead. They saw their immediate duties and did those not vaguely or stupidly, but in an experienced firm way. Then they waited until whatever was going to happen, happened. They sized this up, noted whatever new duties there were, and did those. Their position was that of a chess player

who had in his head no moves beyond the one it was now his turn to make. He would be dumbfounded when, after he had made four or five such moves (each sensible enough in itself) sudden catastrophe, from an unexpected direction by an unexpected means, fell on him, and he was mated. Colonel Ross could not risk it. Somebody would have to look out for Bus, and it mustn't be one of those people. They would do no better than Bus himself. (p. 235)

"Bus" is Major General Beal, the youngest Major General in the Air Corps (p. 5), and one of Cozzens' most fully drawn representatives of the professional soldier. He is neither a fool, like Generals Ripper and Turgidson in *Dr. Strangelove,* nor a Machiavellian manipulator and theorist like General Cummings in *The Naked and the Dead.* Rather, like Marquand's General Goodwin, he is representative of the kind of person who succeeds within the military structure and becomes one of its élite members. Neither a philosopher nor an artist nor a fool, he is one of those men who are "trained to win wars for their country." Cozzens neither idealizes nor condemns him, although, at times, through the eyes of Colonel Ross, he is highly critical.

Janowitz identifies two different types of military leaders in the twentieth century: the traditional warrior-leader and the innovating military manager.

Military managers—in the ground, air, and naval forces—are aware that they direct combat organizations. They consider themselves to be brave men, prepared to face danger. But they are mainly concerned with the most rational and economic ways of winning wars or avoiding them. They are less concerned with war as a way of life. Heroic leaders, in turn, claim that they have the proper formula for the conduct of war. They would deny that they are antitechnological. But for them the heroic traditions of fighting men, which can only be preserved by military honor, military tradition, and the military way of life, are crucial." [17]

On the most obvious level, Colonel Ross, the citizen-soldier, emerges as a type of military manager and General Beal as the warrior-leader; less obviously, General Nichols is the figure who combines the characteristics of both. In any case, Beal is Cozzens' most detailed portrait of the professional and it is to him that the others must be compared.

Frohock adequately describes Beal's situation: "To develop from a good combat commander of combat fliers into the kind of operational commander who can take over the Air Force for the Pacific showdown, General Beal has to grow up and grow up fast. He must, in other words, become less like Carricker and more like Ross." [18] In short, he must change from being merely a warrior-leader who leads by example and become more of a military manager capable of creating and directing large-scale strategic operations. As Janowitz puts it: "The heroic leader has been, and remains, relatively indifferent to politico-military affairs. But the military manager, because he is policy-oriented, develops either an absolute or pragmatic outlook, depending on his military education and professional experience." [19] Cozzens never makes explicit whether Beal succeeds or not, but he does offer a rather full picture of him in the process.

At every turn, Cozzens emphasizes Beal's youth, and it is not mere physical or chronological youth with which he is concerned. Beal, in some ways, is the embodiment of a careless American innocence and immaturity, and his reactions to complex problems are frequently little better than adolescent. He accepts the Military Academy's values of duty, honor, country without question, and instinctively obeys orders with which he deeply disagrees (pp. 67–68). At moments of crisis, he dumps problems on Colonel Ross and goes flying, either alone (p. 200) or to test his skill against Carricker's—two fighter pilots playing "chicken" in the air (pp. 502–503). When he returns from that particular jaunt, Colonel Ross confronts him by asking if he and Carricker are nuts. Beal answers that, "Boys will be boys" (p. 503).

His comment affirms Ross's earlier observation: "Beyond question General Beal had been tried by emergency and not found wanting; but as far as Colonel Ross knew or could guess, the emergencies were the soldier's, the man of action's, immediate and personal, well within a simple nature's resources of physical courage and quick sight" (pp. 16–17). Typically, after a strong but brief emotional response to the tragedy of the paratroopers' deaths, his solution to the problem is to relieve a commander, shake up the system (p. 612). But, while he had run from the complexities of the racial confrontation, he deals with the catastrophe of the dead soldiers. Colonel Ross examines why:

> . . . this trouble, though bad, was a good deal better suited to Bus's tastes and talents. Bus, not any less Bus than Benny, there, was Benny, reacted hard; but with assurance. The high strung gamut ran free from a fast simple emotional response to the uncomplicated thought of the brave, the brave who are no more (in quaint, grim truth, all sunk beneath the

wave!); through the explosion, simple and emotional, too, of anger rushing into natural patterns—no indecisive repinings about dear, dead days with that comical bastard Woody; no plaguing nonsense put on him by whoever gave their cry-baby prerogatives to a bunch of touchy colored boys, or by the finicking policies some Public Relations nut sold the Air Staff —of a known role to play, orders to be given; then, with no real checks or crosses, on into the evening's wearing-out of anger, a subsiding, still simple, toward a common sense of mere regret, an acceptance (what else could one do with it?) of accomplished fact. (PP. 572–573)

In other words, in this situation involving clear-cut issues of tactical mismanagement and men's deaths, Beal finds himself at home and is much more capable of functioning well, than he is when dealing with the essentially civilian, sociological problem of American racial attitudes and conflicts. Then again, Cozzens suggests that perhaps it is not imperative that the general should possess great concern for such problems. American racism is a problem for civilians to solve—civilians like Ross; Beal's commitments are to American weapons and how much damage they can inflict on an enemy. In fact, there are indications that Beal knew precisely what he was doing when he disappeared and left Ross to handle the racial incident. He recognized that the judge would handle it and handle it in a manner better than he. This is at least suggested when the two confront each other after the general's return from flying with Carricker:

"Do you wonder what went on here while you left me and Pop running the Army?"

"Nope," said General Beal, smiling at him. "I know what went on, Judge. You fixed everything."

"Maybe I did; and maybe I didn't," Colonel Ross said. "I certainly split my old gut trying. You gave a few orders you don't know about; and I want them to stick. We're not going to court-martial those colored boys. Lieutenant Willis is back on duty as acting commander of the tentative group."

"O.K." (p. 506)

"O.K.," the general seems to say, "now let's get on to more important things."

The structure of *Guard of Honor* is subtle, particularly if one places full faith in the viewpoint of Colonel Ross and in his ability to decipher the truth. For while his is the consciousness through which most of the action filters, nevertheless Cozzens introduces a character whose objectivity exceeds Ross's. Brigadier General J. J. Nichols, Deputy Chief, Air Staff, on a mission of evaluation, penetrates all surfaces with a cool and critical eye. He is the epitome of the successful organization man, unaffected by personal feelings and interested solely in the efficiency of the Air Corps. Colonel Coulthard, Beal's brother-in-law, introduces a solemn note suggesting Nichols' dehumanization:

"Funny kind of comedy, you'll find; if you see much of him. Before you finish laughing, if he decided that was the best thing, you might hear him say: 'Take that man out and shoot him.' He'd mean you. I knew him at Selfridge a good many years ago. He was Adjutant. He really ran the place. He runs every place he is. You know; the other people are horsing around, interested in different things; they

get tired, they get sick of it all, they don't pay attention. Not Jo-Jo. He just drives right on. And, Norm,
he isn't here for fun; don't think he is." (pp.
273–274)

Ross does not underestimate Nichols. In fact, he analyzes him as fully as his limited impression allows, seeing
in Nichols the leader who fuses some of the qualities of
the warrior-leader with the objectivity of the ideal military manager. At one point, studying the general's face,
Ross sees a man who has given up faith in any political
or sociological or religious truths—a man who, originally
innocent, has seen through all of the illusions of belief
and faith and is now only concerned with action and
process. Ross continues his examination:

> Though not certain of all that these marks and
> signs portended, Colonel Ross could recognize their
> most important meaning. They showed a man past
> that chief climacteric, the loss of his last early invol-
> untary illusions. A time of choice had come and
> gone. At least in a limited sense, it had been up to
> him whether he adopted, as soon as he could learn or
> invent them, new versions of his boy's eye views; or
> whether he tried to go on without them. Colonel
> Ross was impressed; for if he was right about General
> Nichols, General Nichols had chosen the hard way,
> and went on without them. (pp. 396–397)

The judge imagines how Nichols evaluates Mowbray,
Beal, and Ross himself, and concludes that to this inspecting general they must all seem to be children. Comforting
himself with the possibility that Nichols regards him as
the least childish, Ross continues his evaluation:

General Nichols and the never large number of
men like him could watch them with calculating detachment—not underrating these persistent children,
nor even despising them. They were boys in mind
only. They had the means and resources of man's
estate. They were more dextrous and more dangerous
than when they pretended they were robbers or
Indians; and now their make-believe was really serious to them. You found it funny or called it silly at
your peril. Credulity had been renamed faith. Each
childish adult determinedly bet his life and staked
his sacred pride on, say, the Marxist's ludicrous substance of things only hoped for, or the Christian
casuist's wishful evidence of things not so much as
seen. Faiths like these were facts. They must be taken
into account; you must do the best you could with
them, or in spite of them. (p. 397)

Nichols, then, is the disenchanted American, believing in nothing save the proper functioning of the power
structure that he serves. Like Cozzens himself, he accepts
a world full of ideas and ideology, but, to him, as to
Cozzens, ideologies are facts—simplistic illusions, really,
and important as facts because people believe in them,
act upon them, and so affect the social structure. It is
interesting that Cozzens includes the phrase, "Colonel
Ross thought," when presenting Nichols' analysis of all
the "superannuated children" whom he inspects, for, by
so doing, he implies that Nichols merely regards Ross as
a cog in the structure. He may be one of the more important moving parts but a part he is.

Despite the racial problem, the deaths of the paratroopers, and Beal's obvious shirking of responsibility,
Nichols, in the final analysis, seems satisfied with what he
sees at Ocanara. General Beal will be successful as a com-

mander in the Pacific primarily because he possesses a
personal mystique which makes men loyal to him. From
the absurd Mowbray to the destructive Carricker to the
reasonable Ross, everyone respects, worries about, and
works for him. He is the heroic leader who leads through
the presence and example of his own personality. Before
revealing that no one in Washington seriously considers
Beal an administrator (p. 405), Nichols cites the central
characteristic of the warrior leader who commands a combat unit: " 'There's this about Bus—there always was,
Judge. There's you, and there's Pop; and you know him
and you work for him and you go to bat for him. And if
you will, other people will. They did; they have. The
Old Man knows that' " (p. 402).

So, on the evening of the third day, Nichols, most of
his thoughts still to himself, prepares to leave Ocanara.
On the flight line, General and Mrs. Beal, as usual, look
and act young—perpetual child adults. Back on the right
track in their marriage, they are happy as they playfully
bid goodbye to Nichols. The deaths, the violence, the
racial tension, the revelation of personal strengths and
weaknesses—all these things had occurred and were now
over. The final conversation between Ross and Beal reveals that nothing has changed. Beal, admitting that he is
no "master mind," asks the colonel to watch for problems
and, particularly, to pick up Mowbray's mistakes (p. 631).

As he watches Beal and Nichols on the flight line,
Ross sums up, and in his summing up is the sense of his
immediate frustration but also a sense of his total acceptance of the absurd universe with which one is faced:

> General Beal continued to grin. With his grin,
> Bus wrote off, it seemed, all that formidable tale of
> worries so heavy on everyone over the last couple of

days. General Beal had been, it seemed, in no special danger of sinking under them; so those who fell over themselves trying to lift the load could have their trouble for their pains. The not-unmoving picture of the simple soldier, fatefully set-on in his still unfamiliar high place by a host of mischances; dogged by disaster not his fault; threatened with ruin by staggering irrelevancies—by Colonel Woodman, his bottle, his pistol in his mouth; by Benny persisting as Benny, the unreconstructable two-fisted fighting man; by the unrelated intrusion of a little history and sociology in the sullen contention of some colored boys that they were as good as anybody else; by a flustered jump master in a C-46 who hadn't sense enough to stop a drop and so got them in the papers again—well, it seemed, that picture was overdrawn. The only people who ever took the danger seriously were Colonel Mowbray, a simple dotard, and Colonel Ross—well, what was he? (pp. 626–627)

The answer is that Colonel Ross is the perfect staff officer who brings with him from civilian life skills and attitudes which free the professional warrior from the distasteful tasks that arise during large-scale operations. He has sat at the general's desk beneath the general's flag and has played the role of commanding officer in Beal's absence (p. 570), but only in matters pertaining to personnel and support. General Nichols likes Colonel Ross— he is good for General Beal, and General Beal, the youngest Major General in the Air Corps, has a future waiting for him in the Pacific. Bracher, the best critic of Cozzens, sums up what appear to be the novelist's final conclusions:

General Beal with his boyish unlimited integrity that accepted as the law of nature such elevated concepts as the Military Academy's Duty-Honor-Country is morally admirable; and it is made clear at the end of the book that his type, with its innocent single-mindedness of purpose, is absolutely essential to the winning of the war. But without the direction of the disillusioned publicans like General Nichols or the loyal backing of Colonel Ross, Beal would not be very effective.[20]

Thus, unlike John William De Forest, Cozzens makes no moral judgment concerning the professional versus the citizen-soldier; unlike the World War I novelists, he does not regard warfare as immoral or as a selling-out of the Christian tradition; unlike Mailer and Jones, he does not view the military élite as self-consciously pursuing power. He most closely resembles those other World War II novelists who accepted warfare as a brutal but normal human experience. But, unlike them, he does not deal with the traditional material of a fighting unit engaged in battle. Rather, like Haines and Marquand, Cozzens is concerned with that special group of people whose stature in American society has increased constantly since World War II—the military élite. He neither makes judgments nor oversimplifies; he accepts and elucidates. His attitudes and his work seem to fit Millgate's description of the tone of an increasing number of sociological novels written by Americans: "With the obvious exception of *exposé* novelists, much of whose work is of a sub-literary kind, the more widespread attitude among contemporary social novelists seems to be one of conservatism or of simple acceptance." [21]

While acceptance may be an identifiable trend, it is nevertheless by no means universal. The most obvious exception is Joseph Heller's *Catch-22*. The apotheosis of the protesting military novel, it also goes far beyond anything previous to it both in terms of the extensiveness of its criticism and the quality of its satire.

Notes

1. Millgate, *American Social Fiction: James to Cozzens*, p. 184.
2. Morris Janowitz, *The Professional Soldier: a Social and Political Portrait* (New York, 1960), pp. 86, 242, 83. (Subsequent references are indicated by page numbers in parentheses.)
3. Boston, 1951, p. 140. (Subsequent references are indicated by page numbers in the text.)
4. *The Power Elite* (New York, 1956), p. 7. (Subsequent references are indicated by page numbers in the text.)
5. Walter Millis, *Arms and Men: A Study in American Military History*, pp. 309, 358, 360.
6. William Wister Haines, *Command Decision* (Boston, 1947), pp. 218–219. (Subsequent references are indicated by page numbers in the text.)
7. Janowitz, p. 5.
8. Bracher, p. 24.
9. Millgate, p. 186.
10. Bracher, p. 9.
11. *Ibid.*, p. 9.
12. *Ibid.*, p. 6.
13. *Ibid.*, p. 20.
14. James Gould Cozzens, *Guard of Honor* (New York, 1948), p. 615. (Subsequent references are indicated by page numbers in the text.)
15. Bracher, p. 26.
16. Frohock, *Strangers to This Ground: Cultural Diversity in Contemporary American Writing*, p. 75.
17. Janowitz, p. 35.
18. Frohock, *Strangers to This Ground*, pp. 76–77.
19. Janowitz, p. 277.
20. Bracher, p. 225.
21. Millgate, p. 181.

7.

Joseph Heller's Catch-22:
Satire Sums up a Tradition

"I wonder what he did to deserve it," the warrant officer with malaria and a mosquito bite on his ass lamented after Nurse Cramer had read her thermometer and discovered that the soldier in white was dead.

"He went to war," the fighter pilot with the golden mustache surmised.

"We all went to war," Dunbar countered.

"That's what I mean," the warrant officer with malaria continued. "Why him? There just doesn't seem to be any logic to this system of rewards and punishment. Look what happened to me. If I had gotten syphillis or a dose of clap for my five minutes of passion on the beach instead of this damned mosquito bite, I could see some justice. But malaria? *Malaria?* Who can explain malaria as a consequence of fornication?" The warrant officer shook his head in numb astonishment.

"What about me?" Yossarian said. "I stepped

out of my tent in Marrakech one night to get a bar of candy and caught your dose of clap when that Wac I never saw before hissed me into the bushes. All I really wanted was a bar of candy, but who could turn it down?"

"That sounds like my dose of clap, all right," the warrant officer agreed. "But I've still got somebody else's malaria. Just for once I'd like to see all these things sort of straightened out, with each person getting exactly what he deserves. It might give me some confidence in this universe.[1]

Yossarian, the hero of Joseph Heller's *Catch-22* has little confidence in the universe but he would like to make some sense out of it. In effect, the very structure of the novel itself, resembling Lawrence Sterne's *Tristram Shandy,* suggests a chaotic world in which the perceptive intellect must impose order to find survival. Like a host of other American heroes, Yossarian is the single and somewhat rebellious consciousness in search of order amidst chaos, sanity amidst insanity, the meaningful life amidst a host of meaningless ones. In the process, he inspects the United States Army Air Corps as it functioned during World War II, American society as it is embodied in the fighting unit, western world culture at large, and the God that that culture claims for its own. Invariably, his conclusions rest in the discovery of the absurd: absurd men pursuing absurd prestige and power, absurd nations fighting wars for absurd reasons, an absurd Christianity that no longer has meaning, and an absurd God who turns out to be the ultimate bungling authority figure. But, of course, if a system of values and beliefs is to be so inspected, some basis for judgment must be established.

In *Catch-22,* Heller offers Yossarian and his ulti-

mately achieved value system as such a basis. In the last
analysis, he is a pleasure-seeking animal who finds commitments to causes involving death and destruction irrational, particularly when the few in power prosper
from such death and destruction that the masses suffer.
He wants to make love; eat and drink well; have sensible
friends; and, perhaps, like Holden Caulfield, save another
soul or two from absurdity. Most of all, he wants to stay
alive as long as he can. Yossarian, along with his companion, Dunbar, constantly stresses the fact that this life
is the only one he has. To give it away to a cause that
does not benefit him directly is an expression of the absurdity he abhors. The concentration upon the pleasures
and happiness of this life and the acceptance of the idea
that there is no continuation of the ego into another
existence are at the heart of Yossarian's fascination for
what he regards as the sensibleness of life in Sweden:

> He would certainly have preferred Sweden, where
> the level of intelligence was high and where he
> could swim nude with beautiful girls with low, de-
> murring voices and sire whole happy, undisciplined
> tribes of illegitimate Yossarians that the state would
> assist through parturition and launch into life with-
> out stigma. . . . (p. 303)

While Heller suggests that this utopia of pleasure
and nonresponsibility may be out of reach, he also suggests that there is nothing in the western world tradition
that makes sense to his hero. Finally, Yossarian has faith
only in his own existence and hope only in a more
rational life in another country: a country that he feels
exists outside the mainstream of western world capitalism

and Christianity. Just as the World War I writers rejected commitments to duty, honor, country, Heller rejects commitments to the various faiths of his culture.
From almost every angle of approach, Yossarian questions
why he should die for an economic system in which he
reaps few benefits or for a religious tradition he thinks is
meaningless. Although Heller does not state it as baldly
as Dalton Trumbo, his hero resembles one of the "little
men" who, throughout the history of the western world,
have fought and died for faiths from which they gained
nothing. After making love to the wife of Lieutenant
Scheisskopf, Yossarian considers the source of much of the
faith of the western world: the benevolent God of
Christendom.

> "And don't tell me God works in mysterious
> ways," Yossarian continued, hurtling on over her
> objections. "There's nothing so mysterious about it.
> He's not working at all. He's playing. Or else He's
> forgotten all about us. That's the kind of God you
> people talk about—a country bumpkin, a clumsy,
> bungling, brainless, conceited, uncouth hayseed.
> Good God, how much reverence can you have for a
> Supreme Being who finds it necessary to include such
> phenomena as phlegm and tooth decay in His divine
> system of creation? What in the world was running
> through that warped, evil, scatalogical mind of His
> when He robbed old people of the power to control
> their bowel movements? Why in the world did He
> ever create pain?" (p. 178)

For the most part, Yossarian is surrounded by pain,
the death and destruction of the western world at war,
and it is clear that Heller uses the microcosm of an

American fighting unit as the means of pointing out the absurdity of that world and its values. Yossarian learns, for instance, that the ultimate product of war is the soldier in white whom the men are discussing in the hospital. Helpless, emasculated, defeated, he is the direct descendant of Faulkner's Mahon and Trumbo's Johnny. "An unrolled bandage with a hole in it" (p. 166), he appears twice in *Catch-22* and represents the pointless waste of warfare.

In a sense, *Catch-22* sums up a tradition. It is the clearing in the woods, the meeting ground, for almost all the themes and ideas developed along the various paths followed by novelists dealing with Americans at war and Americans within the military structure. Like Melville, the first in the tradition to use the military world as a microcosm of a larger social order, Heller uses the base at Pianosa as a mirror of the culture of the United States. Like Melville and Crane, he presents his hero in danger of being emasculated in the totalitarian system: without recourse to justice and unable to assert his individuality within the corporate or command structure. Like De Forest, he is critical of professional officers, viewing them as men in love with warfare and its results: death, destruction, pay and promotion. Like most of the World War I novelists and some from World War II, he uses his work as a vehicle for criticism of an entire culture. But, while he may condemn the concepts of honor, glory, and patriotism just as much as Hemingway and Dos Passos, he does not follow along the path established by them. In fact, at several points, Heller seems to satirize the element of sentimentality in the war novels that precede his. Particularly noteworthy is his presentation of the relationship between Yossarian and Luciana, the beautiful Italian girl permanently scarred by an American bombing raid.

In a situation in which Hemingway might have had the lovers attempt an escape to an idyllic life in the mountains, Heller merely debunks the entire concept of romantic love (pp. 152–163).

Although *Catch-22* contains most of the characteristics of the lengthy tradition, one must step outside its limited domain to find Heller's predecessor in terms of its ultimate world view. Clearly, his is not the spirit of the protesters of World War I: serious, concerned, and hopeful about change. Rather, he seems more like Mark Twain in *The Mysterious Stranger* or in some of the selections Janet Smith has gathered in *Mark Twain on the Damned Human Race*. Here it is, he tells the reader, in all its irrationality and hopelessness, announcing that man's capacity to laugh at it may be the only indication of his sanity. In short, Heller introduces a new element into a major novel in the tradition—the element of satire. He directs its thrust at everything in the culture that is destructive, death-dealing, or authoritarian—those things that the rational mind regards as irrational. In another context, just as Twain provided an escape for his most representative hero, Huck Finn, from an American society he satirizes in *Adventures of Huckleberry Finn,* so too, Heller provides escape for his hero from a culture which would destroy him. For Huck there was still the territory, the vast virgin land of hope that the continent provided. For Yossarian there is no territory of freedom in an already established America. For him there is Sweden and the hope for a more rational life. As a highly individualistic hero, he must flee an increasingly rigid and corporately structured America in order to pursue that individuality. Interestingly, the America he flees closely resembles the America General Cummings predicts in *The Naked and the Dead*. There, Cummings had warned Lieutenant Hearn that the totalitarianism of the military system was a prelude to future life in the United States. As discussed in Chapter Five, the general views World War II as the event that will transform the nation's potential energy and power into fearsome reality, and he foresees the American people marching out of the war with an acceptance of organization, authority, and aggressive foreign commitments. Germany, he tells Hearn, provided an inadequate power base for the total development of fascism, but, he suggests, the United States would be the ideal environment for such development. In fact, he forecasts the death of American liberalism and its replacement by a corporate "ladder of fear" in a totalitarian framework. Liberalism, to the General, is childish, naïve, and unable to comprehend the realities of the human condition. In a world of massive organized power, it must pass away.

Samuel P. Huntington, in *The Soldier and the State: The Theory and Politics of Civil-Military Relations,* presents an analysis of trends in American culture which confirms Cummings' predictions. The book is of particular interest because the writer, unlike Mills, Coffin, Cook, or even Millis, is not dismayed by the growth of military influence in national decision making since World War II. In fact, Huntington cites Hamilton and Calhoun as early figures who shared a more enlightened view concerning standing armies than did Washington, Jefferson, Madison, or the Congress at large.[2] Also, very much like Mailer's fictional general, he sees World War II as the critical event in the emergence of military institutions and a military definition of reality in the United States—a definition that Yossarian must reject.

Before tolling the death knell of liberalism, Huntington describes it in its opposition to the military conservatism he sees in the nation's future:

> The heart of liberalism is individualism. It emphasizes the reason and moral dignity of the individual and opposes political, economic, and social restraints upon individual liberty. In contrast, the military ethic holds that man is evil, weak, and irrational and that he must be subordinated to the group. The military man claims that the natural relation among men is conflict; the liberal believes that the natural relation is peace. Liberalism holds that the application of reason may produce a harmony of interests. For the liberal, success in any enterprise depends upon the maximum release of individual energies; for the military man it depends upon subordination and specialization. The liberal glorifies self-expression; the military man obedience. Liberalism rejects the organic theory of society. In contrast to the military view, liberalism holds that human nature is pliable and may be improved through education and proper social institutions. The liberal normally believes in progress and minimizes the significance of history. (p. 90)

Threatened from abroad by Communism, the United States, according to Huntington, must give up beliefs in individualism and self-expression, the hope of international accord, and the possibilities of human progress and ultimate perfectibility. In their stead he would call for obedience, subordination, and belief in the application of force to solve problems. "The requisite for military security is a shift in basic American values from liberalism to conservatism. Only an environment which is sympathetically conservative will permit American military leaders to combine the political power which society thrusts upon them with the military professionalism without which security cannot endure" (p. 464).

Near the conclusion of *The Soldier and the State*, Huntington envisions the ideal American community once the nation has accepted the ultimate truth of the military definition of reality, and, one assumes, totalitarian rule. Interestingly enough, his model is the "ordered serenity" of the United States Military Academy at West Point. There, all buildings and all people "stand in fixed relation to each other, part of an over-all plan, their character and station symbolizing their contributions, stone and brick for the senior officers, wood for the lower ranks" (p. 465). There, Huntington finds peace and security in the individual's subjection of self to the established social order—"the harmony which comes when collective will supplants individual whim" (p. 465). He concludes:

> There join together the four great pillars of society: Army, Government, College, and Church. Religion subordinates man to God for divine purposes; the military life subordinates man to duty for society's purposes. In its severity, regularity, discipline, the military society shares the characteristics of the religious order. Modern man may well find his monastery in the Army. (p. 465)

Not Yossarian. No ritualistic militarism cloaking death and destruction for him. In fact, the rage for corporate order and collective will which he witnesses at Pianosa is death-dealing, cruel, and, in Yossarian's view, insane. Unable to subject himself to the structure which Cummings regards as the predecessor of life in the United States and which the social scientist Huntington identifies as necessary for national security, he is the antithesis of the organization man. Intensely individualistic, he is a rationalist, a skeptic, a nonbeliever. As a member of a long line of perceptive, intuitive, and lonely American heroes, he shouts a howl of protest at being ordained a priest in a religion of destructiveness, and, one assumes, he would not believe such slogans as "Aerospace Power for Peace" and "Peace is Our Profession." With humor, sensitivity, and the disarming ability to admit his own lack of traditionalist ideals, Yossarian for most of the novel is a perfect hero for the purposes of satire. Simple and intuitive, he cuts through cant and ritual to dissect the reality of his own experience and the world that surrounds him.

In its structure, *Catch-22* builds toward a climax that represents Yossarian's discovery of the final truth concerning human existence. Mentioned at key points throughout the novel, the actual description of the discovery occasioned by Snowden's death appears in Chapter Forty-One—just before the catch-all of the concluding chapter in which Heller provides for his hero's escape. It is in this discovery of Snowden's last moments that Heller places the important final impetus in Yossarian's rejection of the culture and the people responsible for the young man's death. In his helplessness in the face of Snowden's agony, Yossarian learns the importance of life and the absurdity of commitments to abstract ideals of a religious or economic or political nature.

Yossarian ripped open the snaps of Snowden's flak suit and heard himself scream wildly as Snowden's insides slithered down to the floor in a soggy pile and just kept dripping out. A chunk of flak more than three inches big had shot into his other side just underneath the arm and blasted all the way through, drawing whole quarts of Snowden along with it through the gigantic hole in his ribs it made as it blasted out. Yossarian screamed a second time and squeezed both hands over his eyes. His teeth were chattering in horror. He forced himself to look again. Here was God's plenty, all right, he thought bitterly as he stared—liver, lungs, kidneys, ribs, stomach and bits of the stewed tomatoes Snowden had eaten that day for lunch. (p. 429)

In an American bomber over Italy, he discovers, indeed, what had happened to all the Snowdens of yesteryear.

> Yossarian was cold, too, and shivering uncontrollably. He felt goose pimples clacking all over him as he gazed down despondently at the grim secret Snowden had spilled all over the messy floor. It was easy to read the message in his entrails. Man was matter, that was Snowden's secret. Drop him out a window and he'll fall. Set fire to him and he'll burn. Bury him and he'll rot like other kinds of garbage. The spirit gone, man is garbage. That was Snowden's secret. Ripeness was all. (pp. 429–430)

The nature of the discovery, hinted at earlier in the novel, had triggered one of Yossarian's outbursts of passive resistance. Much as Bartleby confronts the businessman-narrator of Melville's story, Yossarian confronts the symbol of American business and western world capitalism in *Catch-22*, Milo Mindenbinder. Yossarian has refused to wear the uniform, symbol of his membership and complicity in the system, and, instead, sits naked in a tree where he contemplates the absurdity that surrounds him and wishes for escape from it. He indirectly accuses Milo of being ultimately responsible for Snowden's death, but Mindenbinder is too concerned with dumping a load of Egyptian cotton to consider the matter. In fact, he has climbed out on Yossarian's tree limb to find out if Yossarian thought the masses could be convinced that chocolate-covered cotton would be good for them, and his final thought in rejecting the accusation that he shares some responsibility for Snowden is: " 'A strong Egyptian-cotton speculating industry means a much stronger America' " (p. 260). Recognizing Yossarian's abnormal behavior as a threat to the system, Mindenbinder urges him to play it smart and begin playing the game again— in other words, get in uniform and shut up. In a response similar to Bartleby's "I prefer not to," Yossarian answers "I don't want to" or "I don't think so" (p. 257). Heller's hero finally learns that this kind of passive resistance within the system is not enough. Because he refuses the road of violent revolution when he refuses Dobbs's plan to murder Colonel Cathcart (pp. 223–224), his only possible course is escape.

Besides the similarity between Bartleby and Yossarian as passive resisters and the elusive debt that Heller owes Melville in using the military world as a microcosm, there are other similarities between the two writers. Of minor interest is the fact that Chief White Halfoat's hilarious vision of death by pneumonia seems a satirical recasting of Queequeg's foreknowledge of his impending doom. More important, Melville was the first American writer to see justice in the military as merely a device for organizational expediency, hinting at it in *White Jacket*

and developing it fully in *Billy Budd;* in *Catch-22,* Heller
views justice within the system in exactly the same way,
and, with satirical thrust, reveals it in all its irrationality.
In *White Jacket* Melville indicated that there was little
fear of military rule and military justice in the United
States. Norman Mailer, through General Cummings, predicted in 1948 that growing militarism in the nation was
a good possibility. In 1957 Samuel Huntington wrote a
sociological-political study extolling the idea of military
ascendance. From the vantage point of 1961, providing,
as it does, a view of subsequent trends in American life,
Heller looks back to what justice has been like in the
military structure.

Early in the novel, he presents the trial of Clevinger:
a young, idealistic lad not entirely unlike Billy Budd.
Because he had spoiled the appearance of Scheisskopf's
squadron by stumbling in ranks, he is charged with
" 'breaking ranks while in formation, felonious assault,
indiscriminate behavior, mopery, high treason, provok-
ing, being a smart guy, listening to classical music, and
so on' " (p. 74). In a hilarious extension of the role
played by Vere at Billy's court-martial, Heller suggests
how military justice operates: "As a member of the Action Board, Lieutenant Scheisskopf was one of the judges
who would weigh the merits of the case against Clevinger
as presented by the prosecutor. Lieutenant Scheisskopf
was also the prosecutor. Clevinger had an officer defending him. The officer was Lieutenant Scheisskopf" (p. 74).

The ranking member of the Action Board, a bloated
colonel, reveals to Clevinger what justice is:

"Justice is a knee in the gut from the floor on the
chin at night sneaky with a knife brought up down
on the magazine of a battleship sandbagged under-

handed in the dark without a word of warning. Gar-
roting. That's what justice is when we've all got to
be tough enough and rough enough to fight Billy
Petrolle. From the hip. Get it?"

"No, sir."

"Don't sir me!"

"Yes, sir."

"And say 'sir' when you don't," ordered Major
Metcalf.

Clevinger was guilty, of course, or he would not
have been accused, and since the only way to prove
it was to find him guilty, it was their patriotic duty
to do so. (p. 79)

The similarity between Clevinger and Billy Budd is
most evident when Heller reveals the hatred that the
officers of the board feel toward the accused's honesty and
innocence—a hatred similar to Claggart's:

They would have lynched him if they could. They
were three grown men and he was a boy, and they
hated him before he came, hated him while he was
there, hated him after he left, carried their hatred for
him away malignantly like some pampered treasure
after they separated from each other and went to
their solitude.

Yossarian had done his best to warn him the
night before. "You haven't got a chance, kid," he
told him glumly. "They hate Jews."

"But I'm not Jewish," answered Clevinger.

"It will make no difference," Yossarian promised, and Yossarian was right. "They're after everybody." (pp. 79–80)

Clevinger's trial is not the only example of military justice in the novel. Later, in a situation designed to suggest the helplessness of primitive Christian instincts in a command structure, Heller presents the trial of the chaplain. He is accused of forging letters, of stealing a plum tomato from Colonel Cathcart, and of not believing in God (p. 377). After the court hears the charges, one of the board of officers—a stout colonel—suggests that they just knock his brains out. " 'Yes, we could knock his goddam brains out, couldn't we?' the hawk-faced major agreed. 'He's only an Anabaptist' " (p. 378). An Anabaptist is, by definition, a believer in simplicity, nonresistance, and mutual help rather than competition. Persecuted in the early sixteenth century by the power structure of the Catholic Church, he is here persecuted by the power structure of the United States Army. Charged with being Washington Irving, the debaser of censorship, the chaplain is asked how he pleads:

"Innocent, sir." The chaplain licked dry lips with a dry tongue and leaned forward in suspense on the edge of his chair.

"Guilty," said the colonel.

"Guilty," said the major.

"Guilty it is, then," remarked the officer without insignia, and wrote a word on a page in the folder. "Chaplain," he continued, looking up, "we accuse you also of the commission of crimes and infractions we don't even know about yet. Guilty or innocent?"

"I don't know, sir. How can I say if you don't tell me what they are?"

"How can we tell you if we don't know?"

"Guilty," decided the colonel.

"Sure he's guilty," agreed the major. "If they're his crimes and infractions, he must have committed them."

"Guilty it is, then," chanted the officer without insignia, and moved off to the side of the room. "He's all yours, Colonel." (p. 379)

Near the end of the novel Heller has a representative of the ineffectual liberal tradition, Major Danby, offer an explanation to Yossarian concerning the need for expediency within the system. His presentation of the problem is reminiscent of the situation in *Billy Budd,* since, like Vere, Danby possesses the right instincts concerning individual liberty and the right to justice but he values the system as it exists and fears chaos as the aftermath of its destruction. Yossarian, filled with doubts about the deal he has made with Cathcart and Korn, is considering not going through with it. Danby, like Mindenbinder earlier, pleads with him to be smart, to take advantage of their offer. In the process he explains that Cathcart could easily convict Yossarian of any number of charges in the military courts by merely convincing other members of the structure that their perjury would be for the good of the structure and the nation. And, Danby, adds, perhaps it *would* be for the good of the country. "If you were court-martialed and found innocent, other men would probably refuse to fly missions, too. Colonel Cathcart would be in disgrace, and the military efficiency of the unit might be destroyed. So in that way it *would* be for the good of the country to have you found guilty and put in prison, even though you *are* innocent" (p. 433).

As the conversation develops, Danby reveals that in civilian life he is a university professor, and Heller insists that the major does have a deep commitment to the truth. He sees that truth as terribly complex, however, and the complexity all but immobilizes him. ". . . Yossarian felt sorry for the gentle, moral, middle-aged idealist, as he felt sorry for so many people whose shortcomings were not large and whose troubles were light" (p. 434).

In the closing pages of the book much of the caricature and satire disappear; at one point Heller has Danby voice the essential problem that a deserter in the war against fascism must face:

> "I mean it, Yossarian. This is not World War One. You must never forget that we're at war with aggressors who would not let either one of us live if they won."
>
> "I know that," Yossarian replied tersely, with a sudden surge of scowling annoyance. "Christ, Danby, I earned that medal I got, no matter what their reasons were for giving it to me. I've flown seventy goddamn combat missions. Don't talk to me about flying to save my country. I've been fighting all along to save my country. Now I'm going to fight a little to save myself. The country's not in danger any more, but I am."
>
> "The war's not over yet. The Germans are driving toward Antwerp."
>
> "The Germans will be beaten in a few months. And Japan will be beaten a few months after that. If I were to give up my life now, it wouldn't be for my country. It would be for Cathcart and Korn. So I'm turning my bombsight in for the duration. From now on I'm thinking only of me." (pp. 435–436)

Heller hedges here on the universal issue of pacifism and conscientious objection, but he clearly approves of his hero's decision to strike out on his own and thus abandon the absurd structure of which he is a part. The note of optimism at the close of the novel rings false and is generally out of tune with the satirical savagery of most of it. Had Heller continued in a satirical vein, perhaps Yossarian would have kept his deal with Cathcart and Korn. As it is, from Chapter Thirty-Nine—"The Eternal City"—forward, the tone of the work changes radically. It seems evident that in the face of the horrors of the western-world past represented by Rome, the eternal city, and the affirmation of the savage present in Snowden's death, Heller wishes to express some hope in the future. By permitting Yossarian at least to attempt escape from the insane world of the United States Army Air Corps in the Mediterranean to the hope of a better world in Sweden, he moves from the tone of Twain's *The Mysterious Stranger* to the closing hopeful gesture of *Huckleberry Finn*. He also leaps out of the pessimism of such twentieth-century novelists of the military as Hemingway, Faulkner, and Dos Passos. Their inspectors of United States and western world values—in the military novels and in others—are almost exclusively caught and victimized by the culture. For Jake Barnes, Frederick Henry, Harry Morgan, Robert Jordan, Robert Cantwell, Donald Mahon, John Andrews, and others, there was no chance of escape. All end in death or defeat. In fact, Huck Finn's most obvious twentieth-century counterpart, Holden Caulfield, finds no place to escape in America except to a rest home. But, if Heller violates the tone of his work by returning to a nineteenth-century hopefulness about the young American hero, he has prepared the way for it within the context of *Catch-22* itself. For, while Yossarian is typically a twentieth-century American product insofar as he is from a large urban center, New York, and embodies some urban sophistication and skepticism, there exists in the novel a character who is as rural, as practical, and as alone as Huck himself. Combining the pragmatism of Huck with the individualism of a Thoreau, the inscrutable Orr looks as innocent as Alfred E. Neumann as he cunningly and quietly plans his escape from Pianosa to Sweden. When the chaplain brings word that Orr has landed his raft in Sweden and in so doing has restored the religious man's faith in God, Yossarian is ecstatic. The rural, simple, innocent American has shown him the way.

> "Danby, Orr planned it that way. Don't you understand—he planned it that way from the beginning. He even practiced getting shot down. He rehearsed for it on every mission he flew. And I wouldn't go with him! Oh, why wouldn't I listen? He invited me along, and I wouldn't go with him! Danby, bring me buck teeth too, and a valve to fix and a look of stupid innocence that nobody would ever suspect of any cleverness. I'll need them all. Oh, why wouldn't I listen to him. (p. 439)

Thus, it is the representative of an earlier and simpler America who shows Yossarian the way to the territory and to possible freedom and happiness.

Ralph Waldo Emerson, in describing the rejuvenating effects of intuitive contacts with natural surroundings, announced: "Give me health and a day, and I will make the pomp of emperors ridiculous. The dawn is my Assyria. . . ." [3] With all his faith in the individual's capacity to find truth, in his rejection of rituals of all sorts and of ritualistic Christianity in particular, in his call for individual self-reliance and for American independence from imitation of European manners and social structure,

Emerson raised his voice in the hope for a unique and enlightened American experience. Perhaps with an intuitive sense of America as Eden, he called, as Whitman would do as well, for a nation of mighty individuals, free from the restrictions of social structure and inhibition. The perceptive, intuitive American could make the pomp of emperors ridiculous and the dawn would be his Assyria.

Yossarian is Assyrian, a rather odd nationality to claim in the twentieth century, and Heller calls attention to the fact:

> "Yossarian? Who the hell is Yossarian? What the hell kind of a name is Yossarian, anyway? Isn't he the one who got drunk and started that fight with Colonel Korn at the officers' club the other night?"
>
> "That's right. He's Assyrian."
>
> "That crazy bastard."
>
> "He's not so crazy," Dunbar said. "He swears he's not going to fly to Bologna."
>
> "That's just what I mean," Dr. Stubbs answered. "That crazy bastard may be the only sane one left."
> (p. 109)

Just as the Assyrians were a threat to the Hebrew nation, the source of western world religious belief and of the God Yossarian calls "a country bumpkin," so too Yossarian is a threat to the power morality embodied in the military structure of the United States. His ultimate refusal to fly on more bombing missions is a threat to the system. In Marquand's novel, General Melville Goodwin describes life in the army in terms of religious commitment to a large corporation. In order to succeed, he says, one must have simple loyalties to a commander, learn to be obedient. Neither Marquand nor Cozzens presents the effects of such an organizational approach to existence when it involves men in actual combat. Heller, with some satirical exaggeration, does so throughout most of *Catch-22* and the results are frightening. For it is clear that the brunt of his specific satire is borne by an América that since the war had moved in the direction predicted in Mailer's *The Naked and the Dead* and John Horne Burns' *The Gallery*: increasingly monolithic; increasingly reliant upon the military, and, hence, upon military spending to support its industries; increasingly conservative politically; and increasingly committed to a military definition of reality and to the use of its force and power as a means of resolving international differences. In Huntington's terms, it is a nation moving toward a culture in which a man might find his monastery in the army.

With devastating satire, Heller deals with the potential military monks he finds at Pianosa, and it is clear that he intends them to be representative of American culture at large. In fact, until the change in tone that occurs in Chapter Thirty-Nine, the primary direction of the novel is toward the satirical destruction of an American life Heller clearly regards as immoral and absurd. Using the military unit as a microcosm, he takes on American business, education, medicine, organization men, and religion. Caught in the frenzy of a nation geared for war, Yossarian faces them all.

The military structure at Pianosa parallels the totality of a corporate America, and one of its most ambitious members, Colonel Cathcart, reacts to Yossarian as a threat to the system:

Yossarian—the very sight of the name made him shudder. There were so many esses in it. It just had to be subversive. It was like the word *subversive* itself. It was like *seditious* and *insidious* too, and like *socialist, suspicious, fascist,* and *Communist*. It was an odious, alien, distasteful name, a name that just did not inspire confidence. It was not at all like such clean, crisp, honest, American names as Cathcart, Peckem and Dreedle. (p. 207)

Cathcart is the commander of Yossarian's group: a man so valorous that he would volunteer his men for anything, and a man so ambitious that he keeps increasing the number of missions his men must fly in order to prove his efficiency to his commanders. The epitome of the organization man, and, in David Riesman's terminology, completely "other-directed," his only *raison d'être* is to rise within the military structure to ever higher ranks:

Colonel Cathcart was impervious to absolutes. He could measure his own progress only in relationship to others, and his idea of excellence was to do something at least as well as all the men his own age who were doing the same thing even better. The fact that there were thousands of men his own age and older who had not even attained the rank of major enlivened him with foppish delight in his own remarkable worth; on the other hand, the fact that there were men of his own age and younger who were already generals contaminated him with an agonizing sense of failure and made him gnaw at his fingernails with an unappeasable anxiety that was even more intense than Hungry Joe's. (p. 185)

In order to gain promotion, he will try anything—even religion, and, like Colonel Mowbray in *Guard of Honor,* he thinks of religious faith as a useful tool of the power structure. Because some possible publicity in *The Saturday Evening Post* might enhance his chances of making the rank of Brigadier General, he browbeats the chaplain into leading the men in prayers during the briefings prior to every mission. It is clear how subservient the representative of religion is to the structure when Cathcart vetoes every one of the chaplain's suggestions and finally commands him to pray for tighter bomb patterns (pp. 189–190). When the chaplain suggests that the commander could fittingly do that himself, Cathcart is enraged, and, in effect, accuses him of not knowing his place:

> "I know I could," the colonel responded tartly. "But what do you think you're here for? I could shop for my own food, too, but that's Milo's job, and that's why he's doing it for every group in the area. Your job is to lead us in prayer, and from now on you're going to lead us in a prayer for a tighter bomb pattern before every mission. Is that clear?" (p. 190)

The chaplain, who lives by himself in a clearing in the woods, who is afraid to enter the Officers' Club for fear of disturbing the men, and whose job is gradually being taken over by an atheist enlisted man who understands that religion is primarily public relations, must acquiesce to the colonel. After all, he is only a captain.

Clearly, this is not merely an attack on Y.M.C.A. representatives or promiscuous Red Cross workers. This is an attack on the role played by religion in the United States. In presenting the relationship between commander and underling, Heller presents it as a tool of the structure—providing ritualistic trappings for anything that the power élite desires. Certainly, the satiric thrust of having a representative of Christianity pray for destructive bombings is a successful gesture in conveying the absurdity of what was going on during World War II: Christians throughout the western world praying for the deaths of their fellow Christians.

In reminding the chaplain of his position within the structure, Cathcart describes Milo Mindebinder's job as just purchasing food. It is clear that in Heller's eyes he is much more than that. He is, ultimately, the representative of the capitalist spirit in fullest flowering· in America. Cathcart may reap personal benefits from the war in terms of prestige and status, but Mindenbinder is making the money. He tries to convince everyone at Pianosa that they, as shareholders, reap much of the benefits from his syndicate. Heller makes it clear that Milo is the only real winner and reveals the businessman's moral position in a number of ways.

Milo had been earning many distinctions for himself. He had flown fearlessly into danger and criticism by selling petroleum and ball bearings to Germany at good prices in order to make a good profit and help maintain a balance of power between the contending forces. His nerve under fire was graceful and infinite. With a devotion to purpose above and beyond the line of duty, he had then raised the price of food in his mess halls so high that all officers and enlisted men had to turn over all their pay to him in order to eat. Their alternative—

there was an alternative, of course, since Milo de-
tested coercion and was a vocal champion of freedom
of choice—was to starve. When he encountered a
wave of enemy resistance to his attack, he stuck to
his position without regard for his safety or reputa-
tion and gallantly invoked the law of supply and
demand. And when someone somewhere said no,
Milo gave ground grudgingly, valiantly defending,
even in retreat, the historic right of free men to pay
as much as they had to for the things they needed to
survive. (pp. 361–362)

Milo does business with everyone except the Communists even though the Soviet Union is allied with the
United States (p. 249). He does not view the Germans as
the real enemies. After all, he states, they are good busi-
nessmen and good members of the syndicate. At one
point, in order to close a profitable deal with them, Milo
bombs his own base (p. 252). Earlier, again in order to
make a profit, he alerts the Germans about an imminent
American bombing raid—the raid in which Yossarian's
prospective tent-mate, Mudd, is killed. When confronted
by Yossarian over the moral issue involved, Milo offers an
explanation:

Milo shook his head with weary forbearance.
"And the Germans are not our enemies," he declared. "Oh, I know what you're going to say. Sure,
we're at war with them. But the Germans are also
members in good standing of the syndicate, and it's
my job to protect their rights as share-holders. Maybe
they did start the war, and maybe they are killing
millions of people, but they pay their bills a lot
more promptly than some allies of ours I could
name. Don't you understand that I have to respect

the sanctity of my contract with Germany? Can't you see it from my point of view?"

"No," Yossarian rebuffed him harshly. (p. 251)

Yossarian says "no" to a lot of things, including, in this case, an economic system which has no social commitments and whose single objective is the opportunistic amassing of wealth. For, just within the context of this situation, the system is responsible for Mudd's death, and, by extension, the deaths of all the unknown soldiers. Although Mindenbinder is the foremost representative of the capitalist ethic, such opportunism, according to Heller, runs through the whole fabric of American society. In the figure of Doc Daneeka he satirizes the American doctor-businessman in general and the American Medical Association in particular. Since no money is involved, Daneeka does not care about his patients at Pianosa. Instead of treating them himself, he sets up a system whereby two enlisted men handle all the cases. When Yossarian confronts him concerning his professional attitudes, he offers the following explanation:

"It's not my business to save lives," Doc Daneeka retorted sullenly.
"What is your business?"
"I don't know what my business is. All they ever told me was to uphold the ethics of my profession and never give testimony against another physician." (p. 173)

The doctor may be unsure about the nature of his business but Heller makes it clear that it is merely the amassing of wealth by any means possible. Early in the

novel, Daneeka exclaims: "I don't want to make sacrifices. I want to make dough' " (p. 32). Later, reminiscing
about his practice before he was drafted, he talks about
the war:

> "It was a godsend," Doc Daneeka confessed
> solemnly. "Most of the other doctors were soon in
> the service, and things picked up overnight. The
> corner location really started paying off, and I soon
> found myself handling more patients than I could
> handle competently. I upped my kickback fee with
> those two drugstores. The beauty parlors were good
> for two, three abortions a week. Things couldn't
> have been better, and then look what happened.
> They had to send a guy from the draft board to look
> me over. I was Four-F. I had examined myself pretty
> thoroughly and discovered that I was unfit for mili-
> tary service. You'd think my word would be enough,
> wouldn't you, since I was a doctor in good standing
> with my county medical society and my local Better
> Business Bureau. (pp. 40–41)

He had it made, he tells Yossarian, pulling down fifty
grand a year with the strongest trade union in the world
backing him up (p. 51). Like the chaplain, this professional man, this authority figure, also worries about cross-
ing the men who control the ultimate corporate power
in this ladder of fear—Colonel Cathcart and his executive
officer, Colonel Korn (p. 342). When Doctor Stubbs bucks
the command system, Daneeka comments: 'He's going to
give the medical profession a bad name by standing up
for principle. If he's not careful, he'll be blackballed by
his state medical association and kept out of the hospi-
tals' " (pp. 342–343).

Although Heller spends less time on American education than he does on other aspects of the culture, he does hint at a system which discourages questions and encourages conformity and adjustment to the existing social structure. Quite early in the novel, Yossarian attends educational sessions set up by the command structure with the rightist Captain Black ultimately in charge insofar as the lessons are held in his Intelligence Tent. After the men begin to ask such questions as "Who is Spain?" "Why is Hitler?" "When is right?" and "Where are the Snowdens of yesteryear?" the authorities recognize that some control is necessary. "Group Headquarters was alarmed, for there was no telling what people might find out once they felt free to ask whatever questions they wanted to" (pp. 34–35). So, Colonel Korn develops the rule that the only people permitted to ask questions are those who never do. Soon, it is no longer necessary to hold the sessions (p. 35).

Throughout his consideration of the products of American colleges and universities, Heller makes clear that the primary role of the institutions is to prepare young men and women for participation in the corporately structured world in which they live. According to him within the context of *Catch-22,* the education is absurd because the world for which it prepares the student is insane and in need of radical redirection. He emphasizes the cruelty and destructiveness of it when he has a psychiatrist in an Army hospital try to persuade Yossarian to adjust to his culture.

"The trouble with you is that you think you're too good for all the conventions of society. You probably think you're too good for me too, just because I arrived at puberty late. Well, do you know what you are? You're a frustrated, unhappy, disillusioned, undisciplined, maladjusted young man!" Major Sanderson's disposition seemed to mellow as he reeled off the uncomplimentary adjectives.

"Yes, sir," Yossarian agreed carefully. "I guess you're right."

"Of course I'm right. You're immature. You've been unable to adjust to the idea of war."

"Yes, sir."

"You have a morbid aversion to dying. You probably resent the fact that you're at war and might get your head blown off any second."

"I more than resent it, sir. I'm absolutely incensed."

"You have deep-seated survival anxieties. And you don't like bigots, bullies, snobs or hypocrites. Subconsciously there are many people you hate."

"Consciously, sir, consciously," Yossarian corrected in an effort to help. "I hate them consciously."

"You're antagonistic to the idea of being robbed, exploited, degraded, humiliated, or deceived. Misery depresses you. Ignorance depresses you. Persecution depresses you. Violence depresses you. Slums depress you. Greed depresses you. Crime depresses you. Corruption depresses you. You know, it wouldn't surprise me if you're a manic-depressive!"

"Yes, sir. Perhaps I am."

"Don't try to deny it."

"I'm not denying it, sir," said Yossarian, pleased with the miraculous rapport that finally existed between them. "I agree with all you've said."

"Then you admit you're crazy, do you?"

"Crazy?" Yossarian was shocked. "What are you talking about? Why am I crazy? You're the one who's crazy!" (pp. 297–298)

To be a sane man in an insane environment means that one must be judged insane by the caretakers of that environment. In specifically American military terms, Yossarian inhabits a world in which justice has become a joke, in which money and profit mean more than lives, and in which religion and psychiatry are in the service of a unitary state. For it is clear that Yossarian's world at Pianosa is Heller's microcosm for life in the United States. He takes a more destructive view of that culture than any other American military novelist and presents it as an environment in which pyramid-climbing sharpies and money-hungry entrepreneurs thrive and rule.

If Huntington views men finding peace and serenity in the ordered life of the military world, Heller sees them becoming human defectives in such a structure. Suggesting essentially the same idea concerning the organization man that Burns voices in *The Gallery,* he is careful to establish that almost all the successes within the system are either completely sexless or at least incapable of love. For instance, Cathcart maintains a villa where the men imagine he engages in orgiastic weekends in the country. He cultivates that image but actually spends his time there shooting birds. The most ominous success, and, in Heller's view, the most typical of an identifiable military mentality, is Scheisskopf. Perfectly named, he rises from Lieutenant to Colonel, and, surpassing Cathcart, to General during his climb of the corporate pyramid. A military martinet, his monomaniacal desire is to have men march: mechanically, uniformly, in step. As a lieutenant, he devises a method by which his unit's marching will be better than any of the other squadrons. In order to have their arms move in unison, he wishes to have "a friend of his in the sheet metal shop sink pegs of nickel alloy into each man's thighbones and link them to the wrists by strands

of copper wire with exactly three inches of play. . . ."
(p. 72). In the pursuit of such order, Scheisskopf neglects
his wife; the training cadets do not. When she informs
her husband that she might be pregnant, he replies that
he does not have time for such nonsense: " 'Don't you
know there's a parade going on?' " (p. 70). Later, when he
needs a live model and asks her to march for him, she asks
hopefully if he wishes her to march in the nude. "Lieutenant Scheisskopf smacked his hands over his eyes in
exasperation. It was the despair of Lieutenant Scheisskopf's life to be chained to a woman who was incapable
of looking beyond her own dirty, sexual desires to the
titanic struggles for the unattainable in which noble man
could become heroically engaged" (pp. 71–72): such as,
Heller implies, making men march. The last view that
the reader has of Scheisskopf reveals that he has attained
the rank of general and has broadened his horizons as a
result. He wants *everybody* to march (p. 383).

Again, not Yossarian. As Heller completes his creation of a microcosm of a culture in which men are
emasculated by their reliance upon authority and by their
pursuit of wealth, prestige, and power, he increasingly
moves his hero along a path of ultimate rejection of that
culture. But it is not only the capitalist-Christian-authori-
tarian structure of the United States which Yossarian rejects. Heller sees in that society merely the inevitable and
tragic repetition of the absurdity of European history:
its warfare, its class structure, its monomaniacal pursuit
of wealth; its childish reliance upon authority in matters
of religion and politics. Yossarian, the individualistic
rationalist, rejects it all.

In the critical chapter "The Eternal City," in which
he becomes less like Candide and more like Hamlet,
Yossarian walks the streets of Rome, the city in *Catch-22*

which becomes the symbolic source of western world culture. Reminiscent of Raskolnikov's walks through the
streets of St. Petersburg and his dream of Mikolka beating the horse to death because it is his private property,
Yossarian inspects the horrible reality of a degraded
human condition. As he walks, he views some of the
representatives of massive poverty: "the shivering, stupe-
fying misery in a world that never yet had provided
enough heat and food and justice for all but an ingenious
and unscrupulous handful" (p. 403). He sees men torturing other men and making jokes about it—everywhere
the powerful or the many violating the meek or the good.
Against the ancient fluted Corinthian columns of 'the
Ministry of Public Affairs, he witnesses a group of soldiers
raping an Italian girl (p. 405). He sees men beating dogs
and children, and he watches a mob of police brutalizing
a man with an armful of books (p. 406). As he walks, he
thinks: "The night was filled with horrors, and he thought
he knew how Christ must have felt as he walked through
the world, like a psychiatrist through a ward full of nuts,
like a victim through a prison full of thieves" (p. 405).
A monk, obviously suggesting both the ineffectuality and
the irresponsibility and guilt of the Church and Christendom, walks with his head down and notices nothing
(p. 407). When Yossarian arrives at his destination, the
apartment for the officers from his Group at Pianosa, he
discovers that Aarfy, in many ways a typical American
boy who is anxious to pursue success in a corporate structure, has raped and killed the helpless, simple, ugly, and
innocent maid whom the men had always left alone.

It is the face of this past that Yossarian rebels against
its ultimate product in the present—the corporately con-
structed war machine of the western world. After his discovery in Rome he absolutely refuses to fly any more

bombing runs in a war that makes money for the Minden-binders and Daneekas and provides status and prestige for the Scheisskopfs and Carthcarts. In so doing, he becomes a threat to the system of corporate control. Heller sums up the situation: "Morale was deteriorating and it was all Yossarian's fault. The country was in peril; he was jeopardizing his traditional rights of freedom and independence by daring to exercise them" (p. 396). But at this point Yossarian is neither a Quixote nor an Orr. Interested in his own happiness and comforts, he agrees to the deal proffered by Cathcart and Korn. If he will keep quiet and not spread his dissent to the other members of the bomb group, they will send him home as a hero. Call me Blackie, says Korn; call me Yo Yo says Yossarian (p. 418). In making the deal, Yossarian follows the dictates of the cynical old man who sits in the direct center of the garish and pathetic whorehouse which the men frequent. By defeating every argument that the idealistic but misguided American boy, Nately, could offer, it seems the old man gains ultimate victory. Indeed, within the context of their conversation, Nately had seemed absurd when he shouted that anything worth living for was worth dying for (p. 242). But, absurd or not, the spirit of that kind of idealism lives on in Yossarian, and a series of events prevents him from accepting Cathcart and Korn's arrangement.

First of all, Nately's whore, performing the function of *deus ex machina,* turns on the traitor as he leaves Cathcart's office, and stabs him several times.

> Yossarian thought he knew why Nately's whore held him responsible for Nately's death and wanted to kill him. Why the hell shouldn't she? It was a man's world, and she and everyone younger had every

right to blame him and everyone older for every un-
natural tragedy that befell them; just as she, even in
her grief, was to blame for every man-made misery
that landed on her kid sister and on all other children behind her. Someone had to do something
sometime. Every victim was a culprit, every culprit a
victim, and somebody had to stand up sometime to
try to break the lousy chain of inherited habit that
was imperilling them all. (pp. 396–397)

Then, the helplessness he feels at the hands of the operating doctors suggests the helplessness of the individual
once under the anesthesia of complicity in the system (p.
420). Finally, the news of Hungry Joe's death and the
remembrance of the lesson Snowden taught him seal Yossarian's fate. He cannot become a part of an organizational structure whose last resort of control is Catch-22,
the catch that suggests that the use of power is the answer
to all questions and that one must always obey one's
superiors regardless of what their orders are (p. 58).

Because of the satirical tone throughout most of the
novel, *Catch-22* is by no means a typical example of the
American military novel. Nor is it even representative of
most of the fiction that emerges from World War II.
Published sixteen years after the close of the war, the
book is more about the United States in the postwar era
than about the conflict itself. It is clear, for instance, that
Captain Black's Glorious Loyalty Oath Crusade is direct
satire upon McCarthyism and the anti-Communist hys-
teria he bred. And Heller is surely satirizing the military-
industrial complex that grew during the fifties when he
has Major Danby comment on the relationship between
Mindenbinder and Cathcart: " 'Milo and Colonel Cathcart are pals now. He made Colonel Cathcart a vice-

president and promised him an important job after the war' " (p. 438). In a larger context, *Catch-22* is concerned with the general direction the country has taken since 1945: a direction that has caused concern for such political and sociological analysts as Mills, Lasswell, Coffin, Cook, Millis, and William H. Whyte. An advocate of the trend, Samuel Huntington, describes it as one which will bring about the ultimate death of the liberal tradition and replace it with a military conservatism in which one will learn subservience and control: the "ordered serenity" of the West Point community. Such acceptance of authoritarianism is, to Heller, debilitating and destructive. Snowden taught Yossarian that "The spirit gone, man is garbage." Heller in *Catch-22*, takes his readers on an inspection tour of a world in which the spirit of individualism and freedom has been drained from its members in the name of security and obedience. If one is to survive, then, in General Cummings' words, one must learn to fit into a "ladder of fear."

Since Yossarian is a representative of the traditional questing spirit of the liberal American, it is perhaps Heller's statement of ultimate hopelessness that his hero must seek rationality in another country and in another sociopolitical framework. While it is true that the change in tone near the close of the novel provides hope for the hero, his symbolic dismissal of the United States indicates a complete denial of the values of that culture for, if Huntington is correct and the nation is moving toward the kind of authoritarianism Melville envisioned in *White Jacket*, then the hero representative of a liberal optimism must disappear. Perhaps the fact that Heller uses such a figure, Yossarian, for most of *Catch-22* as a device to satirically expose the culture is the first step toward a situation in which the liberal American hero will go underground. It seems less alarmist, however, to suggest that Yossarian will not be the last of those idealistic heroes whose discovery of the realities of American and western world values leads them either to escape or to cynical acceptance. Even in the character of Colonel Ross in *Guard of Honor* one senses even the "adjusted" man's disappointment with what seems to be his conception of ultimate knowledge: that it is for children to concern themselves with absolutes and that the mature man finally must concern himself with processes and with the ultimate problem of keeping an organization or a culture afloat. In fact, Cozzens' world in *Guard of Honor* is somewhat similar to Heller's in *Catch-22*. In both, men are destructive, insensitive, self-seeking, and for the most part unconcerned with any transcendent cultural values. Certainly, Mowbray's arrangement of a party for a General which results in wholesale death is as gruesome as Cathcart's constant volunteering of his men for more missions or Scheisskopf's desire to make his charges march. Both books are ultimately concerned with a social structure which dwarfs its members and controls their lives. Cozzens, with some resignation, announces that, after all, this is the way it is; Heller, despite the bitterness of his view of the culture, holds out hope in the transcendent figure of Yossarian. It remains an open question whether this affirmation, involving as it does, a complete shift of tone in the novel, is merely a device enabling Heller to avoid an ultimate blackness which is totally destructive. Although he may recognize that Sweden represents only another illusion, his final statement in *Catch-22* may be the insistence that such illusions and such ideals are the means by which men and cultures survive.

Criticism of *Catch-22* is varied and for the most part disappointing. Douglas Day in the *Carolina Quarterly*

views the novel as "hopelessly confused," "banal," "sentimental," and "trite," but he seems to give himself away
when he suggests that "most critics of fiction will be unable to classify *Catch-22,* so they will probably end by
scorning it." [4] Hopelessly misreading the novel, he even
accuses Yossarian of cowardice.[5] Joseph Waldmeir agrees
in general with Day, suggesting that the work is chaotic
and endlessly repetitive and that Heller has no central
point of view through which to focus his social criticism.[6]
Others, most of whom at least comment on the problem
of the work's structure, seem more perceptive. John
Wain, in a review that is generally favorable, thinks the
book evasive about ultimate political issues; John M.
Muste and Alex Cockburn point out that Heller is critical of the entire culture and not merely the military;
Frederick R. Karl is helpful in his discussion of the
chapter "The Eternal City" when he suggests that "the
center of western religion is godless"; and David Littlejohn perceptively identifies Heller with Samuel Beckett
and others whom he terms "the anti-realists." [7] Sanford
Pinkser sees a similarity between Heller and Beckett and
extends the sense of shared technique and thought to
Ionesco and Albee as well.[8] One hesitates, however, to
agree with Pinkser when he suggests that *Catch-22* lacks
any deep philosophical content.[9]

Most recent is Josh Greenfield's article in *The New
York Times Book Review.* While Greenfield admits that
the novel may be transcending its time, he hedges his bet
by later asserting that it is really "a fifties cop-out." [10] In
so doing, it seems that his concept of a work's universality
is to make it from one decade into the next: into a decade more activist than the fifties during which Heller
conceived and wrote most of the book. In short, it is
not Heller but Greenfield who is incapable of seeing

beyond the immediate pressures of various groups and organizations and movements. For it seems evident that Heller's view extends beyond the absurdities of any particular time or place. The world at Pianosa is an indictment of the western-world past, but it is also, regretfully, a clue to the future—the kind of future that also disturbed Melville: a future in which the individual must sacrifice himself to mass movement regardless of its political direction or philosophical commitment. In any environment which makes such demands, Yossarian will be a figure critical and rebellious. In his last conversation with the two people who finally urge him to freedom, the university professor and the chaplain, he reveals that he will probably be uncomfortable in any structure:

> "Let the bastards thrive, for all I care, since I can't do a thing to stop them but embarrass them by running away. I've got responsibilities of my own now, Danby. I've got to get to Sweden."
> "You'll never make it. It's impossible. It's almost a geographical impossibility to get there from here."
> "Hell, Danby, I know that. But at least I'll be trying. There's a young kid in Rome whose life I'd like to save if I can find her. I'll take her to Sweden with me if I can find her, so it isn't all selfish, is it?"
> "It's absolutely insane. Your conscience will never let you rest."
> "God bless it." Yossarian laughed. "I wouldn't want to live without strong misgivings. Right, Chaplain?" (p. 441)

Thus Yossarian, who earlier in the novel provided the chaplain with a religious vision by sitting naked in a tree, emerges as a symbol of humanistic faith. Never to be satisfied with the human condition, he takes off for the undiscovered country.

Notes

1. Joseph Heller, *Catch-22* (New York, 1961), pp. 168–169. (Subsequent references are indicated by page numbers in the text.)
2. Huntington, p. 194. (Subsequent references are indicated by page numbers in the text.)
3. "Nature," in *The Complete Works of Ralph Waldo Emerson with a Biographical Introduction and Notes by Edward Waldo Emerson and a General Index*, Vol. I, p. 17.
4. Day, *"Catch-22:* A Manifesto for Anarchists," *Carolina Quarterly* (Summer, 1963), p. 87.
5. *Ibid.*, pp. 92.
6. Waldmeir, "Two Novelists of the Absurd: Heller and Kesey," *Wisconsin Studies in Contemporary Literature*, V (1964), 195.
7. Wain, "A New Novel about Old Troubles," *Critical Quarterly*, V (Summer 1963), 173; Muste, "Better to Die Laughing: The War Novels of Joseph Heller and John Ashmead," *Critique: Studies in Modern Fiction*, V (Fall 1962), 24; Cockburn, "Catch-22, a Review," *New Left Review*, XXVIII (January–February 1963), 91; Karl, *"Catch-22:* Only Fools Walk in Darkness," *Contemporary American Novelists*, ed. Harry T. Moore, p. 141; Littlejohn, "The Anti-realists," *Daedalus* (Spring 1963), pp. 250–264.
8. Pinkser, "Heller's *Catch-22:* The Protest of *Puer Eternis,"* *Critique: Studies in Modern Fiction*, VII (Winter 1964–1965), 150–162.
9. *Ibid.*, p. 152.
10. Greenfield, "22 Was Funnier than 14," *The New York Times Book Review* (March 3, 1968), p. 53.

8.

The Military Novel
in the Nuclear Age

The Korean conflict, a limited war fought for specific political objectives, seems an event that the United States is anxious to forget; for the most part, the fiction that emerges from that war will not prohibit the process. Just as the conflict itself, in terms of tactics such as the landing at Inchon, seems a continuation of the war in the Pacific during World War II, the men writing about it follow the examples of the novelists of that war. They do not, however, produce any work comparable to *The Naked and the Dead, Guard of Honor,* or *Catch-22.*

Thomas Anderson's *Your Own Beloved Sons* and Pat Frank's *Hold Back the Night* are straightforward, matter-of-fact studies of American combat units in crisis situations, and they contain nothing beyond Harry Brown's 1944 work, *A Walk in the Sun.* Frank G. Slaughter, in an extremely poor novel, *Sword and Scalpel,* offers caricature and cliché in a narrative that includes a nasty and devious regular officer, a Hollywood starlet in a North Korean prison camp, a humane and suffering hero, and an all-knowing priest who understands everyone's problems at a glance. Naturally, the starlet, Kay Storey, shares her imprisonment with her hero-sweetheart, Dr. Paul Scott, and later gives up her chance for stardom by testifying at his court-martial. In the last analysis, the book is slick, absurd, and completely devoid of ideas.

In some ways, unfortunately, the same description fits a novel that could have been much better, James A. Michener's *The Bridges at Toko-Ri*. Writing with the serious intention of presenting an apologia for United States involvement in Korea, Michener tries to create sympathy for both his regular officer, Admiral Tarrant, and his recalled reservist, Lieutenant Brubaker. Like Slaughter, in the process he falls into cliché and caricature. Tarrant is little more than a glorified representative of the radical right. Drawn with a great deal of sympathy, he sentimentalizes American civilization and pictures liberals as people who would give the Communists the continent west of the Mississippi. Envisioning the latter's eventual occupation of the United States, he objects to the policy of fighting the war for limited political purposes (p. 57), thinking, evidently, that the enemies of the United States ought to be annihilated.[1] Michener glamorizes Tarrant and seems to share this conservative military definition of reality. Certainly, he presents no conflict between the admiral and the citizen-soldier, Brubaker. Brubaker is not happy about being recalled to fight in Korea, but soon Tarrant regards him as a replacement for his lost son and their relationship rests on a basis of intimate understanding. In fact, Brubaker becomes a vehicle with which Michener criticizes those Americans who oppose the war, even using his death as a means of communicating such criticism.[2]

This element of propaganda in *The Bridges of Toko-Ri* extends to his treatment of class structure within the military. Michener's enlisted men are as happy and complacent, and as oversimplified, as Cooper's are in *The Spy*. One, Beer Barrel, an expert at guiding landings of jets on aircraft carriers, is a mischievous but happy rulebreaker whom Tarrant loves: "In his [Admiral Tarrant's] life he had seen many fine and stirring things: his wife at the altar, Japanese battleships going down, ducks rising from Virginia marshes and his sons in uniform. But nothing he knew surpassed the sight of Beer Barrel bringing home the jets at dusk" (p. 15). One wonders what his wife or dead son would think of the admiral's preference. Another enlisted man, Forney, a natural hater of Communists, gets involved in brawls over women, drinks a great deal, and is, in the last analysis a caricature of the common man similar to Cooper's Sergeant Hollister.[3] Whereas Cozzens, in *Guard of Honor,* reveals a conservatism which is steeped in rational skepticism and which is expressive of an orderly and intellectual view of the human condition, Michener, in *The Bridges at Toko-Ri,* is little more than a propagandist for United States involvement in the war.

In contrast, James Salter's *The Hunters* is a peculiarly effective book. Following in the tradition established by Harry Brown, Salter makes no overt ideological statements as he presents in detail the closed world of an F-86 fighter squadron in Korea. With great objectivity and insight into the workings of a combat unit at war, he reveals the effects upon men of an environment in which the only standard of excellence becomes the number of enemy planes they destroy. Unlike Michener, he does not editorialize when his central figure, Cleve, is killed. In-

stead, he coolly offers the description of the enemies who
have downed him: "Their heavy shots had splashed into
him, and they had followed all the way, firing as they
did, with that contagious passion peculiar to hunters." [4]
Interested in the mentality and the environment of the
American pilot, he thus hints that there would be little
difference if he could dissect a Chinese or North Korean
fighter squadron. Purveyors of violence and destruction,
all professional soldiers are hunters.

In *The Arm of Flesh,* a later book and one not
directly concerned with Korea, Salter clarifies the neeα
for destruction that many of his characters possess. Like
John Hersey in *The War Lover,* he suggests sexual in-
adequacy as its source. For instance, Major Clyde, the
squadron commander, is a magnificent fighter pilot but
he is unable to satisfy his wife who sleeps instead with
some of his lieutenant underlings. A contrasting character, Cassada, is not an outstanding pilot but is capable
of an idyllic and most fulfilling love relationship.[5] As in
The Hunters, Salter creates in *The Arm of Flesh* a prob-
ing and revealing analysis of a group of men under the
pressures of military competition. His vision is narrow,
however, and his novels do not measure up to the levels
achieved by the best writers of World War II.

While the novels concerned with the Korean War
have followed in the paths established by their immediate
predecessors, a good amount of fiction concerned with the
military in the nuclear age has deviated sharply from
that tradition. Concerned with the new military power
élite or with the dangers of nuclear war, these works are
often undeniably slick and journalistic but they do express concern about issues of the greatest topical importance. In general, such novels as *Seven Days in May,*
Fail-Safe, and *Dr. Strangelove, or: How I Learned to Stop*

Worrying and Love the Bomb parallel in fiction the concerns of Mills, Cook, and Coffin in nonfiction. Often glib
and superficial in their treatment of issues and their
creation of character, they most closely resemble the least
scholarly of the sociological works: Coffin's *The Passion
of the Hawks* and Cook's *The Warfare State.*

Coffin, after commenting on the attitudes and activities of Major General Edwin A. Walker, cites the
possibility of a military *coup d'état* in the United States:

> The time may come, though, when the officers
> in rebellion will be tougher and more realistic, when
> the people will be more disillusioned. Time is run-
> ning out on our crusade to regenerate the world. Our
> enemies are growing more numerous and stronger.
> This is not because we are less lovable, but that we
> have dared to occupy the place of Rome in the
> ancient world. Beleaguered by enemies springing up
> in a hundred places, some of them close by, weary of
> the debate and hesitation of a democratic society, we
> may be ready for a Caesar.
> Is he now a plebe sitting taut on the edge of his
> chair at Annapolis, a captain in South Vietnam, or a
> bright young major sent on to postgraduate school? [6]

Cook concurs with this prediction, suggesting that "in a
moment of crisis the wild men of the Pentagon or the
Central Intelligence Agency may take matters into their
own hands." [7] For the purposes of this study it is beside
the point whether or not such conjecture will be borne
out by subsequent events. What is important is the fact
that in a country which Melville described a century ago
as having no need to wonder about a military takeover,
there are now a number of intelligent and well-informed

people worried about just such a prospect. In fiction, Fletcher Knebel and Charles W. Bailey's *Seven Days in May* is the best example of a work dealing with such a concern.

An easily read piece of journalistic fiction, the book concentrates on a simple narrative development. President Lyman, a well-intentioned and capable liberal, negotiates a test ban treaty which sets off negative reactions from the military élite, American industrialists dependent upon defense spending, and some politicians of the radical right. "The Senate debate on ratification gave every member of the lunatic fringe plenty of chance to rant. People started to worry about their jobs, as if the United States couldn't prosper without making bombs. As if Marx and Lenin and Khrushchev had been right." [8] The President's primary political opponent to the treaty is a senator from California. Considering all the forces lined up against him, Lyman offers the following explanation for Senator Prentice's reaction: "Think of all the defense contracts in California. Almost all our missiles and planes are made there. And it's not just big industry, it's the unions too. You turn on disarmament full steam and there'd be ghost towns all around Los Angeles for a while." Thus, Knebel and Bailey make clear the extent of industry's dependence upon defense spending. They also make clear the supposition that forces in industry and elected government could not accomplish a *coup* without the cooperation and even leadership of the military—those people whom Mills describes as most accustomed to making important daily decisions and who have the greatest access to classified information. [9]

Providing the leadership in *Seven Days in May* is General James Mattoon Scott, Chairman of the Joint

Chiefs. Described as a combination of Generals Eisenhower and MacArthur, he lies to the President and to a congressional committee in order to facilitate his plan to rise to ultimate power. Opposed to democratic practices, he voices the alarmist view that " 'Unless the country is rallied by a voice of authority and discipline, it can be lost in a month.' " The ultimate development of such fictional military figures as De Forest's Colonel Carter and Mailer's General Cummings, Scott is the embodiment of the kind of dangerous innocence whose simple answer to international problems is to " 'start assembling more warheads. . . .' " [10] One assumes that in 1970 he would be presented as an advocate of MIRV and the ABM.

Scott and the group he leads are ultimately defeated by a political task force hastily organized by the President, but it is clear that the authors have a great deal of respect for their military creation. Strong-willed, competent, and with good intellectual capability, Scott is the transcendent figure in the novel. The only military man in the President's line-up of opposition to Scott is a Marine, Colonel Jiggs Casey. Doubtful about the treaty and concerned with the advantage the Soviets may gain from it, he is nevertheless dedicated to the Constitution and to constitutional authority. Of interest is the fact that in placing a Marine in opposition to the Air Force general, Knebel and Bailey also parallel the views of Coffin and Cook. In both *The Passion of the Hawks* and *The Warfare State,* the Marine, particularly General Shoup, emerges as the traditional American soldier: confident, competent, and obedient to civilian authority; in contrast, in both books the Air Force officer, particularly General LeMay, emerges as a power-seeking revisionist in conflict with civilian policy and chafing at civilian rule.[11]

In *The Professional Soldier,* the objective Janowitz offers a possible explanation for such an attitude. He suggests that the leader of ground forces has become in the nuclear age much more flexible and pragmatic in his approach to warfare. On the other hand, "The Air Force, because its primary mission is the delivery of strategic weapons, tends to be committed to an absolute doctrine." [12] Coffin, in his impressionistic manner, goes further: "The Air Force, in the decade after World War II, became obnoxious. It was too rich, too powerful, too fawned over. And it believed it was the divine instrument. A Secretary of the Air Force told me earnestly that there was no need to spend any great amount of money on the Navy or Army. The Air Force, he said, could 'fulfill America's destiny in the world' without outside assistance." [13] Of course, it is also important that the Marine Corps is the only major United States fighting unit that does not presently possess in its arsenal a nuclear armed missile with a strategic capacity. In an age wherein the military man becomes almost mythic in the fact that he possesses at his fingertips the awesome capability to inflict more destruction upon the world than all of his predecessors combined, it is understandable why the tactically oriented rather than strategically oriented Marine appeals to the civilian worried about nuclear war. Walter Millis, after making some comparisons between the present arms race and the arms race in Europe prior to World War I, states the problem that is at the heart of much of the worry: "Civilization still remains, it would seem, at the mercy of a slip or miscalculation. If no one today either wants or expects a war, neither did more than a few in 1914; yet we have set up a hair-trigger mechanism for universal catastrophe vastly more sensitive

and more lethal than that created by the general staffs in
the early years of the century." [14]

While Millis concentrates on the historical parallel,
Coffin merely suggests: "Two questions jab at the mind
in the early morning hours of lucidness when all the
world is still. How safe from accidents or human mean-
ness is our great apparatus for destruction. Not very." [15]
Among others, two works of fiction deal with this possibility of man-made apocalypse. *Fail-Safe* deals with the
problem of mechanically induced catastrophe, and *Dr.
Strangelove* with the human madness which might pre-
cipitate ultimate nuclear destructiveness and destruction.

Gordon Milne, in *The American Political Novel,*
sees *Fail-Safe* as essentially a political novel but insists
that it is not a particularly good one.[16] If one looks at it
in the tradition of the American military novel, one must
draw much the same conclusion. It is, after all, merely a
journalistic venture which generates interest solely on the
basis of its timeliness. However, it is interesting that Burdick and Wheeler, unlike Knebel and Bailey, do not
present the military élite in a villainous role. Characters
like Colonel Cascio may crack under pressure and others
may appear as smug automatons,[17] but the more important
military characters such as Generals Bogan and Black
emerge as heroic figures. Rather, the villain of the piece
is the civilian scientist, Groteschele—a kind of Merlin of
nuclear age mathematics and electronics. The authors depict him as a power-hungry, pyramid-climbing technocrat
whose theories concerning nuclear warfare lead the nation to the brink of its destruction. While still in college
he recognizes that the nation will be at war or ready for
war for generations to come and that in a nuclear age the
scientist will be more important to military operations

than the traditional fighting man. His Ph.D. dissertation, *The Theory of Counter-Escalation Postures in a Thermonuclear World,* "provided a respectable language and theory within which the 'first strike' or 'preemptive war' could be discussed" (p. 113), and his rise to fame is based on his advocating a first strike (pp. 116–117). In lecture tours around the country he is an apostle of violence and death, fascinating audiences with his descriptions of the horrors of a nuclear exchange between the United States and the Soviet Union. "There was a morbidity about his subject matter which somehow flowed over onto Groteschele and gave him an aura" (p. 117).

In presenting the scientist, Burdick and Wheeler delve into some facile Freudianism—a practice not uncommon in this kind of literature. For instance, after completing *Counter-Escalation,* he no longer makes love to his wife—he impersonally ravishes her (p. 119), and, through an encounter with a woman he meets at a party, Evelyn Wolfe, his interest in destruction is identified with his sexual attitudes: "It was not he, Groteschele, the physical man, who was attractive to women. It was Groteschele, the magic man, the man who understood the universe, the man who knew how and when the button would be pushed. He was a master of death and somehow that gave him potency" (p. 123). The "cobra-like" Miss Wolfe is fascinated by Groteschele's potential power and gets him to talk about it:

> "Knowing you had to die, imagine how fantastic and magical it would be to have the power to take everyone else with you," Groteschele said, spinning out what he had never said to himself. "The swarms of them out there, the untold billions of them, the beautiful ones, the artful ones, the friends, the

enemies . . . all of them and their plans and their
hopes. And they are murderees: born to be murdered
and don't know it. And the person with his finger
on the button is the one who knows and can do it."
(p. 124)

After hearing this hymn to his power, Miss Wolfe pro-
ceeds to ravish the ravisher (pp. 124–125). As if the situation were not obvious enough, Burdick and Wheeler
cannot resist the temptation to close with a moral: "Groteschele realized that he had never in his life distinguished between sex and love. And now it was too late"
(p. 125).

In the last analysis, *Fail-Safe* contains little or no
criticism of the military establishment. In fact, Brigadier
General Warren A. Black provides the moral focus in the
novel, and, in the face of the horror of nuclear war, his
is the voice of reason. In contrast to Groteschele, he is
much concerned about the effect the cold war is having
on the fabric of life in the United States, and despite his
love of the Air Force, he considers resigning his commission as a gesture against a world-wide militarism which
is leading to world-wide catastrophe (p. 153). He is certainly deeply troubled by the arms race:

Black often had the sensation in a meeting that
they had all lost contact with reality, were free-float-
ing in some exotic world of their own. It was not just
SAC or the Pentagon, Black thought. It was the
White House, the Kremlin, 10 Downing Street, de
Gaulle, Red China, pacifists, wild-eyed right-wingers,
smug left-wingers, NATO, UN, bland television
commentators, marchers for peace, demonstrations
for war . . . everyone. They were caught in a fantastic

web of logic and illogic, fact and emotion. No one
seemed completely whole. No one could talk complete sense. And everyone was quite sincere. (pp.
151–152)

Interestingly, he is pragmatic about Soviet intentions and United States responses, regarding the Soviet
Union as a country pursuing its national interests; in
contrast, Groteschele is absolutist, viewing the pattern of
world conflict as a simple bifurcation of evil Communists
and good Americans (p. 183). It is Black who most per-
suasively opposes the scientist's faith in a system that has
obviously broken down (pp. 154–156), and, finally, he is
the figure who must drop nuclear weapons on New York
in compliance with the agreement reached by the President and his Soviet counterpart. Realizing the nature of
the act he has performed and knowing too that his family
was in the city when the bombs detonated, Black commits
suicide. In contrast, Groteschele thinks only of his future
in the wake of the catastrophe: "If there were drastic
cutbacks in military expenditures many businesses would
be seriously affected; some of them would even be ruined.
A man who understood government and big political
movements could make a comfortable living advising the
threatened industries. It was a sound idea, and Groteschele tucked it away in his mind with a sense of reas-
surance" (pp. 270–271).

Clearly, in *Faile-Safe,* the villain of a protesting novel
concerned with a military situation has changed from the
calculating general such as Cummings or Scott to the
ruthless and self-seeking scientist. With some reservations,
the same can be said of the best of the pieces of fiction
dealing with a "doomsday" theme: *Dr. Strangelove.*

In *Fail-Safe,* Black feels a particular dedication to

the Strategic Air Command even though his doubts about American defense policy make him a heretic in the organization (p. 153). Janowitz clarifies some of the mystique surrounding SAC:

> To be a member of SAC, living apart from the rest of the military community, entrusted with the most important mission, and rotating through a cycle of alerts, is something special for an officer. The resulting pressures pervade the entire organization, up to the highest commander, and condition its outlook. Living with these tensions, the men retain the fighter spirit, even though the element of personal combat has disappeared.[18]

In *Dr. Strangelove* this mystique is satirized in a manner similar to the satirization of the military in *Catch-22*. If the tone of *Fail-Safe* was highly serious in presenting a possible nuclear holocaust caused by a technical malfunction, *Dr. Strangelove* is a wildly funny treatment of the human madness expressed in the arms race and of the universal absurdity of the human condition. With a devastating sequence of caricatures of political, military, and scientific figures, the book constantly points to the idea that it is not man's machines that are broken down but man himself.

The history of the text of *Dr. Strangelove* is an interesting one. Based on a rather undistinguished "doomsday" novel by Peter George, *Red Alert,* it was converted into a screen scenario by Stanley Kubrick and Terry Southern. While they followed the basic narrative created by George and included many of the incidents found in *Red Alert,* they introduced an element which radically changed the impact of the work—the element of satire.

When reconverted into the form of the novel for publication under the title, *Dr. Strangelove, or: How I Learned to Stop Worrying and Love the Bomb,* the work retained all of the satirical elements introduced in the scenario.

Like Joseph Heller, the authors of this novel satirize military types. For instance, the commander of the SAC B-52 who ultimately precipitates the end of the world, Major King Kong, is a caricature of the type of military man Janowitz defines as the heroic leader. In a literary tradition of southern military aristocrats begun by De Forest's Colonel Carter, Kong is anxious for combat, pay, and promotion. A warrior-leader, he munches a sandwich and studies the pictures in *Playboy* as his aircraft, *The Leper Colony,* cruises on auto-pilot. An unfulfilled trained killer, he feels incomplete: " 'It's something I never had an' I don't guess I ever will have now. *Combat!*' " [19] But his urge for activity is fulfilled when General Jack D. Ripper orders *The Leper Colony* beyond its fail-safe point on a first strike against the Soviet Union:

> When King spoke, it was with great dignity. "Well, boys, I reckon this is it."
> "What?" Ace Owens said.
> "*Com*-bat."
> "But we're carrying hydrogen bombs," Lothat Zogg muttered.
> King nodded gravely in assent. "That's right, *nuclear com*-bat! Toe-to-toe with the Ruskies." (p. 19)

It is clear that Kong never realizes the full implications of his mission of destruction. Trained to accomplish predetermined objectives in a mechanical way, he merely sets out to follow orders to the best of his ability.

Unfortunately, that ability is quite high. Using all of his "American know-how," he does his duty expertly, and, with an air of uncomprehending gamesmanship, steers *The Leper Colony* through Soviet radar and defenses in order to drop his lethal payload. Finally, in a last heroic gesture, he descends with one of his bombs, *Lolita,* to her target (p. 137). It is clear that Kubrick and Southern intend Kong as a caricature of the military man whose sense of courage and duty and honor is even much more absurd in the nuclear age than it was for Hemingway in World War I.

While Major King Kong is a caricature of the heroic leader, General Buck Turgidson, the Chairman of the Joint Chiefs, is a caricature of the military manager. The first time the reader meets him he is performing a function which Cook, in *The Warfare State,* suggests the Pentagon has been inflicting upon the State Department ever since the end of World War II: he is violating Miss Foreign Affairs (p. 23). As he leaves her to rush to the War Room because of the crisis caused by Ripper and Kong, he offers her some Pentagonese: " 'Look, you start your countdown right now and old Buckie will be back up here before you can say re-entry' " (p. 25). He brings this mentality with him to the crisis. Like Kong, he never fully recognizes the ultimate consequences of nuclear warfare, and both seem like dangerously innocent boys playing at being adults. In the face of catastrophe, he is coolly efficient as he announces to the President: " 'Yes, sir, seems like General Ripper of Burpelson Air Force Base—one of our finest bases, sir—decided to go for the Russians with his planes' " (p. 35). To the President's anguished outcry that only he has the authority to use nuclear weapons, the general replies: " 'I hate to judge before all the facts are in, but it's beginning to look like

General Ripper kind of exceeded his authority'" (p. 35). The master of the managerial platitude, he advises the President to let his military staff handle everything (p. 39) and suggests that the whole system should not be condemned because of one slip-up. When it becomes apparent that *The Leper Colony* will accomplish its mission and so detonate a Doomsday machine which will destroy the world, Turgidson laments his fate: " 'It's all so pointless. I mean, a man works his whole life fighting for something, and this is what he gets. You know, I can see twenty, forty, a hundred million dead, but everybody? It's just a damned shame, and I don't mind saying so'" (p. 139).

The boy-man who breaks the rules of the game and so causes the crisis, General Jack D. Ripper, is both a comic fascist figure and the embodiment of most of the shiboleths of the radical right. Because he sees Communists and saboteurs everywhere, he demands that his men be absolutely obedient to him and to his beliefs: "These included: (a) To defend the Constitution of the United States whatever may be the outcome of this defense. (b) To obey without question the orders of the commanding officer and him alone. (c) To suspect and to fire upon saboteurs, however friendly they may appear to be. (d) To hold our belief in God and rely on the purity of our bodily essences" (p. 27).

Like Groteschele in *Fail-Safe,* Ripper feels that the only way to defeat the Communists is through the use of the preemptive strike (pp. 45–46), and this reasoning provides the basis for his unleashing of the B-52's in his command. Also, just as Burdick and Wheeler suggest that Groteschele's fascination with destruction may be the result of a sexual maladjustment, Southern and Kubrick suggest the same thing concerning Ripper. Groteschele, as he is ravished by Miss Wolfe, expresses his fear of the woman: "She would, without mercy and as if it were her due, draw the energy and juices and fluids and substance from his body through the inexhaustible demands of pure sex." [20] While one might at first glance think the statement one of Norman Mailer's, it turns out that it more closely resembles some of Jack D. Ripper's. Worried that fluoridation is a Communist plot to sap his precious bodily fluids and, hence, his manhood, Ripper reveals his fear of love-making and of sexual activity in general:

> Ripper's eyes slowly turned toward Mandrake. He said, "Have you ever loved a woman, Group Captain? Physically loved her?"
> Mandrake had no chance to reply before Ripper went on. "There's a feeling of loss, a profound sense of emptiness. Luckily, however, I was able to interpret the signs correctly. It was a loss of essence. But I can assure you it has not recurred, Group Captain. Women sense my power, and they seek me out. I do not avoid women, Group Captain." His voice became louder. "But I deny them my life essence." (p. 81)

The man to whom Ripper speaks, Group Captain Mandrake, functions as a symbol of cool British rationalism inspecting an America gone mad with weaponry and anti-Communism. As he tries to sort out the pieces of a code that would permit him to recall *The Leper Colony*, he is confronted by another American military representative, Colonel Bat Guano. Guano, a Special Forces officer, is less sophisticated than his Air Force counterpart but offers essentially the same point of view as Ripper's. Immediately suspicious of Mandrake because of his long

hair and his different uniform, Guano sums up his outlook: "Perverts let their hair grow long, he knew. They
liked to dress up in fancy clothes, too" (p. 103). Janowitz
has suggested that the military mind recognizes in private
property the only basis for a stable political order;[21] yet
one is hardly prepared for Guano's refusal, with the entire
world in the balance, to rifle a Coca Cola machine in
order that Mandrake might make a call to the President.
" 'That's private property, Group Captain,' " says Guano,
and he can only be persuaded to help when Mandrake
suggests that failure to do so might hurt his career
progression.

Although Kubrick and Southern satirize members of
the military establishment, it is clear that in *Dr. Strangelove* as in *Catch-22* the military figures are mere buffoons
in the hands of shrewder and more sinister operators: in
Catch-22 the American businessman, Milo Mindenbinder,
and in *Strangelove* the scientist who creates the weapons
and controls the environment, Dr. Strangelove himself.
The embodiment of a morally bankrupt technical and
scientific competence, he explains that the Doomsday
Machine, about to destroy the world as he speaks, is the
logical outgrowth of American and Soviet defense policies: " 'Deterrence is the art of producing in the mind of
the enemy the fear to attack. And so because of the auto-
mated and irrevocable decision-making process which
rules out human meddling, the Doomsday Machine is
terrifying, simple to understand, and completely credible
and convincing' " (p. 98). Thus, Strangelove is the ultimate demonic villain in an American tradition including
such scientists as Hawthorne's Rappaccini and Melville's
Bannadonna. In addition, one is reminded of the prediction made by Mailer's General Cummings when it
seems that the doctor may accomplish in mineshafts be-

neath the United States what he failed to accomplish in Nazi Germany. For, in those shafts he plans to create a completely controlled environment and perhaps a master race.

> Strangelove said, "Offhand, I should say that in addition to the factors of youth, health, sexual fertility, intelligence, and a cross section of necessary skills, it would be *absolutely vital that our top government and military men* be included, to foster and impart the required principles of leadership and tradition."
>
> The arrow had not missed its mark, and around the table there was an outbreak of sober, nodding heads. Attention was concentrated more than ever on Doctor Strangelove.
>
> Strangelove went on. "Naturally they would breed prodigiously, eh? There would be much time and little to do. With the proper breeding techniques, and starting with a ration of say, ten women to each man, I should estimate the progeny of the original group of two hundred thousand would emerge a hundred years later as well over a hundred million. Naturally the group would have to engage in enlarging the original living space. This would have to be continuous. They would have to do it so long as they stayed in the mine shaft."
>
> General Turgidson said quietly to his aide, "You know, I'm beginning to think this Kraut has really got something." (p. 143)

Thus, the American man seems ready again to follow the voice that has led him once to doomsday, and, despite some profound words by the normally ineffectual President Muffley, Kubrick and Southern offer little hope that

man will get off the treadmill leading to ultimate destruction. Instead, they indicate that the very power and
technology that western man worships will bring about
his doom.

Although *Dr. Strangelove* is probably the best of the
novels dealing with the explosiveness of the cold war,
there are others that provide suspense and adventure.
For instance, Mark Rascovich's *The Bedford Incident,* a
book modeled on *Moby-Dick,* presents a monomaniacal
Navy captain in pursuit of a Soviet submarine nicknamed
"Moby-Dick." Embodying the military definition of reality concerning the inevitability of conflict, he manages
to destroy the sub. Then, in a situation similar to that in
Fail-Safe, Rascovich provides for the destruction of the
United States vessel in order to avoid a nuclear war over
the incident. The captain, Finlandu, is a stern and re-
ligiously dedicated man whose actions prompt a German
NATO officer to suggest " 'that we Germans are not the
only ones guilty of breeding submissive militarists.' " [22]
John Castle's *The Seventh Fury* offers still another portrait of an American officer who possesses a military definition of reality, and is, in general, little more than a
slick adventure story.[23] The same description fits such
novels of espionage or nuclear holocaust as Pat Frank's
Forbidden Area and *Alas, Babylon,* and Philip Wylie's
Triumph and *Tomorrow!* Edward Stephens' *Blow Negative!* is merely a glorification of Admiral Rickover, and
Ed McBain's *The Sentries* is a presentation of a right
wing attempt to overthrow the government which contains few military references but has enough sex, suspense, and sadism to appeal to a popular audience.

In beginning with the historical novel of the American Revolution and ending with the current crop of
journalism dealing with the nuclear age, the study in

some ways comes full cycle. Like Cooper and Lancaster
and Brick, most of the cold war novelists deal in caricature rather than characterization and in adventure
rather than in ideas. In addition, just as in many of the
historical novels, one is tempted to play the game of
attempting to identify actual historical figures in the
fictional characters. If one wonders early in *The Spy*
whether or not Harper is Washington, or in *The Pilot*
whether Mr. Gray is John Paul Jones, so, too, one
wonders if Dr. Strangelove is intended as a caricature of
Dr. Edward Teller or General Ripper as a caricature of
General Edwin Walker. In *Fail-Safe* there is some similarity between the fictional Secretary of Defense, Swenson,
and Robert McNamara, and one wonders if John F. Kennedy is the president who "coolly lopped a half-dozen
oldtimers from the White House staff and told them
bluntly it was for incompetence." Certainly, Burdick and
Wheeler use the late Senator Everett Dirksen as their
model for this political figure: "A midwestern Republican
with a vigorous shock of white hair, sanguine complexion,
and Falstaffian girth, he orated like William Jennings
Bryan and generally looked like a musical-comedy senator.
But under that shock of white hair operated one of the
finest minds in Washington." [24] Finally, in a book that
propagandizes for a mixed strategic force of missiles and
bombers, Anthony Gray's *The Penetrators,* there appear
a defense secretary, Charles Van Ness, who is obviously
patterned after McNamara; an Air Force Chief of Staff,
General Halstead Norwood, who, like Le May, has
molded SAC and who is fighting a rear-guard action for
a manned bomber force; and a new SAC commander,
General Hub Younger, who greatly resembles the "missile general," Bernard Schreiver.

In the last analysis, the American military novels in

the nuclear age are, thus far, disappointing. Interested in neither complexity of character nor complexity of themes or ideas, they titillate the reader with fast-moving narratives concerned with subjects of the utmost topical importance: the survival of American democracy and the survival of the world. From a literary point of view, except for *Dr. Strangelove,* they are hardly worth considering; however, coupled with the nonfiction dealing with the same problems, they contribute to a composite of concern about national and human survival unprecedented in the history of American culture. For the first time in the history of the United States, American novelists are suggesting that specific national policies are leading in the direction of national destruction. Quite often, at the heart of that concern is the explicit or implicit condemnation of an economy that has come to rely too heavily on defense spending. Fred J. Cook in *The Warfare State* sums up the feeling:

> The time has come when we can see clearly and unmistakably before us our chosen destiny. The Pied Pipers of the Military and Big Business, who have been drumming into our ears the siren song of "peace through strength," can no longer quite conceal the brink toward which they lead us. The A-bomb that could decimate a city has given place to H-bombs that can vaporize entire islands and turn entire states into radioactive wastes. And the end is not yet in sight. In our search for "peace through strength," we must continue to pursue the ever more ultimate and ever more horrible weapons, which our prospective enemies must also continue to pursue; and we both are promised, since scientists assure us there is virtually no limit to nuclear power, that we shall

find the treasure we seek. Let us examine some of the glories it is promised we shall find.

First there is the Doomsday Machine. The RAND corp. [sic] has described this pithily in its *Glossary of Terms on National Security* as: "A reliable and securely protected device that is capable of destroying almost all human life and that would be automatically triggered if an enemy committed any one of a designated class of violations." (p. 340) [25]

To the authors of *Dr. Strangelove* this kind of thinking is mad and will finally lead to ultimate destruction, and they make it clear that it is not limited to American culture. Their Soviet representative in *Strangelove,* De Sadeski, is as childishly insane as his counterparts in the United States. The novel is concerned with the madness of man in a world in which his technical and scientific capabilities have so outstripped his moral capacity to handle them that he jeopardizes his own existence; but although this general intention is present, it can be said that the satire is aimed primarily at the military and conservative definition of reality. For, if in a nuclear world armed conflict among nations remains inevitable, then, in the last analysis, there is little hope for survival.

Perhaps because of the very immensity of the problem, dwarfing, as it does, the human beings who grapple with it, satire may be the best vehicle in fiction for expressions of concern. If *Catch-22* includes most of the elements present in the tradition of the American military novel and employs satire to sum up American culture, then *Dr. Strangelove* applies the same view to attitudes and a world view that may bring about ultimate destruction. In commenting about the widespread military definition of reality, Cook comments: "Mad? It certainly is. But with the all-consuming passion of the Warfare State for the tensions and gadgets of war, insanity had become no drawback to reality. It has, indeed, become our way of life." [26] Cook's suggestion that the values of the culture are insane parallels in nonfiction the attitudes of Heller and of Kubrick and Southern in fiction. On the other hand, Walter Millis' attitude seems closer to that of Cozzens or Marquand:

> Presumably the human race will in the future, as it has done throughout the past, find means of getting along somehow, probably for the better rather than for the worse. But just how it will do so seems impossible to predict; while the old certainty of military action as the final answer to every problem—a certainty that has remained with us since the dawn of history—seems no longer available. It may be that for final sanctions in our human affairs we shall have to look toward other factors.[27]

Unlike the pursuit of perfection evinced in Heller's satire, there is present in this statement a sense of a calm acceptance of the difficulties and degradation of the human condition. Dealing with the ultimate challenge of a world in which man finally possesses the means to bring about his own total destruction, perhaps practical men like Cozzens' Colonel Ross will be able to forestall catastrophe and provide the guidance for man to muddle through. In the meantime, it is clear that work like Heller's serves to remind man of his need to dream of the possibilities of the future and to be critical of the inadequacies of the present.

Should Millis' hope concerning the extinction of

warfare be realized, then, of course, the tradition of the American military novel will come to an end. Unfortunate in its breeding ground of violence, death, destruction, and totalitarianism, it includes nevertheless a number of works that are excellent both in terms of their achievement as art and as statements concerning American political and sociological situations. Even more unfortunate, however, is the probability that the tradition will be a continuing one, and that the United States will continue to participate in wars of various kinds and intensities. Barring the possibility of one of ultimate intensity, it is certain that some men and women who participate in them will write about their experiences in fiction. For, if warfare continues to be inevitable, then inevitable too are man's attempts to represent it and to interpret it in art. Despite the nightmare of history, in the words that follow war there is always the hope that man may better understand the condition of his own humanity.

Notes

1. Michener, pp. 57, 44, 57.
2. *Ibid.*, pp. 33, 35; 142.
3. *Ibid.*, pp. 15; 64–71, 78–79.
4. Salter, *The Hunters*, p. 244.
5. *The Arm of Flesh*, pp. 104–111, 176–178.
6. Tristram Coffin, *The Passion of the Hawks: Militarism in Modern America*, pp. 112–113.
7. Fred J. Cook, *The Warfare State*, p. 165.
8. Knebel and Bailey, p. 44.
9. *Ibid.*, p. 48. Cf. C. Wright Mills, *The Power Elite*, p. 199, cited in Chapter Six.
10. *Ibid.*, pp. 33, 302, 300.
11. Coffin, pp. 190, 125–137; Cook, pp. 164, 308.
12. Morris Janowitz, *The Professional Soldier: A Social and Political Portrait*, p. 296.

13. Coffin, p. 177.
14. Millis, *Arms and Men: A Study in American Military History,* p. 358.
15. Coffin, p. 242.
16. Milne, pp. 123–124.
17. Eugene Burdick and Harvey Wheeler, *Fail-Safe* (New York, 1962), pp. 238–245, 69–75. (Subsequent references are indicated by page numbers in the text.)
18. Janowitz, p. 305.
19. Peter George (Peter Bryant), *Dr. Strangelove, or: How I Learned to Stop Worrying and Love the Bomb,* based on the Screenplay by Stanley Kubrick, Peter George, and Terry Southern (New York, 1964), pp. 5–9. (Subsequent references are indicated by page numbers in the text.)
20. Burdick and Wheeler, p. 125.
21. Janowitz, p. 243.
22. Rascovich, pp. 74, 166; 258.
23. Castle, pp. 35, 74.
24. Burdick and Wheeler, pp. 22; 92.
25. Cook, p. 340.
26. *Ibid.,* p. 349.
27. Millis, p. 365.

Bibliography

Adams, Henry. *The Education of Henry Adams: An Autobiography*. New York, 1918.

Alden, John Richard. *The American Revolution: 1757–1783*. New York, 1954.

Aldridge, John W. *After the Lost Generation: A Critical Study of the Writers of Two Wars*. New York, 1951.

Allen, Gay Wilson. *The Solitary Singer: A Critical Biography of Walt Whitman*. New York, 1955.

Allen, Hervey. *It Was Like This: Two Stories of the Great War*. New York, 1936.

Anderson, Charles Robert. "The Genesis of *Billy Budd*," *American Literature*, XII (November 1940), 329-346.

Anderson, Thomas. *Your Own Beloved Sons*. New York, 1956.

Andrews, Mary Raymond Shipman. *Her Country*. New York, 1918.

———. *His Soul Goes Marching On*. New York, 1922.

———. *Joy in the Morning*. New York, 1919.

———. *Old Glory*. New York, 1917.

———. *The Three Things*. New York, 1915.

Arvin, Newton. *Herman Melville*. New York, 1950.

Atkins, John. *Ernest Hemingway: His Work and Personality*. London, 1952.

Baker, Carlos. *Hemingway: The Writer as Artist*. Princeton, N.J., 1963.

Balakian, Nora, and Charles Simmons, ed. *The Creative Present: Notes on Contemporary American Fiction*, Garden City, N.Y., 1963.

Beach, Edward L. *Run Silent, Run Deep*. New York, 1955.

271

Beach, Joseph Warren. *American Fiction, 1920–1940*. New York, 1960.

Bellamy, Edward. *The Duke of Stockbridge: A Romance of Shay's Rebellion*. New York, 1900.

Bernstein, John. *Pacifism and Rebellion in the Writings of Herman Melville*. The Hague, 1964.

Berryman, John. "Stephen Crane: *The Red Badge of Courage*," in *The American Novel from James Fenimore Cooper to William Faulkner*, ed. Wallace Stegner. New York, 1965.

Bewley, Marius. *The Eccentric Design: Form in the Classical American Novel*. New York, 1959.

Bierce, Ambrose. *The Collected Writings of Ambrose Bierce*. New York, 1946.

――――. *Collected Works of Ambrose Bierce*. 12 vols. New York, 1909–1912.

Bolander, Louis H. "The Naval Career of James Fenimore Cooper," *United States Naval Institute Proceedings*, LXVI (April 1940), 541–550.

Bourjaily, Vance. *The End of My Life*. New York, 1947.

Bowen, Merlin. *The Long Encounter: Self and Experience in the Writings of Herman Melville*. Chicago, 1960.

Boyd, James. *Drums*. New York, 1926.

Boyd, Thomas. *Through the Wheat*. New York, 1923.

Bracher, Frederick. *The Novels of James Gould Cozzens*. New York, 1959.

Branch, Edgar Marquess. *The Literary Apprenticeship of Mark Twain*. Urbana, Ill., 1950.

Braswell, William, "Melville's *Billy Budd* as 'An Inside Narrative'," *American Literature*, XXIX (May 1957), 133–146.

Brelis, Dean. *The Mission*. New York, 1958.

Brick, John. *The King's Rangers*. Garden City, N.Y., 1954.

――――. *The Rifleman*. Garden City, N.Y., 1953.

――――. *The Strong Men*. Garden City, N.Y., 1959.

Brinkley, William. *Don't Go Near the Water*. New York, 1956.

Brown, Harry. *A Walk in the Sun*. Philadelphia, 1944.

Brown, Joe David. *Kings Go Forth*. New York, 1956.

Burdick, Eugene, and Harvey Wheeler. *Fail-Safe*. New York, 1962.

Burns, John Horne. *The Gallery*. New York, 1947.

Cady, Edwin H. *The Road to Realism: The Early Years of William Dean Howells*. Syracuse, N.Y., 1956.

Calmer, Ned. *The Strange Land*. New York, 1950.

Campbell, William E. March (William March). *Company K*. New York, 1958.

Carpenter, Frederick Ives. *American Literature and the Dream.* New York, 1955.

Castle, John. *The Seventh Fury.* New York, 1961.

Cather, Willa. *One of Ours.* New York, 1922.

Catton, Bruce. *America Goes to War.* Middletown, Conn., 1958.

Chamales, Tom T. *Never So Few.* New York, 1957.

Chase, Richard. *The American Novel and Its Tradition.* Garden City, N.Y., 1957.

————. *Herman Melville: A Critical Study.* New York, 1949.

Churchill, Winston. *Richard Carvel.* New York, 1903.

Coates, Robert M. *The Bitter Season.* New York, 1946.

Cobb, John. *The Gesture.* New York, 1948.

Cockburn, Alex. "*Catch-22,* a Review," *New Left Review,* XXVIII (January-February 1963), 87–92.

Coffin, Tristram. *The Passion of the Hawks: Militarism in Modern America.* New York, 1964.

Cook, Fred J. *The Warfare State.* New York, 1962.

Cooke, John Esten. *Surry of Eagle's Nest: Or, the Memoirs of a Staff-Officer Serving in Virginia.* New York, 1894.

Cooper, James Fenimore. *The History of the Navy of the United States of America.* 2 vols. Philadelphia, 1839.

————. *The Pilot.* New York, 1872.

————. Review in *Proceedings of the Naval Court Martial in the Case of Alexander Slidell Mackenzie, a Commander in the Navy of the United States, &c Including the Charges against Him by the Secretary of the Navy. To Which is Annexed, an Elaborate Review, by James Fennimore [sic] Cooper.* New York, 1844.

————. *The Spy: a Tale of the Neutral Ground.* New York, 1871.

Cooperman, Stanley. *World War I and the American Novel.* Baltimore, 1967.

Cowie, Alexander. *The Rise of the American Novel.* New York, 1951.

Cowley, Malcolm. *Exile's Return: A Literary Odyssey of the 1920's.* New York, 1951.

————. *The Literary Situation.* New York, 1954.

Cozzens, James Gould. *Guard of Honor.* New York, 1948.

Crane, Stephen. *The Collected Poems of Stephen Crane,* ed. Wilson Follett. New York, 1962.

————. *The Complete Stories and Sketches of Stephen Crane,* ed. Thomas A. Gullason. Garden City, New York, 1963.

————. "The Red Badge of Courage" in *Stephen Crane: An Omnibus,* ed. Robert Wooster Stallman. New York, 1958.

————. *Wounds in the Rain.* New York, 1900.

Cummings, E. E. *The Enormous Room.* New York, 1922.

———. *Poems: 1923–1954.* New York, 1954.

Dabney, Virginius. *The Story of Don Miff as Told by His Friend John Bouche Whacker: A Symphony of Life.* Philadelphia, 1886.

Davidson, David. *The Steeper Cliff.* New York, 1947.

Davidson, James. *J. W. De Forest and His Contemporaries: The Birth of American Realism.* Unpublished Ph.D. Dissertation, New York University, 1958.

Dawson, Coningsby. "Insulting the Army," *New York Times Book Review* (October 2, 1921), pp. 16–17.

Day, Douglas. "*Catch-22:* A Manifesto for Anarchists," *Carolina Quarterly* (Summer 1963), pp. 86–92.

De Forest, John William. *Miss Ravenel's Conversion from Secession to Loyalty,* ed. Gordon S. Haight. New York, 1957.

———. *A Volunteer's Adventures: A Union Captain's Record of the Civil War,* ed. James H. Croushore with an introduction by Stanley T. Williams. New Haven, Conn., 1946.

De Leon, T. C. *John Holden, Unionist, a Romance of the Days of Destruction and Reconstruction,* St. Paul, Minn., 1893.

Dodson, Kenneth. *Away All Boats.* Boston, 1954.

Dos Passos, John. *First Encounter.* New York, 1945.

———. *Three Soldiers.* New York, 1921.

Edel, Leon. *Henry James: The Untried Years.* Philadelphia, 1953.

Eisinger, Chester E. *The Fiction of the Forties.* Chicago, 1963.

Emerson, Ralph Waldo. *The Complete Works of Ralph Waldo Emerson with a Biographical Introduction and Notes by Edward Waldo Emerson and a General Index.* Boston, 1903.

Fast, Howard. *Conceived in Liberty: A Novel of Valley Forge.* New York, 1939.

———. *The Proud and the Free.* Boston, 1950.

———. *The Unvanquished.* New York, 1942.

Faulkner, William. *Collected Short Stories of William Faulkner.* New York, 1950.

———. *A Fable.* New York, 1954.

———. *Soldier's Pay.* New York, 1926.

Feuchtwanger, Lion. *The House of Desdemona or the Laurels and Limitations of Historical Fiction,* trans. Harold A. Basilus. Detroit, 1963.

Fiedler, Leslie. *Love and Death in the American Novel.* New York, 1960.

———. *Waiting for the End.* New York, 1965.

Finklestein, Sidney Walter. *Existentialism and Alienation in American Literature.* New York, 1965.

Follett, Wilson, ed. *The Collected Poems of Stephen Crane.* New York, 1962.

Fosburgh, Hugh. *View from the Air.* New York, 1953.

Frank, Pat. *Alas, Babylon.* Philadelphia, 1959.

———. *Forbidden Area.* Philadelphia, 1956.

———. *Hold Back the Night.* Philadelphia, 1952.

Fredenburgh, Theodore. *Soldiers March!* New York, 1930.

Frederic, Harold. *The Copperhead.* New York, 1893.

———. *In the Valley.* New York, 1907.

Freeman, F. Barron. *Melville's* BILLY BUDD. Cambridge, Mass., 1948.

Friedman, Norman. *E. E. Cummings: The Growth of a Writer.* Carbondale, Ill., 1964.

Frohock, Wilbur Merrill. *The Novel of Violence in America.* Dallas, Texas, 1958.

———. *Strangers to this Ground: Cultural Diversity in Contemporary American Writing.* Dallas, Texas, 1961.

Fuller, J. F. C. *War and Western Civilization.* London, 1932.

Garland, Hamlin. *Main-Travelled Roads.* New York, 1899.

Gellhorn, Martha. *The Wine of Astonishment.* New York, 1948.

George, Peter (Peter Bryant). *Dr. Strangelove, or: How I Learned to Stop Worrying and Love the Bomb.* New York, 1964.

———. *Red Alert.* New York, 1958.

Gessner, Robert. *Treason.* New York, 1944.

Gray, Anthony. *The Penetrators, a Novel.* New York, 1965.

Greenfield, Josh. "22 Was Funnier than 14," *The New York Times Book Review* (March 3, 1968), 1, 49, 51, 53.

Greever, Garland. Introduction to Sidney Lanier's *Tiger-Lilies and Southern Prose,* eds. Garland Greever and Cecil Abernathy. Baltimore, 1945.

Gullason, Thomas A., ed. *The Complete Stories and Sketches of Stephen Crane.* Garden City, N.Y., 1963.

Hagedorn, Hermann. *The Rough Riders.* New York, 1927.

Haight, Gordon S. Introduction to John William De Forest's *Miss Ravenel's Conversion from Secession to Loyalty,* ed. Gordon S. Haight. New York, 1955.

Haines, William Wister. *Command Decision.* Boston, 1947.

Harris, Joel Chandler. *On the Plantation: A Story of a Georgia Boy's Adventures during the War.* New York, 1915.

———. *Tales of the Home Folks in Peace and War.* Boston, 1898.

Harrison, Charles Yale. *Generals Die in Bed.* New York, 1930.

Hassan, Ihab Habib. *Radical Innocence: Studies in the Contemporary American Novel.* Princeton, N.J., 1961.

Hatcher, Harlan. *Creating the Modern American Novel.* New York, 1965.

Hayes, Alfred. *The Girl on the Via Flaminia*. New York, 1949.

Heggen, Thomas. *Mr. Roberts*. Boston, 1946.

Heller, Joseph. *Catch–22*. New York, 1961.

Hemingway, Ernest. *Across the River and into the Trees*. New York, 1950.

———. *A Farewell to Arms*. New York, 1929.

———. *Green Hills of Africa*. New York, 1935.

———. *In Our Time*. New York, 1958.

———. *The Short Stories of Ernest Hemingway*. New York, 1955.

———, ed. *Men at War: the Best War Stories of All Time*. New York, 1955.

Hergesheimer, Joseph. *Balisand*. New York, 1924.

Hersey, John. *A Bell for Adano*. Garden City, New York, 1945.

———. *The War Lover*. New York, 1959.

Heym, Stefan. *The Crusaders*. Boston, 1948.

Hoffman, Frederick J. *The Modern Novel in America*. Chicago, 1963.

———. *The Twenties: American Writing in the Post-War Decade*. New York, 1962.

House, Kay Seymour. *Cooper's Americans*. Columbus, Ohio, 1965.

Howard, Leon. *Herman Melville: A Biography*. Berkeley and Los Angeles, 1951.

Howe, Irving. *William Faulkner: A Critical Study*. New York, 1962.

Humes, H. L. *The Underground City*. New York, 1958.

Huntington, Samuel P. *The Soldier and the State: the Theory and Politics of Civil-Military Relations*. Cambridge, Mass., 1957.

Janowitz, Morris. *The Professional Soldier: A Social and Political Portrait*. New York, 1960.

Jones, James. *From Here to Eternity*. New York, 1951.

———. *The Pistol*. New York, 1958.

———. *The Thin Red Line*. New York, 1962.

Kantor, MacKinlay. *Andersonville*. Cleveland, 1955.

———. *Long Remember*. New York, 1934.

Karl, Frederick R. "Catch-22: Only Fools Walk in Darkness," in *Contemporary American Novelists*, ed. Harry T. Moore. Carbondale, Ill., 1964.

Kazin, Alfred. "Ishmael in His Academic Heaven," *New Yorker* (February 12, 1949), pp. 84–89.

———. *On Native Grounds: An Interpretation of Modern American Prose Literature*. New York, 1942.

Kennedy, Robert F. *Thirteen Days: A Memoir of the Cuban Missile Crisis*. New York, 1969.

Killens, John Oliver. *And Then We Heard the Thunder*. New York, 1963.

Killinger, John. *Hemingway and the Dead Gods: A Study in Existentialism.* Lexington, Ky., 1960.

Kirkland, Joseph. *The Captain of Company K.* Chicago, 1891.

Klotz, Marvin. *The Imitation of War, 1800–1900: Realism in the American War Novel.* Unpublished Ph.D. Dissertation, New York University, 1958.

Knebel, Fletcher and Charles W. Bailey, II. *Seven Days in May.* New York, 1962.

Kreidberg, Marvin A., and Merton G. Henry. *History of Military Mobilization in the United States Army: 1775–1945.* Washington, 1955.

Kubrick, Stanley, Peter George, and Terry Southern. See George, Peter.

Lancaster, Bruce. *Blind Journey.* Boston, 1953.

——. *Guns of Burgoyne.* New York, 1939.

——. *Phantom Fortress.* Boston, 1950.

——. *The Secret Road.* Boston, 1952.

Lanier, Sidney. *Tiger-Lilies and Southern Prose,* eds. Garland Greever and Cecil Abernathy. Baltimore, 1945.

Lasswell, Harold D. *National Security and Individual Freedom.* New York, 1950.

Lawrence, D. H. *Studies in Classic American Literature.* Garden City, N.Y., 1955.

Lee, Mary. *It's a Great War!* Boston, 1929.

Leisy, Ernest E. *The American Historical Novel.* Norman, Okla., 1950.

Levin, Harry. *The Power of Blackness: Hawthorne, Poe, Melville.* New York, 1960.

Light, James F. *John William De Forest.* New York, 1965.

Littlejohn, David. "The Anti-realists," *Daedalus* (Spring 1963), 250–264.

Lively, Robert A. *Fiction Fights the Civil War: An Unfinished Chapter in the Literary History of the American People.* Chapel Hill, N.C., 1957.

Loshe, Lillie Deming. *The Early American Novel.* New York, 1907.

Lowry, Robert. *Casualty.* New York, 1946.

Ludwig, Jack. *Recent American Novelists.* Minneapolis, Minn., 1962.

Mailer, Norman. *The Naked and the Dead.* New York, 1948.

Malin, Irving. *William Faulkner: An Introduction.* Stanford, Calif., 1957.

Maltz, Albert. *The Cross and the Arrow.* Boston, 1944.

Marquand, John P. *Melville Goodwin, U.S.A.* Boston, 1951.

Mason, F. van Wyck. *Rivers of Glory.* Philadelphia, 1942.

———. *Stars on the Sea.* Philadelphia, 1940.

———. *The Harbors.* Philadelphia, 1938.

Matthews, Brander. *Americanisms and Briticisms: With Other Isms.* New York, 1892.

Matthiessen, F. O. *American Renaissance: Art and Expression in the Age of Emerson and Whitman.* New York, 1941.

Maxwell, D. E. S. *American Fiction: The Intellectual Background.* New York, 1963.

McBain, Ed. (Evan Hunter). *The Sentries.* New York, 1965.

McCarthy, Eugene J. "The Power of the Pentagon," *Saturday Review* (December 21, 1968), pp. 8–10, 44.

Melville, Herman. *Billy Budd, Sailor (An Inside Narrative),* eds. Harrison Hayford and Merton M. Sealts, Jr. Chicago, 1962.

———. *Collected Poems of Herman Melville,* ed. Howard P. Vincent. Chicago, 1947.

———. *Israel Potter: His Fifty Years of Exile.* London, 1923.

———. *White Jacket or the World in a Man-of-War.* London, 1922.

Merk, Frederick. *Manifest Destiny and Mission in American History: A Reinterpretation.* New York, 1963.

Michener, James A. *The Bridges at Toko-Ri.* New York, 1953.

Miller, James E., Jr. *A Reader's Guide to Herman Melville.* New York, 1962.

Miller, Merle. *That Winter.* New York, 1948.

Millgate, Michael. *American Social Fiction: James to Cozzens.* New York, 1964.

Millis, Walter. *Arms and Men: A Study in American Military History.* New York, 1956.

Mills, C. Wright. *The Power Elite.* New York, 1956.

Milne, Gordon. *The American Political Novel.* Norman, Okla. 1966.

Mitchell, Silas Weir. *Hugh Wynne, Free Quaker: Sometime Brevet Lieutenant-Colonel on the Staff of His Excellency General Washington.* New York, 1922.

Moore, Harry T., ed. *Contemporary American Novelists.* Carbondale, Ill., 1964.

Morford, Henry. *The Coward: A Novel of Society and the Field in 1863.* Philadelphia, 1864.

———. *The Days of Shoddy: A Novel of the Great Rebellion in 1861.* Philadelphia, 1863.

———. *Shoulder-Straps: A Novel of New York and the Army, 1862.* Philadelphia, 1863.

Morris, Donald. *Warm Bodies.* New York, 1957.

Mumford, Lewis. *Herman Melville: A Study of His Life and Vision.* New York, 1962.

Muste, John M., "Better to Die Laughing: The War Novels of Joseph Heller and John Ashmead," *Critique: Studies in Modern Fiction*, V (Fall 1962), 16–27.

Myrer, Anton. *The Big War.* New York, 1957.

Nason, Leonard H. *Chevrons.* New York, 1926.

O'Connor, Richard. *Ambrose Bierce: A Biography.* Boston, 1967.

O'Connor, William Van. *The Tangled Fire of William Faulkner.* Minneapolis, Minnesota, 1954.

Paul, Elliot. *Impromptu.* New York, 1923.

Peckham, Howard H. *The War for Independence: A Military History.* Chicago, 1958.

Pennell, Joseph Stanley. *The History of Rome Hanks and Kindred Matters.* New York, 1944.

Philbrick, Thomas. *James Fenimore Cooper and the Development of American Sea Fiction.* Cambridge, Mass., 1961.

Pinkser, Sanford. "Heller's *Catch-22:* The Protest of *Puer Eternis,*" *Critique: Studies in Modern Fiction,* VII (Winter 1964–1965), 150–162.

Podhoretz, Norman. *Doings and Undoings: The Fifties and After in American Literature.* New York, 1965.

Pound, Ezra. *Personae: The Collected Poems of Ezra Pound.* New York, 1926.

Powell, Richard. *The Soldier.* New York, 1960.

Preston, Richard A., Sydney F. Wise, and Herman O. Werner. *Men in Arms: A History of Warfare and Its Interrelationships with Western Society.* New York, 1956.

Quinn, Arthur Hobson. *American Fiction: An Historical and Critical Survey.* New York, 1936.

Rascovich, Mark. *The Bedford Incident.* New York, 1963.

Rideout, Walter. *The Radical Novel in the United States, 1900–1954: Some Interpretations of Literature and Society.* Cambridge, Mass., 1956.

Ridgely, Joseph V. *William Gilmore Simms.* New York, 1962.

Ringe, Donald A. *James Fenimore Cooper.* New York, 1962.

Roberts, Kenneth. *Arundel.* Garden City, N.Y., 1949.

———. *Rabble in Arms.* Garden City, N.Y., 1933.

Rosenberry, Edward. "The Problem of *Billy Budd,*" *PMLA*, LXXX (December 1965), 489–498.

Ross, James E. *The Dead Are Mine.* New York, 1964.

Rosten, Leo. *Captain Newman, M.D.* New York, 1961.

Rovit, Earl. *Ernest Hemingway.* New York, 1963.

Salinger, J. D. *The Catcher in the Rye.* Boston, 1951.

Salter, James. *The Arm of Flesh.* New York, 1961.

————. *The Hunters*. New York, 1956.

Sargent, Epes. *Peculiar: A Tale of the Great Transition*. New York, 1906.

Schiffman, Joseph. "Melville's Final Stage, Irony: A Re-examination of *Billy Budd* Criticism," *American Literature*, XXII (May 1950), 128–136.

Schneider, Robert W. *Five Novelists of the Progressive Era*. New York, 1965.

Shapiro, Lionel. *The Sealed Verdict*. New York, 1947.

————. *The Sixth of June*. New York, 1955.

Shaw, Irwin. *The Young Lions*. New York, 1948.

Shulenberger, Arvid. *Cooper's Theory of Fiction: His Prefaces and Their Relation to His Novels*. Lawrence, Kansas, 1955.

Simms, William Gilmore. *Woodcraft*. New York, 1961.

Slaughter, Frank G. *Sword and Scalpel*. Garden City, N.Y., 1957.

Slote, Alfred. *Strangers and Comrades*. New York, 1964.

Smith, Janet, ed. *Mark Twain on the Damned Human Race*. New York, 1962.

Snell, George. *The Shapers of American Fiction: 1798–1947*. New York, 1961.

Spiller, Robert E. *The Cycle of American Literature: An Essay in Historical Criticism*. New York, 1955.

————. *Fenimore Cooper: Critic of His Times*. New York, 1931.

————, *et al.*, eds. *Literary History of the United States*. New York, 1931.

Stallings, Laurence. *Plumes*. New York, 1924.

Stallman, Robert Wooster, ed. *Stephen Crane: An Omnibus*. New York, 1958.

Statham, Leon. *Welcome, Darkness*. New York, 1950.

Steinbeck, John. *The Moon Is Down*. New York, 1942.

Stephens, Edward. *Blow Negative!* Garden City, New York, 1962.

Stern, Milton R. *The Fine Hammered Steel of Herman Melville*. Urbana, Ill., 1957.

Stevenson, David L. "James Jones and Jack Kerouac: Novelists of Disjunction," in *The Creative Present: Notes on Contemporary American Fiction*, eds. Nora Balakian and Charles Simmons. Garden City, N.Y., 1963.

Stouffer, Samuel A., *et al*. *Studies in Social Psychology in World War II*. 4 vols. Princeton, N.Y., 1949–1950.

Swiggart, Peter. *The Art of Faulkner's Novels*. Austin, Texas, 1962.

Taylor, David. *Farewell to Valley Forge*. Philadelphia, 1955.

————. *Lights across the Delaware*. Philadelphia, 1954.

————. *Storm the Last Rampart*. Philadelphia, 1960.

Taylor, Ward. *Roll Back the Sky*. New York, 1956.

Thane, Elswyth. *Ever After*. New York, 1946.

Thompson, Lawrance. *Melville's Quarrel with God*. Princeton, N.J., 1952.

Thoreau, Henry David. *Walden*. Variorum edition, ed. Walter Harding. New York, 1962.

Thorp, Willard. *American Writing in the Twentieth Century*. Cambridge, Mass., 1960.

Trilling, Diana. "The Radical Moralism of Norman Mailer," in *The Creative Present: Notes on Contemporary American Fiction,* eds. Nora Balakian and Charles Simmons. Garden City, New York, 1963.

Trowbridge, J. T. *Cudjo's Cave*. Boston, 1895.

Trumbo, Dalton. *Johnny Got His Gun*. New York, 1939.

Tyler, Moses Coit. *The Literary History of the American Revolution, 1763–1783*. 2 vols. New York, 1957.

Upton, Emory. *The Armies of Asia and Europe*. Washington, D.C., 1878.

————. *The Military Policy of the United States*. Washington, D.C., 1917.

Uris, Leon M. *Battle Cry*. New York, 1953.

Van Doren, Carl. *The American Novel, 1789–1939*. New York, 1940.

Vickery, Olga W. *The Novels of William Faulkner: A Critical Interpretation*. Baton Rouge, La., 1959.

Wain, John. "A New Novel about Old Troubles," *Critical Quarterly,* V (Summer 1963), 168–173.

Walcutt, Charles Child. *American Literary Naturalism: A Divided Stream*. Minneapolis, Minn., 1956.

Waldmeir, Joseph J. "Two Novelists of the Absurd: Heller and Kesey," *Wisconsin Studies in Contemporary Literature,* V (1964), 192–204.

Walker, Warren S. *James Fenimore Cooper: An Introduction and Interpretation*. New York, 1962.

Wallace, Willard M. *Appeal to Arms: A Military History of the American Revolution*. New York, 1951.

Ward, Christopher, *The War of the Revolution,* ed. John Richard Alden. New York, 1952.

Weir, Charles. "Malice Reconciled: A Note on *Billy Budd*," *University of Toronto Quarterly,* XXIII (April 1944), 276–285.

Wells, Henry W. "An Unobtrusive Democrat: Herman Melville," *South Atlantic Quarterly,* XLIII (January 1944), 46–51.

Westheimer, David. *Von Ryan's Express*. Garden City, N.Y., 1964.

Wiggins, Robert A. *Ambrose Bierce*. Minneapolis, Minn., 1964.

Willett, Ralph W. "Nelson and Vere: Hero and Victim in *Billy Budd, Sailor*," *PMLA,* LXXXII (October 1967), 370–376.

Williams, Stanley T. Introduction to John William De Forest's *A Volunteer's Adventures: A Union Captain's Record of the Civil War,* ed. James H. Croushore. New Haven, Conn., 1946.

Wilson, Edmund. *Patriotic Gore: Studies in the Literature of the American Civil War.* New York, 1962.

Wharton, Edith. *A Son at the Front.* New York, 1922.

White, Theodore H. *The Mountain Road.* New York, 1958.

Woodruff, Stuart C. *The Short Stories of Ambrose Bierce: A Study in Polarity.* Pittsburgh, 1964.

Woods, William. *The Edge of Darkness.* Philadelphia, 1942.

Wouk, Herman. *The Caine Mutiny.* New York, 1951.

Wrenn, John H. *John Dos Passos.* New York, 1961.

Wylie, Philip. *Tomorrow!* New York, 1954.

———. *Triumph.* Garden City, N.Y., 1963.

Young, Philip. *Ernest Hemingway.* New York, 1952.

Index

283

PS
374
M5
M5
1970

Miller, Wayne C.
    An armed America- its face in
fiction.

PS374 M5 M5 1970
+An armed America+Miller, Wayne Ch

0 00 02 0198187 5
MIDDLEBURY COLLEGE